The Animal Trade

'If the animal kingdom is doomed I don't want to be responsible.'

Spike Milligan (Farnes, 2003)

The Animal Trade

Clive J.C. Phillips

Centre for Animal Welfare and Ethics,
School of Veterinary Science,
University of Queensland, Australia
E-mail: c.phillips@uq.edu.au

www.cabi.org

UNIVERSITY OF WINCHESTER
LIBRARY

CABI is a trading name of CAB International

CABI
Nosworthy Way
Wallingford
Oxfordshire OX10 8DE
UK

Tel: +44 (0)1491 832111
Fax: +44 (0)1491 833508
E-mail: info@cabi.org
Website: www.cabi.org

CABI
745 Atlantic Avenue
8th Floor
Boston, MA 02111
USA

Tel: +1 (617) 682 9015
E-mail: cabi-nao@cabi.org

A catalogue record for this book is available from the British Library, London, UK.

Library of Congress Cataloging-in-Publication Data

Phillips, Clive J.C.
   The animal trade / Clive J.C. Phillips.
      pages cm
   Includes bibliographical references and index.
   ISBN 978-1-78064-313-7 (alk. paper)
1. Animal industry. 2. Pet industry. 3. Wild animal collecting. I. Title.

HD9410.5.P495 2015
381'.416--dc23

2015020183

ISBN-13: 978 1 78064 313 7

Commissioning editor: Caroline Makepeace
Assistant editor: Alexandra Lainsbury
Production editor: Tracy Head

Typeset by SPi, Pondicherry, India.
Printed and bound in the UK by CPI Group (UK) Ltd, Croydon, CR0 4YY.

Contents

Preface

Animals have been traded between countries for thousands of years, and this has made a significant contribution to transferring resources from places where animals can be successfully grown to those with greatest demand, as well as to developing trade and communication networks between nations. The animal trade has also assisted in colonization of new lands, created tension over health and quality issues between trading partners, and has been used politically when trade barriers and sanctions are applied. Despite the latter, the trade in animals for meat has grown rapidly in recent years, due mainly to relaxation of trade barriers, increasing demand for food animals, in Asia in particular, and faster and cheaper transport opportunities. This has allowed the rapid growth of multinational companies using intensive animal production techniques, particularly in developing countries such as Brazil and Thailand. Demand is directed especially towards affordable meat products that are produced with minimal land, labour and feed resource utilization, which has favoured chicken meat and pork over beef and sheep meat. The intensive nature of the production systems used, with high stocking densities of animals in cages and pens, short lifespans for the animals and limited opportunity for them to perform natural behaviour, means that there are inherent ethical problems, especially concerning the welfare of the animals but also pollution and the use of feed that could otherwise support human life directly. The growth of such systems implies that an increasing proportion of animal production systems used worldwide have ethical concerns. The concerns are partially mitigated by some regions, most notably the European Union (EU), having agreements with overseas producers relating to animal welfare standards.

The growing intensity of farm animal production for international trade is reducing the biodiversity of the animals used, and hence the gene pool that is available to cope with problems like disease and climate change. The trade in live animals is increasing particularly rapidly, due mainly to better transport opportunities and a polarization of animal production systems in specified regions, which may be distant from the market for the animals. There are more animals being transported and they are travelling further, with poor welfare arising from high stocking densities, limited opportunity to perform natural behaviour and stress from poor handling and movement of the vessel or vehicle. Growth in demand for live animals for slaughter has grown particularly fast in Asia, which is supplied by importing animals from neighbouring regions and by increased production internally. The trade in live animals also brings risks of disease transmission, especially infectious diseases like foot and mouth disease. The World Organisation for Animal Health (OIE) attempts to control such diseases and reduce their spread with a vigorous research and extension programme. Another growth area has been the trade in exotic animals, which are transported long distances to be sold as pets, often illegally, during which time they will sometimes experience severe stress from the unfamiliar thermal environment, noise and severe restriction of movement.

The growth of the animal trade worldwide therefore brings serious concerns for the welfare and ethical treatment of animals, with additional risks created by disease transmission and loss of biodiversity. This book is an attempt to identify the concerns, as well as posing solutions to the problems we will inevitably face in the future.

Acknowledgements

I am grateful to Bidda Jones of RSPCA Australia for information on live export disasters, Eduardo Santurtun for Fig. 6.4, Nationaal Museum van Wereldculturen. Coll. no. TM-60014403, the Netherlands, for permission to reproduce Fig. 6.5, World Animal Protection for permission to reproduce Fig. 6.6, *The Conversation* for permission to reproduce segments of articles published in this online journal and finally my wife, Alison, for proof-reading the Introduction and supporting my interest in this topic.

Introduction

Just as animals migrate to find new food sources, so humans have travelled to exchange goods, or trade, for millennia. That drive to explore has led us to a position in which we dominate ecosystems in most of the habitable parts of the globe. Trade involves sharing goods, offering them in return for other products or money. One of the fundamentals of trade is to increase the welfare of traders by producing goods in regions suited to the purpose so that they can be sent to regions where suitable conditions for production are not available. Such mutual benefit should help to secure peace between traders, but it may also cause discontent if there are attempts to exploit the importers or consumers in the importing nation, or if prices for the products are undermined in the recipient country. In international trade the threat of exploitation was very real historically because people have little tribal allegiance to those far distant from them. Early colonizers utilized this extensively; in the East Indies, China and many other parts of the globe, Western Europeans in particular used their military superiority to subject people in other parts of the globe to enforced trading for their own benefit.

Trade often ignores the externalities of production – the cost of pollution of the environment, for example. In addition the true costs of the commodities used to produce livestock products may not be taken into account. The water requirements may be from long-term aquifers that are not replenished and the nitrogen used as fertilizer is based on fossil fuels.

The first scientific book I ever read, *Animal Travellers*, described the remarkable feats that wild animals perform in their migrations around the globe (Vérité, 1961), and the book helped me to develop a keen respect for, and interest in, the natural world. Little did I know that these beautiful natural movements of animals would over the next 50 years become overshadowed by a massive growth in the movement of animals, dead and alive, for human consumption. Much of this expansion has come about since the time that *Animal Travellers* was written: the number of food animals exported annually has increased massively, pigs from 2.6 to 36.5 million, sheep from 6.5 to 15.2 million, cattle from 4.9 to 10.4 million and chickens from 0.8 to 1.4 million (FAOSTAT, 2014). In 2011, live agricultural animals worth US$19.9 billion were exported worldwide, more than double the value of animals exported 10 years previously (FAOSTAT, 2013). In the face of such major expansion of the animal trade, it is timely to examine its impact on our economies, diet, health and culture. This growth in the value of live animal exports is accelerating (Fig. I.1), and the keen observer will notice that:

1. The trade is a recent phenomenon, emerging in the 1970s.
2. The growth in the trade is not linear, but curvilinear.
3. There are cycles of increasing magnitude, of approximately 10 years' duration, with restraints to the growth in the mid-1970s, the early 1980s and finally the late 1990s. The magnitude of these cycles appears to be increasing, at the same time as growth increases exponentially, at least in recent years. This trend suggests that growth may be checked at some time in the near future. The causes of restraint to growth are many and varied – the oil crisis in the early 1970s, for example.

Livestock are not the only trade to have emerged from virtually nothing in recent times: the export from Kenya to the European Union (EU) of about 0.5 million t of vegetables, fruit and flowers, worth €1 billion, has emerged just within the last 20 years (Reiter, 2010). However, the livestock trade has a major impact on animal welfare and the diseases of humans and animals, which the plant trade does not have. Understanding the impact of the livestock trade on the welfare of animals is difficult, since we have a limited understanding of animal responses.

Humans have through the course of history had periods when they learned to exploit particular aspects of the natural world: the Stone Age, the Iron Age, etc. As well as standing out for its exploitation of fossil fuels, the current era also stands out for exploitation of animals. However, there is a subtle difference between the two resources we are most actively using at present. Fossil fuels will run out, but the potential for us to continue exploiting animals is just as certain as the fact that we will continue to use iron in all walks of life. Hence the Animal Age is another

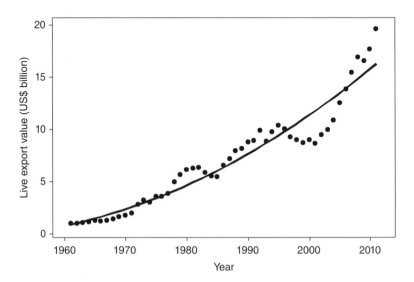

Fig. I.1. Growth in the value of live export animals over the last 50 years.

chapter in human development that singles us out as the most selfish animal species on the planet.

In any trade money is all powerful and the goal of making money can consume those involved. Nothing illustrates this better than the drive of the businessman to make money. In a recent film, *Arbitrage*, about a billionaire trading magnate played by Richard Gere, the climax of the film finds Gere face-to-face with his daughter, who is also his investment manager, to explain the corrupt and failing business dealings that she has just discovered. Gere tries to defend his fraudulent investments: 'We were going broke, everything was finished, we'd have nothing.' He briefly describes the venture, trying to paint a glowing picture:

> we had a great opportunity…we were making a fortune; but I'm not worried about it because it's still springing money, there's so much money coming out of this; you can't believe it; you can't stop it; and yes, I'm the oracle, I've done housing, I've bought credit swaps, I have done it all. Yes, I know how it's outside the charter but it's minting money; it's a licence to print money; for everybody, for ever; IT IS GOD. …'

A moment of silence, then: 'What did you want me to do; did you want me to let our investors go bankrupt? If I sell everything,…at least we'll get to keep the house.' And, raising his voice to fever pitch, 'IT'S MY JOB!' At this point his daughter replies calmly: 'It's illegal.' Gere, in desperation, 'You work for ME, everybody works for me.…I'm on my own path, it's up to you to move with it or against it. I'm a patriarch, that's my role.' Daughter, quietly: 'For a minute I thought you were going to say you were sorry.' She leaves. Gere whispers to himself: 'I'm sorry.'

The scene demonstrates how a billionaire had become obsessed with making money, and was prepared to gamble not just his wealth but also his family. What he did was ethically wrong, but he still compelled himself to do it. In the same way the largest of the animal industries are seen by many as ethically wrong, and all of the reasoning why these industries should continue may be as fraudulent as the billionaire's attempts to explain his own activities in the name of supporting the company, his investors, his job, his assets and even his family. We must never forget that major international companies trading animals exist for one purpose only: to make money.

Changing our use and abuse of animals could come quickly and requires everyone to know the facts; that is partly the purpose of this book. Media stars are increasingly used as the voice of the people in today's ethical debate. In our televisual world, they are regularly called upon to support activist groups' campaigns. For example, the recent attempt by People for the Ethical Treatment of Animals (PETA) to get foie gras[1] banned was supported by Sir Roger Moore, Dame Vera Lynn, Twiggy, Ricky Gervais, Joanna Lumley and Kate Winslet, amongst others. Telling people the facts about our consumption of animal products is one of the most important ways to influence the ethics of animal farming, and telling people about the impact of animal sports on their welfare and populations can also have a major impact on whether they are used or not. Legislation is slow to be enacted, and may be ineffective or unnecessary by the time this happens. For example, the use of animals in circuses and theatres in England became increasingly unpopular over the course of the 20th century, starting with serious activism after the First World War. English legislation did not come until 2015, by which time it was almost unnecessary because only two circuses and no theatres still used animals (Wilson, 2015). The change had been brought about by public pressure. At other times legislation is introduced for largely political motives, for example the banning of bull fighting in Catalonia in 2011, which was an attack on Spanish supremacy over the state. Politicians are reluctant to introduce animal protection legislation because the major beneficiaries are animals, who do not vote, and also because of the financial implications for those with vested interests. Increasingly consumer choice influences animal management practices far more than legislation.

This book begins with the origins of the animal trade, even though this is poorly understood. Were animals traded across Eurasia in the prehistoric period, or did they just accompany nomadic people to provide food and other products? It seems likely that when humans first started trading, their lives were intricately bound with those of animals. Animals fed them, clothed them, transported them, and even heated their houses. It is no wonder that the religious texts of the time attempted to assuage people's concerns about animal use by reassuring them that animals had been placed on the earth for their benefit. Traders went out to exchange animals and their products. James Cook, that most honourable of colonizers, took livestock with him that he thought would be useful, such as goats, to offer to the aborigines in new lands that he visited. In return he wanted meat for his crew – wild pigs usually – water and other essential stores. On his return during subsequent voyages he often found that the animals he had left had been butchered rather than allowed to breed. Systematic animal trade in the modern era continued with the fur trade in North America.

Over the last millennia the capacity to produce animals for the majority of the population to eat has signified a country's degree of development; almost impossible in heavily populated, under-resourced countries like India and China, but increasingly feasible in Europe and North America. Populations, animal and human, were controlled by the availability of high quality feed and food, respectively; hence it was natural for developing nations to seek to expand the availability of meat. Nowadays the population of most Western countries is controlled not by food availability, but by the availability of other resources, land for living, availability of financial resources to raise children, etc. This, coupled with the intensification of animal production in the developed world, has allowed the possibility of exporting animal products to developing countries to meet their growing demand. Hence Australia exports millions of livestock to Asia and the Middle East every year, in particular to the countries with inadequate land for rearing them themselves. Both Australia and New Zealand also send breeding animals, which is helping developing countries to expand their own production to meet internal demand. Some of these, in particular those in South-east and East Asia, are now becoming exporters themselves. Eventually, if intensive production systems continue to transfer from developed to developing countries, the animal production era may come to be seen as just a phase that countries go through on their path to sustainability.

As we plough headlong into stewardship of a world ecosystem that we barely understand, it is clear that the biodiversity that we have inherited is the key to survival. Two hundred years ago, a twinkling of an eye in evolutionary time, we did not even understand the basics of evolution; now we are grappling with the management of an ecosystem, in the Gaia sense of the word, that is not only evidently fragile, but showing all the signs of fraying around the edges. Biodiversity is a response to variation, in time, in space and in complexity. Variation in biodiversity over time is facilitated by reproduction, with longer lives for large animals, which require significant investment, than small.

Our struggle to manage the variation in ecosystems leads us into a quest for uniformity, symmetry, regularity. It is much more difficult to manage grasslands for livestock in the Australian climate than the British one, due to the much greater variation in the former, both within and between years. Hence lower stocking densities are usually adopted in Australia. The various livestock breeds require different management systems and offer different quantities, qualities and types of product. In the short term the most profitable method of utilizing the world's land resources to meet the growing demand for livestock products is to offer a universal blueprint, for the production of milk, for example. Take 100 standard cows of Holstein-Friesian breed; confine them in a building with a lying area and eating area; inseminate them artificially every 21 days until they become pregnant; extract milk mechanically twice a day; organize for a tanker to collect the milk from the farm on a regular basis. Since their inception in Holland, such systems have spread all over the world. Similarly with meat chicken production: take 1000 commercial hybrid chicks, imported at just a few days old from Europe, place them in a sealed commercial building at 0.05 m^2 per bird, with a temperature of 35°C, declining by 3°C per week, and automatic feeders, drinkers and lighting; 32 days later send in a harvesting team and transport product to slaughterhouse. This is easy – or is it? Soaring consumption of fast food, especially chicken, pigs and cheese is causing an explosion of diet-related non-communicable diseases worldwide – diabetes, cancer and cardiovascular, to name but a few. Meanwhile genetic diversity, our armoury against future change in climate, our precious resource accumulated over billions of years to allow fauna and flora to colonize environments sustainably, is disappearing faster than we can identify the very species we should be seeking to preserve.

The animal trade considered in this book is broad-ranging, including the export of live animals (Chapter 6), the trade in meat (Chapter 4) and other animal products (Chapter 5), the trade in companion animals (Chapter 8) and wildlife and exotic animals (Chapter 9). There is a focus not only on the sometimes alarming scale of the trade, but also its ethical and environmental impacts. In many cases the social implications are considered in some detail, as are trade policies (Chapter 2). Our quest for social equality grows day by day, as is necessary in an unsafe and highly populated world, but the movement to control the most unethical practices in the animal trade, such as the export of livestock, bears resemblances to earlier social justice movements. The arguments for controlling the live export trade focus on the pain and suffering by animals during and after the export process, as well as the immorality of the trade. The arguments made to defend the trade focus on the economic benefits that it brings: the people employed, the better opportunity to manage the animals well because the trade is profitable, the benefit to the recipient countries, in terms of procuring a better food supply in developing regions of the world. Very similar arguments were made in relation to the slave trade in the 18th century (Table I.1).

Table I.1. Similarities in the arguments made to defend export of livestock from Australia to Asia and those made to defend the slave trade led by the British in the 18th and early 19th centuries.

Livestock export from Australia to Asia, managed by Australia	Slave trade from Africa to the USA, managed by the British, amongst others
Arguments in favour	
The trade supports agricultural jobs in rural districts of Australia, where there are few opportunities for work.	The trade supported the British economy; without it the country would collapse. The Africans came from local wars and would otherwise have been executed.
The trade is good for the health and well-being of people in the importing countries of Asia.	The trade supported the economy of the agricultural industries in the southern USA.
Animals will be well looked after on farms because the industry is economically viable. Owners protect them, feed them and keep them healthy.	Slaves are morally and physically healthier than their counterparts in Africa. Owners protect them, feed them and keep them healthy.
Cattle and sheep from rangeland produce meat that is unfit for high-quality markets.	Slaves are unfit for any other work.
If we don't do it, others (our competitors) will, e.g. Sudan, and then the animals would be worse off.	If we don't do it, others (our competitors) will, e.g. France and the Dutch, and then the slaves would be worse off.
There are comprehensive Codes of Practice, which ensure the well-being of all animals during live export; it is a crime to mistreat an animal.	There are Codes of Practice, which ensure the well-being of slaves; it is a crime to mistreat a slave, e.g. work them more than 15 h/day.
The welfare of animals on ships is acceptable, mortality is low and declining.	The welfare of slaves on ships is acceptable, mortality is low and declining.
Livestock are property and can legally be traded.	Slaves are property and can legally be traded.
There is a need for inequality between species, the speciesist approach.	There is a need for inequality between races, there must be higher and lower sections of society.
The Bible sanctions humans to have dominion over animals.	The Bible sanctions the use of slaves, which is a natural state of mankind.

Continued

Table I.1. Continued.

Livestock export from Australia to Asia, managed by Australia	Slave trade from Africa to the USA, managed by the British, amongst others
Arguments against	
Economically inefficient to transport livestock, better to trade in carcasses.	Economically inefficient to use slaves, better to use less labour-intensive crops.
Socially detrimental to the country as a whole.	Socially detrimental to the country as a whole.
Morally wrong, whoever does it. Species have equal worth.	Morally wrong, whoever does it. Races have equal worth.
There are alternatives to using Australian rangelands for production of cattle and sheep.	There are alternatives to using slaves for labour-intensive agricultural production in the southern USA.
Damaging to Australian reputation internationally.	Damaging to British reputation internationally.
Bad conditions on the ships: ammonia at pathological levels, animals give up eating, space little more than each animal physically occupies, heat stress common, high mortality (estimated at 1% for sheep and 0.1% for cattle). Evidence of conditions provided by ships' vets.	Bad conditions on the ships: stench intolerable, slaves give up eating, space little more than each slave physically occupies, heat stress common, high mortality (estimated at 3%; Cohn and Jensen, 1982). Evidence of conditions provided by ships' doctors.
Bad conditions before the ship journey, long distance from source (e.g. New South Wales) to port (e.g. Fremantle). Conditions beforehand influence shipboard mortality.	Bad conditions before the ship journey, long distance from source (central Africa) to port (West Africa). Conditions beforehand influence shipboard mortality (Cohn and Jensen, 1982).
The Bible and Koran both support the immorality of animal abuse.	The Bible supports the immorality of slavery.

Such was the importance of slavery to the British economy that it took just over 100 years to eradicate it completely; in 1706 slavery was officially outlawed in England, but it was not until 1807 that it was finally abolished throughout the British Empire, after a century of debate between on the one hand the pro-slavery lobby and on the other the abolitionists (accused by the former of being atheists, socialists and communists). Some countries have banned slavery faster, and some slower; some continue to support it.

Our forefathers fought in the first half of the 20th century on the land, in the air and at sea to preserve a just and civil society, without the tyranny of a few. Following years of post-war prosperity and the emergence of a culture of greed, we must now fight in the hearts and minds of the people to oppose the industrial interests that seek to persuade people that long distance export of livestock is acceptable. These same interests are also supporting an ever-increasing consumption of foodstuffs that we know are destroying our health, our morality and the resources of the planet. Chief amongst these are animal-derived products, although sugar and salt are culpable and also perpetrated by large-scale industry. Let no-one suppose that the personal dangers in our struggle are in any way comparable to those faced by our forefathers, but the risks if we fail are just as great – tyranny by a few, food shortages worldwide, the degradation of our valuable land, air and water reserves and above all our sense of morality towards animals. All this could be accomplished within a few short decades, and is happening now.

The fight to restore sound and safe food production systems will use the social media in all its new forms, exposing the industries that perpetrate immoral exploitation of our precious resources – land, water, air, animal welfare and our rich cultural heritage – to produce foodstuffs that are unhealthy and addictive. Already this battle is being fought on the new lands being developed for intensive agriculture; in the Amazonian region, for example, where virgin forest is destroyed to produce agricultural land for the growing of soybeans and maize to feed chickens for a meat industry (Fig. I.2) that is now producing 12 million t/year, second only to the USA, which produces 17 million t/year (FAOSTAT, 2014). Brazil's chicken meat exports, at 3.6 million t/year, are the largest in the world; and this has all happened within the last 15 years (Fig. I.3). The energetic efficiency of chicken production is much lower than that of the staple foods that it replaces in the diet – rice and cassava mainly; approximately one-tenth of the energy input is harvested in poultry systems, whereas there is 15–20 and 60 times the energy input harvested in rice and cassava,

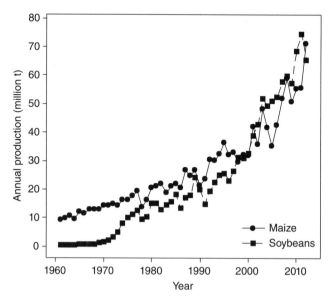

Fig. I.2. Growth in annual Brazilian maize and soybean production, 1960–2011 (FAOSTAT, 2014).

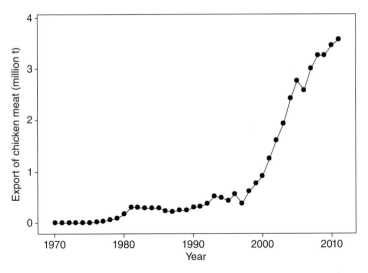

Fig. I.3. Growth in annual Brazilian chicken meat exports, 1970–2011 (FAOSTAT, 2014).

respectively. Comparing food production potential in Brazil, energy output from the land is much less for poultry production (6 GJ/ha/year) than for maize (15–30 GJ/ha/year), which has been known for almost 40 years (Leach, 1976). And poultry production is much more energetically efficient than the production of beef, sheep meat and pork.

The increasing adequacy of food supply for the world's population has meant that the proportion of people that are malnourished has decreased remarkably over the last 50 years, but because of increasing global population the actual number has increased. Hence there is no reason for complacency. In the least developed countries availability of one of the most important staple foods, cassava, has declined, from 46 kg/capita/year to just below 40 kg/capita/year currently (FAOSTAT, 2014). Meanwhile cereals availability increased for these countries from 132 to 149 kg/capita/year. Meat availability increased by just 3 kg, from 10 to 13 kg/capita/year, whereas over the same time period meat availability in the USA increased by 30 kg from 90 to 120 kg/capita/year, in the UK from 70 to 85 kg. In Eastern Europe it increased from 41 to 62 kg, in Asia from 5 to 30 kg. Thus most of the additional meat produced has been for people in the developed or rapidly developing countries, not those in the least developed countries. The gap between those in the USA and those in Asia, in terms of meat consumption, has widened. Furthermore, whereas in 1961 each person in the USA consumed annually on average 80 kg more meat than those in least developed countries, particularly in Africa, in 2009 they consumed 107 kg more. About 18% of the world's population live in extreme poverty and 13% are malnourished. Thus the increased production and trade in livestock is not reaching the world's poor, but is feeding the growing middle-class population around the world. Will this increase still further in future, as global inequality increases and those with a growing income demand a meat-based diet, which is inefficient to produce? This seems likely and we should take steps now to encourage sound agricultural systems that efficiently produce healthy food for the entire global population. This will be easier if the world's population stabilizes this century, as anticipated, with the fertility rate having dropped overall from about 3.0 to 2.5 children per woman in the last 15 years. However, the rapidly escalating trade in animal products brings risks of increased human and animal disease and loss of animal biodiversity (Chapter 7), as well as an unstable food supply (Chapter 3). At the end of this book these trends are analysed to form the basis of an analysis of future prospects and impacts of the animal trade (Chapter 10).

Note

[1] Fatty goose liver produced mainly in France and Hungary and traded as a delicacy around the world.

The History of Animal Trade

1

1.1 Introduction

Our ancestors existed as hunter gatherers, and before that as anthropoid apes. The hunter gatherers had varied diets, which gave them security as a population against climatic extremes that favoured certain plant and animal types (Milton, 2000). The costs and risks of procuring meat and animal products were high and many were primarily gatherers. However, meat, once it was obtained, was a concentrated source of energy and protein, the most important nutrients that they required for survival. Not only did hunter gatherers in different parts of the world have quite varied diets, depending on availability, they were also free to migrate to utilize different fauna and flora sources, depending on the season and weather patterns.

Settled agriculture, adopted over a period of just a few thousand years beginning about 10,000 years ago, offered the opportunity for higher yields from plants and animals that were farmed in small areas. However, the static nature of this activity and the enhanced resource requirements of this form of food production, in the form of a regular water supply and a nutrient-rich soil, increased exposure to climatic and seasonal extremes. The inevitable variation in productivity could only be absorbed into a successful existence if humans cooperated with neighbouring groups, so that food surpluses in one region were transported to others where the need was greater. Thus our cognitive skills in organizing this trade, coupled with our highly social behaviour, combined to make plant and animal raising a viable alternative to hunter gathering when societies cooperated by trading in surplus goods.

In parts of the world characterized by low rainfall, the rainfall is also highly variable. Settled agriculture would have been particularly unpredictable, and in these regions hunter gatherer communities persisted at low density until relatively recently, for example the Aborigines of Australia and !Kung bushmen of the Kalahari desert of southern Africa. Such communities were small, isolated and self-sufficient, without the need or capacity to trade. However, encouragement from the governments of these regions for the nomadic populations to settle and pressure for the land that they occupied to be utilized for extensive livestock ranching has encouraged some to adopt this farming method themselves.

At the same time as animal husbandry spread from the Fertile Crescent of the Middle East to Europe and other parts of the world, an animal-centred mythology developed in the human populations. Myths were their inner language that represented their fears and hopes, which were a living testament to their sense of morality. They came to be associated with religions, again with strong animal-related symbolism. The Old Testament of the Bible and the Koran both contain many admonitions to look after animals well, particularly cattle and sheep, which were the basis of animal agriculture in the Fertile Crescent. In Hinduism gods took mainly animal forms, a strategy to encourage humans to look after animals well and a means of assuaging their concerns about using animals in the way that they did. While it seems likely from the evidence of cave paintings and rock art that animals featured strongly in the aspirations of hunter gatherer societies, and may even have had religious significance, it also seems likely that the inclusion of animals in mythology and religion assumed a new meaning during the establishment and early pursuance of animal agriculture. For example, the ancient Egyptians had a number of gods based on cattle, of which Apis was the most famous. These cattle were revered for their strength and virility, but still ritually sacrificed on a regular basis, demonstrating a combination of dominance over the animals but appeasement of their spirit for taking their life. The Israelites worshipped a golden calf amongst other deities, but were encouraged to adopt monotheism. Crete became an important trading post in the ancient world and it is here that we see some of the first evidence of trading in animal products, dating from the period between 2000 and 1500 BC when woollen textiles were sent to Egypt, then itself a major civilization. As in the Fertile Crescent, Cretan animals were centrally engrained in society's folklore, including a mythical minotaur that had the head of a bull and the body of a man.

The development of an animal trade was predicated upon humans owning animals, or their products. The concept of ownership of animals probably arose originally from our use of animals to assist in hunting, but it achieved much greater significance with the development of animal agriculture. Deeply engrained in human culture, animal ownership was initially respectful, saying prayers for the soul of animals, for example, when they were robbed of their lives in a hunt. Large animals offered more than could be consumed by the hunters themselves and so, as society advanced and humans began to specialize in different tasks, meat would be shared with the rest of the community, in return for work by members of the society that specialized in other tasks – flint knappers, bone carvers, shamans and potters. Crucially, this sharing of tasks enabled knowledge to be passed between generations, and thus skills advanced over time. Such a society is more likely to be successful than a society where everyone is able to perform every task. Thus as society progressed only a proportion engaged in the hunt, and later in animal agriculture an even smaller proportion of society was involved with animals. The domestication of animal and plant species further facilitated settled agriculture and its ability to support a greater population of humans than hunter gatherer societies, but it also made the population more susceptible to climatic extremes. Animals were able to buffer these extremes through their ability to gain and lose body weight. Good weather allowed cereals and grasses to grow well, providing surplus to supplement the livestock. However, in bad weather or in preparation for winter animals had to be slaughtered because of food restrictions, whereas hunter gatherers would continue to take animals, even if this meant following them or encouraging them with food to stay close to the humans. Thus society evolved to domesticated animal keeping from harvesting animals from the native fauna when required, to keeping animals at the homestead, which resulted in surpluses and shortfalls as conditions varied.

Settled agriculture allowed humans to accumulate artefacts that nomadic hunter gatherers could not. As society became more sophisticated goods began to be traded to make best use of resources in different regions. Animal products played a part in this, for example shells formed an early currency in many parts of the world, beginning 3000–4000 years ago. The cowrie shell from the Maldives islands became the first form of Chinese money. About 3000 years ago, ivory from elephants' and other animals' tusks was sent from the Indus valley to be purchased by the Egyptians. The Chinese were the first to learn how to make silk by unravelling the threads of the silk-moth's cocoons, a skill that led to a trade that gave its name to the 4000 km trading road through Asia, the Silk Route. This was a primary trading network across Asia and into Europe. Assisted by the development of pack animals, in particular the camel and the horse, the routes, for there were many, allowed exchange of silk and other goods beginning about 2000 years ago. As well as silk, the ancient trading route from China through the mountains of Nepal and Afghanistan, and eventually to the Mediterranean brought sheep, tallow and other animal products. The price of delivering silk from Asia to Europe was high, but was reduced, and the security of delivery improved, when ships came to be used across the Indian Ocean. However, the trade routes also spread disease, particularly when ships were used, with conditions on board that were perfect for the spread of disease. Most notoriously a bubonic plague called the Black Death was spread by fleas on small rodents travelling from East to West, reaching Europe about 600 years ago.

These forms of long-distance trade in luxury durable animal products may have been matched by local trade in perishable products, but there is little record of this happening. However, the major livestock species were probably traded as they made their way from the centres of domestication, especially south-western Asia, including Mesopotamia, for sheep and goats, and central Africa for the earliest domestication of cattle, to almost all parts of the globe. As an early example of such trade, chickens and camels crossed the Indian Ocean to Africa to be used in agriculture, and probably such trade also introduced zebu bulls to be mixed with the domesticated African taurine cows.

1.2 Early Developments in Livestock Trade

The first opportunities for trade in animal products in the agriculture period would not have been possible without the development of the sail and wheel in the Neolithic period (8th–4th millennia BCE), as well as pot containers in which to hold agricultural products. Initially land was seen as publically owned, but over time specialized areas for animal farming were created, owned by individual families.

However, for most of the history of domestic animal use in agricultural systems, over approximately the last 10,000 years, each farmstead had a small number of animals, cattle, sheep and goats mainly, that directly met their needs. The majority of the population lived on the land and opportunities to trade in farm animals or their products were limited. Where this did occur it is believed to have contributed to diffusion of culture. Mostly however the trade was in low-volume, high-value items such as exotic materials and semi-precious stones. Regrettably, with the development of trade came the advancement of warfare (Rothman, 2004).

One of the main limiting factors was fodder supply in winter. Before the development of techniques to conserve fodder, livestock were often slaughtered before the onset of cold weather, with just a small number of breeding stock retained. Standing fodder was used for winter feed for these remaining animals, often in forest clearances where trampling losses could be controlled better than in large fields. Before the development of the scythe in the 1st century BCE, grass could only be harvested in small quantities with a sickle. The scythe, operated by two hands, could be used to harvest enough grass to be stacked around a pole and left in the field over winter until needed for stock. Shaping the grass stack so that it had a roof allowed most rain to run off, minimizing the leaching losses. Such techniques were increasingly used over the 1st millennium CE and allowed herds and flocks to increase in size. Eventually this allowed surplus animals and their products to be sold in the growing concentrations of the human population in towns and cities.

Continuous cropping of the land, for both grain and straw, reduced its fertility, and livestock were as much valued for their ability to return fertility to the land as their products. Livestock excreta also assisted in the breakdown of straw before its return to the land as farmyard manure. However, the ability to harvest the excreta and transfer it to arable land was limited. Night corralling of livestock was common but transport of the dung to the land was tedious before horses and carts were utilized. Hand cultivation of the soil was slow and it was not until around 1000 CE that animal-drawn ploughs were developed, cementing the essential place of cattle and horses in feudal systems of agriculture. After this major breakthrough in integrated arable and livestock systems, it was not until the development of mechanized agriculture in the 19th century, in particular tractors and metal ploughs, together with artificial fertilizers, that livestock could be dispensed with on arable farms. Stabling was also introduced and eventually conservation of grass as silage, rather than the hay, which had lower nutritional value, further allowed for intensification of livestock farming.

1.3   Expansion of the Role of Livestock in the Ancient Civilization of the Inca Empire

The Inca tribes of South America developed a sophisticated system of agriculture that included livestock in the highlands and crops cultivated on lower land (Mazoyer and Roudart, 2006). At its peak 15 million people were fed from intensive agriculture that stretched from the Pacific Ocean, across the Andean highlands to the Amazonian plains, a distance of 300–400 km, and for 4000 km from north to south. The climate and terrain are challenging, the plains between the sea and the mountains rarely receiving rain and the hilly terrain limiting cultivation, except by hand. What rainfall there is falls irregularly, influenced by weather systems generated in the Pacific, which were even less predictable to the ancient Inca than they are today. Nevertheless, in the 13th–15th centuries a highly specialized system of agricultural production evolved, with livestock on the higher ground and crops lower down, often on terraces and irrigated by a complex system of water conduits. Although the society was largely agrarian based, livestock, in particular llamas, alpacas, guinea pigs and chickens, were used for food, wool, leather, pack animals, fertilizer producers and even as a currency. Livestock accumulation was one of the only methods of growing rich, the society being organized on egalitarian lines.

Given the highly variable climate and challenging terrain, the Inca had worked out a system of food storage in silos to avert hunger in times of adverse conditions. They knew that food had to be transported around the kingdom, otherwise social and political unrest ensued, and pack animals were crucial to this. The main pack animal was the llama, a large camelid with appropriate adaptation to long distance transport, being surefooted, tolerating a varied diet, and easily handled. They can carry 35 kg about 30 km/day. The transport of goods by this early example of a complex society is believed to have contributed to cultural development. Bulky, low-value items, such as food, were transported short distances and it was only high-quality goods, such as the much-prized obsidian, that were transported long distances. One of the items that was extensively traded throughout the empire was textiles, including woollen goods from llamas and alpacas. The system was successful, but it eventually failed suddenly on the arrival of invaders from Spain, aided by their horses, swords and exotic diseases, none of which was known to the Incas. These diseases included a mange that afflicted llamas, resulting in the deaths of two-thirds of the population of this vital animal in Inca society (Chepstow-Lusty *et al.*, 2007) and paving the way for the introduction of Old World herbivores: cattle, sheep, goats and horses.

One of the lessons of the collapse of Inca agriculture is that intensification brings risks of the system failing when any part is threatened. The system managed by the Incas worked well in the face of considerable climatic and agricultural difficulties. But new challenges proved too much for it and it collapsed within a few years of the Spanish invasion. Less intensive systems show resilience to outside influences, maintaining a smaller but more sustainable population.

1.4 European Livestock Trade from 1066 to the Modern Day

In Europe development of animal production systems lagged behind that of the Incas until the demise of their empire. However, after that period European systems began to develop rapidly. Europe led the intensification of animal production systems in the 19th and 20th centuries, but first we need to consider animal production before that time and its position in relation to agrarian production.

1.4.1 Animal production and trade in mediaeval times and the Middle Ages in England and continental Europe

Following the Norman invasion of England in 1066, and subsequent installation of many lords of the manor, English village agriculture was initially based on rotation of pasture and arable land. The expanding population favoured the use of land for the latter purpose, to provide cereals for the staple food at the time, bread. The diminishing numbers of sheep and cattle caused the arable land to decline in fertility. In the 13th century successful London merchants often bought country estates, rather than there being merchant dynasties (Chambers and Mingay, 1966, p. 201). Later, the intimate mix of merchant and agricultural interests gave British agriculture a dynamism and entrepreneurial advantage over many of their European competitors when intensification was required. However, in 1348–1350 the Black Death pandemic dramatically reduced the population, and hence the pressure on land use was eased. It took 150 years for Europe to fully recover, but by mediaeval times the expansion of wool and milk production resulted in sheep and cattle, respectively, being traded over considerable distances to replenish stock in English royal manor houses, including some coming from continental Europe (Chambers and Mingay, 1966, p. 8). By the middle of the 16th century sheep farming was transforming from its domination by baronial and monastic organizations to a new breed of yeoman farmers with ownership of the land or long-term tenancies. These farmers developed large flocks throughout Great Britain, with centralized stores so that wool could be traded. Often it was not the cloth that was traded, but the wool itself, with the best weavers to be found not in England but in Flanders. The Hundred Years War with France was in part to protect England's woollen trade with Flanders, and resulted in many Flemish weavers fleeing the hostilities to establish themselves in East Anglia. The wool trade brought prosperity to the best grassland areas of England and continental Europe, which fostered a trade in other animal products. This trade was most prominent in pigs, pork being a favoured food of the ruling classes. The wealth created during the Middle Ages and the trading strengths that developed encouraged merchants to import animal products from overseas. Cattle hides were included in the many goods imported from the Baltic States into London and Amsterdam under the Hanseatic League that controlled trade in northern Europe.

1.4.2 Agricultural intensification in Britain in the 18th and 19th centuries

To meet the growing demand for food for an expanding British population more land was enclosed, facilitating the co-existence of arable and pasturing of livestock.

This renewed the pattern of intensification of production to meet the demands of the growing population. Enclosure facilitated expansion of farm enterprises, and small farms were gradually becoming unsustainable. Enclosure Acts in England legalized the removal of small farmers, producing protestors such as the celebrated agriculturist Arthur Young in England: 'All I know is that I had a cow, and an Act of Parliament has taken it from me' (Chambers and Mingay, p. 98). Soil quality began to be improved by fertilizing with manure, and marling of light land, rather than fallowing. A major problem was the availability of fodder for winter feeding of livestock, but with improved soil fertility and dedicated fields this could be addressed by using suitable leguminous crops, such as clovers, and root crops. These were widely used for winter feeding by the 17th century, which allowed the best livestock to be kept for breeding. By the 18th century the selective breeding of livestock of high genetic potential for beef and wool production was being pioneered by farmers such as Robert Bakewell in England, where the limited land availability meant that improvement of livestock breeds was favoured to increase output. Animal trade began in earnest and 75,000 cattle and 500,000 sheep were sent annually from the rich pastures of the southern counties, East Anglia and the Midlands to the Smithfield market in central London by this time (Chambers and Mingay, 1966, pp. 10, 33). The upland areas of Scotland and Wales also came to be used more intensively for livestock production. The Scottish Highland's sheep population increased from less than 0.5 million in the 1750s to more than 2.5 million in the 1870s (Collins, 1978, p. 17). This was facilitated by both clearance of the land of smallholders by brutal landlords and the breakdown of the clan system as a result of the Napoleonic wars. Roads from the more remote regions, which had hitherto just been used by drovers, were improved to allow more trade. Mining brought prosperity to many remote parts of Britain and for a time it appeared that this would permanently transform the upland economy, 'bringing wealth and people (who would) by consuming the provisions, bring the soil to be cultivated, and its cattel consumed at home' (Collins, 1978, p. 18). However, demand for animals was still relatively elastic compared to cereals, which were required to produce the basic foods of bread, porridge and beer (a safer drink than water, which was often contaminated). This led to more consistent prices for livestock than cereals, whose price fluctuated widely with meteorological conditions. The industrial growth increased demand for livestock near the busy mining districts. Livestock were, however, subject to regular disease outbreaks, such as rinderpest of cattle, which diminished supply. For most of the 18th century the improvement of land and livestock production was not sufficient to keep pace with the increasing population in Europe, leading to ever increasing prices. Increased prosperity in the urban population led to a growing demand for meat and milk, a trend mirrored by increased demand in Asia in the late 20th and early 21st centuries. However, by the late 18th and early 19th centuries Europe was at war, which resulted in rapid price escalation in the UK due to suspension of the animal and grain trade with continental Europe.

Regular famines were commonplace, especially in wartime, and there was little time or money for trade in goods other than food for the majority of the population. In northern Europe the growing population of cities such as London promoted the animal trade. Pigs were often produced on dairy units, fattened on skimmed milk and whey or with the use of brewing by-products. Cattle brought in from Wales, Scotland, Ireland and even continental Europe were fattened nearer to London on pastureland. They would be required to walk 10–20 miles per day and were shod to protect their hooves. Sea and rivers had to be swum across, and cattle were tied nose to tail and had a noose around their lower jaw to keep their heads above water (Chambers and Mingay, 1966, p. 31). Occasionally they crossed in barges. They were often bled to provide sustenance for the drovers. In the early 18th century Daniel Defoe reported while on a tour of England that there were about 40,000 cattle coming annually from Scotland for fattening, mostly around London, but increasingly to the north of England during the Industrial Revolution. He also observed hundreds of thousands of store sheep being sent to the southern downlands for fattening from the more northerly counties of England. Turkeys and geese were driven on foot or in carts from East Anglia to the capital. Animal products were largely transported on England's waterways, including Stilton cheese with its accompanying maggots and mites, and across to continental Europe in times of peace. Better roads allowed animals to be driven further to market, including in winter, which encouraged specialization across the country. Mutton began to be replaced by lamb as the main meat from sheep.

At the start of the 19th century most animal production was as a component of a mixed farming feudal system, with landlord and tenants, who were often little better off than serfs. The growth of trade in agricultural animals was a response to industrialization and the development of the cities. Eggs and meat started to be brought in from neighbouring farmlands. In Europe this process developed slowly with the gradual change in agricultural systems of the 19th century. Feudal systems gave way to more widespread land ownership or proper tenancy agreements. This process was initially led by northern Europe, in particular Great Britain, Belgium, northern France and Germany, with the rest of the world remaining predominantly self-sufficient rural societies. Fertilizers and animal improvement in the 19th and early 20th centuries increased output so that surpluses could be marketed. In the period from 1840 to 1870 large volumes of guano, or accumulated bird excreta, were extracted by indentured Chinese labourers from the Pacific islands off Peru and shipped to Europe and the USA for use as fertilizer (Chambers and Mingay, 1966, p. 174). Restricting the volume sold to British merchants artificially inflated the price and made a small number of Peruvian businessmen wealthy, especially those close to the president, who had nationalized the industry (CHA, 2011). However, it was not long before exhaustion of supplies, development of a nitrate industry in the Atacama region and global recession together cemented a rapid collapse of the industry and eventually plunged Peru into poverty and war. This example serves as a reminder of the danger of plundering of resources that was all too common in the 19th century (recently a sustainable guano mining industry has emerged in the region, with indigenous labour, decent wages and sustainable extraction).

Back in European rural communities, most food and clothing were home-made and meat consumption was rare. Meat was reserved for holidays, if at all, and even bread was largely baked at home. Milk from sheep, goats or a house cow provided the main source of animal-based protein. Eggs were the main animal product that could be sent to market, with refrigeration technology not yet developed to allow the preservation of meat. Some Irish salted beef began to be marketed as corned beef as early as the 17th century for the benefit of the British naval fleets and North American armies. However, hides and tallow were the main tradable products from the keeping of cattle, and meat was for home consumption; sheep were kept primarily for their wool. Malnutrition and nutritional deficiencies were common and often followed the weather patterns and quality of the harvest. Emergence from this peasant economy was desperately slow.

In the 18th and early 19th centuries, Britain led the first agricultural revolution that changed the fabric of society, largely in response to increased demand for food following industrial development and growth of cities. Fields were enclosed, which gave greater control of their use and reduced overstocking of common grazing lands, which had seriously limited the production of livestock. Early maturing breeds of sheep and cattle were developed that could be fattened in one or two seasons, respectively. These were smaller, more rotund animals, such as the down sheep breeds that emerged in southern England and the Hereford cattle from central England. By reducing the size of the animal and the time taken to get the offspring to an adequate fat cover, the number of breeding animals that had to be maintained to produce marketable animals in a specific time could be diminished. This released land for fattening livestock. The fat content of the meat was more valued than nowadays, because of the use of tallow in candles and because of its high energy content that manual workers needed.

The first half of the 19th century in Britain was a time of agricultural revolution from another perspective. Protectionist policies for agricultural products were tested and found wanting. Rapid fluctuations in agricultural product prices during the war in Europe at the beginning of the century led the British government to attempt to guarantee fixed prices for the most erratically priced commodity, cereals. A sliding scale of taxes on imported cereals, dependent on the home price, was introduced through a series of Corn Laws. This encouraged farmers to grow cereals rather than produce livestock and supported the income of the landed gentry, who were politically much more influential then than now, at the expense of affordable food for the masses, who were politically less important. Landowners commanded two-thirds of the seats in Parliament and were more numerous in the Tory than Whig party (Chambers and Mingay, 1966, p. 153). However, the demand for free trade grew with the evident iniquities of such a tax and it became a political issue. In France the inequalities between rich and poor had led to a widespread purge of the aristocracy during the Revolution, and British politicians were wary of a repeat of this at home. Supported by such radicals as Jeremy Bentham, a notable utilitarian at the time, the Corn Laws were eventually repealed in the mid-19th century, encouraged by a depressed economy and famine in Ireland. For a few years, cereal prices dropped sharply, but inclement weather for a few years restricted supply and livestock flooded on to the market. Lean times were unsurprisingly accompanied by disease outbreaks in the cattle – rinderpest and pleuropneumonia in particular – and the government experimented with movement restrictions and compensation payments for slaughtered stock. However, the market stabilized somewhat within a decade and many arable farmers turned increasingly to livestock production and, at a time of expanding home market, actually saw an increase in their profits. Imports from the New World grew, mainly of cereals, with livestock products being difficult to transport, at least until the last quarter of the 19th century when refrigerated transport made it possible for South America and South Africa to export meat to Europe, with the inevitable reduction in price. Between 1850 and 1900 exports of wheat from the USA to Europe expanded fivefold, at the same time as the wheat price fell by more than one half (Mazoyer and Roudart, 2006, p. 369). Oils, fats and wool also flooded into Europe, with devastating effects on home production. Wool and cereal production in England reduced by one-half, even though it was efficient compared to other countries. The sheep flock in France and Germany was reduced by one-half between 1870 and 1914 as a result of growing wool imports from Australia. The rest of the century saw an increase in agricultural commodity transport, with European farmers being unable to resist the competition from areas with the best soil, lowest labour costs and most innovative farmers. The competition resulted in widespread intensification, often led by the younger generation of farmers, many of whom had been educated in the new methods in agricultural colleges established in the second half of the 19th century. Mechanization increased and this began to compensate for the high labour costs that had previously required the involvement of women and children at times of peak labour requirement, such as harvesting.

This was an early example of the impacts of free trade in agricultural products and its benefits for the consumers. Advocates of free trade argued that it would lead to cheaper food, more employment, more exports and increased prosperity. The middle class industrialists in particular were afraid that the high cost of food would render the meagre wages paid to factory workers inadequate. Opponents of free trade argued that there was instability of income for the landed gentry at home, which reduced their capacity to employ, and feed, the rural population. In Britain the issue pitted the landed gentry against the industrialist, and on this occasion the latter won. It was also a class issue, an attack on the aristocratic landowners by the rapidly expanding middle classes, and an early stage in the process of globalization of food markets.

In a foretaste of prominent debates of the 20th and 21st centuries, Richard Cobden, a prominent free trade advocate at the time, lobbied for a free trade in land, as well as corn, which he hoped would lead to a land-owning peasantry. A lesson of the Corn Laws and their Repeal was that fixed prices were generally undesirable. A free trade in livestock and their products had been created, which expanded from 1875 to 1900 by 300% in the case of British meat imports (Chambers and Mingay, 1966, p. 209). Increased prosperity raised the demand for meat and dairy products, with reduced consumption of bread. Not everywhere was aided by the industrial growth. Areas of upland Britain without mining growth saw unprecedented decline because the free market policies adopted allowed food products to enter from the continent without restriction. Poor soil and weather prevented farmers in the remote parts of Britain from improving their production, with low returns from use of fertilizers and intensive cultivation. Improved transport, particularly with the coming of the railways, facilitated competition to supply nearby towns and cities with their food requirements, aided by peace in Europe through most of the 19th century. Thus the more mobile elements of livestock production – capital, labour and entrepreneurship – migrated from the upland areas. Mining areas too went into decay in the late 19th century, accelerating the upland decay. Thomas Telford, the engineer who orchestrated improved transport to remote parts of Britain, berated the Scottish landowners that had cleared the crofters from the land to make way for sheep and hoped that improved transport to the region would prevent the decline. It was not to be and local interests were subsumed by national interests.

Similarly land leasing was under scrutiny, with short-term leases and restricted farming methods, for example a fixed 4-year rotation in Norfolk, England, failing to encourage investment. Free trade was again advocated, leading to greater flexibility in production and an ability to meet changing market demand. The ability of the land to feed a growing population was a popular topic in the early 19th century, with Thomas Malthus famously predicting an ever increasing gap between food production and world population of humans. Nearly 200 years later, the debate is still not concluded. The agricultural revolution of 1750–1880 in the UK highlighted tensions between landowner and industrialist, whereas in reality the latter, and the population as a whole, were dependent on the former to invest in their land to increase food production. Such investment could only be justified over a long period of time.

High rents, disease outbreaks and income taxes encouraged many British farmers to emigrate, mainly to North America. But British colonization was also spreading further afield. The lost access to America in 1776 following the War of Independence started a search for other territory in which to deposit their criminals. Australia, discovered 12 years later by Cook, and occupied by an indigenous population of just 300,000 living in about 500 disparate small tribes, provided the perfect solution. In the biggest land annexation since the 16th century, British convicts were given land on which to produce grain, cattle and sheep. The Aboriginals had no legal redress as they were unable to give evidence in court, not being recognized as a civilized people. The competitive individualism of the white settlers, otherwise known as squatters, benefited them when compared to the communal ownership and reciprocal rights philosophies of the Aboriginals. The settlers even believed that they had divine instruction to till the land and that agriculture had civilizing virtues, the latter being a belief that had some validity since most of the crime existed in the relatively lawless towns at that time.

In 1808 George III was shown a coat made from the wool of Merino sheep taken originally to Australia from his own flock in 1805. The Napoleonic wars had made it desirable for Britain to find a reliable source of wool from outside Europe. Britain was industrializing and its woollen manufacturing factories in the north needed a constant supply of high quality wool to produce garments for the burgeoning middle class. Increasing from just 8% of Britain's wool for manufacturing in 1830 to almost 50% in 1850, Australian wool production grew as fast as squatters could clear the land. Capital was readily supplied from Britain. Surplus sheep carcasses were boiled down to produce tallow, which was then returned to Britain in drums to make candles.

1.4.3   Animal trade in the 20th century

In Europe the First World War brought rapid changes in land ownership as a result of high male mortality in many countries. At its simplest level, the war increased demand for animal products, which supplied high quality food for the troops. This brought a temporary restraint to the depopulation of the upland areas of Britain that had been suffering decline for about 30 years. At the same time the proletariat revolution in Eastern Europe resulted in the creation of cooperatives and land banks, which assisted peasants to buy their own land, purchase equipment and market products. In 1906, 80% of Russian peasant land was held communally (Wasserstein, 2007, p. 23). However, in 1929–32 forced collectivization of the farms brutally transformed the Russian countryside, with expulsion of many peasant farmers to Siberia and removal of others to work in the heavy industry that was being developed in and around the cities. In much of the rest of the world subsistence farming was still common at the beginning of the 20th century and trade was often by barter. In the more prosperous parts of Europe, English country towns for example, shops emerged where people could buy animal products and other necessities. In the cities department stores were established, led by such notables as Harry Selfridge, who opened his first store in London in 1909, and Charles Harrod, who opened a small store in Knightsbridge in 1840, which by 1911 employed 6000 staff. In continental Europe cafés became established, 30,000 in Paris alone in the early 20th century. By 1914 annual meat consumption in Germany and England had risen to 50 kg per person (Wasserstein, 2007, p. 27), not far short of the 80 kg per person that it is today. Elsewhere markets were the main trading opportunity, other than itinerant pedlars.

In the New World, trade in basic commodities, such as animals, proceeded even more rapidly than in the Old World. In Quebec, for example, there was strong growth following the harmonization of British–French relations and development of the fur trade in the late 18th and 19th centuries, which was made possible in part by the ready supply of eggs, poultry and the meat of deer, caribou and moose from the farmlands of the Levis area on the opposite shores of the St Lawrence (Porter, 1961). Horses, oxen and even dogs were used to pull the goods on sleds to the city on the hill.

Back in Europe, because of its propensity to deteriorate rapidly, milk was initially produced in the cities from small numbers of cows kept in yards within the city confines. The development of refrigeration and rail travel enabled milk to be produced in farms that were remote from their market. For example, in England, rather than being produced in the city, the 19th-century development of a widespread rail network enabled milk to be increasingly produced from cows grazing the rich pastures of the western part of the country, Somerset and Gloucestershire in particular. Livestock could also be brought to market by rail, ship and barge with less loss of live weight than if they were droved. The accompanying intensification of animal production included importation of high quality supplements for livestock feeding, use of more fodder crops, yard feeding and the recycling of livestock bonemeal as fertilizer. The British government made low cost loans available for agricultural improvement, payable over long periods; a wide variety of dependent industries benefited when livestock products were readily available: shoe and harness makers, soap boilers, candle makers, cutlers and glue manufacturers. Developments in steam transport also affected the fishing industry. It made trawling more effective, with larger boats driving the small boats out of business and decimating the inshore fishing grounds. Employment in the fishing industry of the Scottish Highlands declined from 30,000 in 1900 to only 13,400 by 1938 (Collins, 1978, p. 23).

The majority of the lower classes in Europe had existed on a diet consisting largely of home-grown food in the early 19th century: staples such as bread and butter and potatoes. However, over the course of the century meat importation from Argentina and Australia grew, providing high quality protein in the diet. Britain was the world's largest trader when the animal trade, along with other trades, developed during the 19th century. That process was aided by a largely free trade with low interest rates (Wasserstein, 2007, p. 8). Although Britain's share of world trade fell in the lead up to the First World War, from 20% in 1876–1880 to 14% in 1911–1912 (Wasserstein, 2007, p. 11), her merchant fleet was the largest in the world and represented one-half of all motor and steam tonnage. Her shipyards launched twice as much tonnage as the rest of the world put together. She was ahead of the rest of Europe in the development of railways and an interurban road network was beginning to be developed.

By the beginning of the 20th century can openers had been invented and tinned food was widely traded. Beef was salted (corned) or boiled (bully-beef) and was particularly important for the troops in the world wars of the first half of the 20th century. During the First World War, the numbers of livestock kept in Britain were restricted in order to increase the land devoted to cropping. Towards the end of the war shortages of meat and lard resulted in escalating prices and led to rationing. In addition to meat and lard, cheese and butter were also imported, but the German U-boat activity that devastated merchant shipping in the middle of the war came close to bringing the war to an early close (in Germany's favour) by starving the British of their food importations; 111 submarines aimed to deprive Britain of food in this way. However, after a large number of the merchant ships had been sunk in early 1917, the British, with their superior naval forces, developed a system of using convoys of ships, and sometimes also used aircraft to chaperone their merchant ships on their routes, largely transatlantic, to Britain. This safe passage, together with the entry of the USA to the war after the damage done to their shipping became intolerable, changed the course of the war (Wasserstein, 2007). Ironically, these merchant ships also devoted space to the transport of performing animals, so important were animals to the entertainment industry in the UK (Wilson, 2015, p. 27).

The animal trade, and the trade in other important food commodities such as grain for bread, played a role in the outcome of the First World War, but on a broader scale it was also implicated in the reasons why such an apparently futile war was fought. Britain had been amassing colonies at a rapid rate throughout the 18th and 19th centuries and these had become successful trading partners. Amongst these, Australia and New Zealand had developed a highly successful trade in meat, wool and butter, which supported the growing industrialized population in Britain. In time of war Australian animals also had their role to play, with about 136,000 horses being sent with the First World War troops to assist in transporting them and hauling supplies, equipment and ammunition. France had also colonized much of Africa and that other major European power, Spain, had long held territories throughout Latin and South America. Germany, by contrast, had little territory abroad to support its industrial growth at home, yet it was to some extent at the intellectual and regal heart of Europe. Hence the major reason for this most wasteful of wars was the territorial ambitions of Central European states, led by Germany. Indeed the entry of minor partners into the war was usually determined not by the considered moral rectitude of the action, but by potential territorial gains for the partner should they prove to be on the winning side. The Second World War followed the first because of the humiliation of the Germans at the end of the First World War and the punitive reparations imposed by the allies. Even at the start of the final year of the First World War, 1918, it had looked like it might end in Germany's favour, yet the Allies showed little mercy in the treatment of their foe and widespread starvation ensued.

The First World War was accompanied and succeeded by socialist revolutions in Russia and spreading across much of Eastern and Central Europe. Food shortages led to the old monarchies and their bourgeois followers being largely thrown out in favour of proletarian rule. In Russia the development of agriculture along Western capitalist lines had involved expanding farming by individual families, developing agricultural education, focusing on land improvement and developing credit lines for farmers. By the first decade of the 20th century this was reversed. Surplus products had to be surrendered to the government for a fixed price, initially just bread and fodder, but later in 1919/20 including meat. Private sales were prohibited.

A major drought in Russia in the early 1920s halved the grain harvest and, humiliatingly for the Russian leaders, the USA provided relief aid to the beleaguered peasants. However, the situation had eased by the mid-1920s and by the middle of the decade the losses in livestock that had occurred since 1913 had ceased (Wasserstein, 2007). An easing of the transformation of agricultural land ownership allowed some return to private enterprise, which was Lenin's final legacy before his death in 1924.

Communism and the collectivization of agricultural production

Communism, with its collective farming principles developed under Stalin in the late 1920s, spread across much of Central and Eastern Europe where the proportion of the population engaged in agriculture was in excess of 75%, compared with less than 50% in most of Western Europe. Release of the Russian peasantry from serfdom in the late 19th century, even though requested by the peasants themselves, had led to an inequitable distribution of land. The Russian government took this as an opportunity to experiment with collectivization of both land and the peasants' livestock, aggregating them into commonly owned units of 5000–10,000 ha, with little regard for traditional villages. This they believed would provide opportunities for more mechanized production, increasing output, as well as quelling any potential political dissent from a troublesome sector of society. The result was exactly the opposite. It was strongly resisted by the peasants, who slaughtered their livestock for food and hoarded the grain, which resulted in mass deportation of 'kulaks', or the most affluent and successful farmers, to distant agricultural labour camps.

Although the world wars did nothing for Germany's territorial ambitions (in fact they lost significant territory), they did heighten the tension surrounding the politics of the commercial food production sector in a way that was to set the pace for the 20th century. The Germans fiercely opposed collectivization, releasing land from this mantle, that was perceived by many Russians as coming from the devil himself whenever their temporary territorial gains allowed it. Communism embraced cooperative farming principles, whereby workers contributed to mass food production in huge cooperative, or communally owned, farms. However, salaries were meagre and many peasants hoarded the grain they produced or resisted the forced labour schedules, viewing the new system as just a new form of serfdom. The Soviet leaders had grandiose, and to many unrealistic, ideals, and through the course of the first half of the 20th century collective farms increased in size, from an average of 3500 acres in the 1940s to 16,000 acres in 1960. State control too was increased after the Second World War in a further attempt to make them sustainable.

Although the collective farms were considerably larger than the peasants' holdings, even larger State Farms were also created, either from struggling cooperative farms or using spare land and landless workers. These were essentially run as factories, set up mostly in the period from 1960 to 1980. Most were specialized for production of a particular commodity, e.g. milk or meat. Each worker played his (or her, for women were involved equally) part, men taking more mechanical roles, women usually responsible for jobs that involved animals, milking, cleaning animal sheds, etc. Workers sometimes had small plots themselves to allow them to produce extra commodities, many of which would be taken to local markets for sale. However, during the peak periods of collectivization even this was forbidden as it was seen to promote individual production, which was supposed to be forfeited for the benefit of common good. The Communist system prided itself on full employment, and ideology was essentially egalitarian, with the farming system organized by a central committee. Planning and forecasting was introduced on a grand scale, but often the targets were unrealistic and led at times to neglect of the environmental considerations of land management. Massive fields were constructed and machinery to match, leading to soil erosion; herbicides and pesticides were used indiscriminately, sometimes with dangerous consequences.

Communism embraced mechanized production, which was seen as one of the advantages of the massive farms that had taken the place of small family units. An inevitable consequence of this wide-scale system of production was increased trade, at least internally, including animal products. In theory at least, products could be made in parts of the Soviet Union where they could most efficiently be produced, milk from the lush pasture of the Baltic States for example, and transported around the empire. Forced transmigration of peoples around the Soviet states enabled workers to be placed where it was most strategic to do so; however, this was also driven by a desire to reduce nationalist tendencies by mixing the various races in the vast area dominated by communism.

In the late 1920s agricultural trade was badly hit by a severe drought in the USA. The hardship was exacerbated in Europe by political instability following border changes after the First World War and economic disparity as a result of the high level of reparations from Germany to Britain and France and from Britain to the USA for First World War costs. International trade slumped by 60% in 1929/1930 and wool prices, for example, declined by 46% (Wasserstein, 2007). Many farmers had to revert to self-sufficiency, especially the peasants in Central and Eastern Europe. They relied on horsepower, a single house cow and had little access to capital that would enable them to invest in mechanized production, as for example could those in Britain (Wasserstein, 2007). Meat largely disappeared from the peasant diet. Transfer of land tenure in the central and eastern states was frustrated by nationalistic tendencies following border changes after the end of the First World War. Governments preferred to transfer land to their own nationals in the new territories, even though they often had not the skills to efficiently farm the land. Many countries retreated from democracy, for example in Italy where Mussolini led the country to embrace Fascism and a totalitarian government.

Free trade was progressively challenged in the late 1920s with a creeping protectionism that was used to safeguard markets. By the 1930s free trade was largely abandoned, with import duties often averaging 50% (Wasserstein, 2007). Britain was one of the last to change, but increasingly adopted an imperial preference for trade with its colonies. Import duties had a beneficial effect on Britain's upland livestock industries, which had been suffering from European competition in the latter part of the 19th century. International institutions were not sufficiently well developed to control the situation. The League of Nations, the forerunner to the United Nations, was in its infancy and the international monetary conferences that preceded the founding of the International Monetary Fund had little useful outcome. National boards were established to regulate supply and pricing, such as the Milk Marketing Board in the UK, established in 1934.

The massive experiment with collective farming in Central and Eastern Europe and much of Asia continued almost unchecked until the later stages of the 20th century. In it workers were responsible not to themselves, or their families, but to the state. It was present not only in the Soviet empire; communist ideology of forced collectivization also spread to other regions, from Albania in the south, to Lithuania in the north, and eastwards spreading across the Asian continent to Mongolia, China and Vietnam. Collective farms often were turned into state farms and enlarged.

However, it was becoming increasingly clear that workers' diminished responsibility to their family for their work led to low levels of commitment and massive inefficiencies. Collectivization was associated with high levels of bureaucratic controls, often with little regard to local conditions. Goals were set for production over 5-year periods (the notorious Five Year Plans), but these were often unreasonable and unattainable. Achieving targets was not helped by the infiltration of corruption deep into the managerial system.

Livestock-keeping systems that had evolved over hundreds of years in central Asia were replaced by collectivized agriculture. In Tibet a nomadic system of keeping yak, Bactrian camels, cattle and sheep on the highlands of the Tibetan plateau had proved efficient at utilizing the scant resources available. Pastoral nomadism, or transhumance, ensured a transfer of animals from low ground to high ground in summer and on return surplus animals were sold, which enabled the pastoralists to buy essentials such as wheat flour for bread making (Kreutzmann, 2013).

The impact of communism on pastoral nomadism over the last half century has varied between regions of Asia (Anon., 2011a). In Kirghiz there has been forced settlement of much of the high ground pastures, including the erection of fences to contain stock and create identifiable 'farms'. At the same time there have been townships built to facilitate marketing of livestock products and provision of services, including agricultural extension. This has been supported by external subsidies from central administration. Another approach has been settling the nomadic pastoralists into low lying areas between the mountains and desert, with transfer of stock between high and low ground by vehicle, rather than the traditional movement on foot. Production in the low-lying areas is supported by animal housing and the availability of stored fodder, in the form of silage or hay. Arguments made to support the transition include the modernization of livestock keeping, including better health care for their stock, and the opportunities to limit grazing of degraded pastures, allowing them to regenerate. In addition, the lifestyle of the herders is generally improved, with access to basic resources, such as health care, electricity, clean water, housing, schools, cultural centres and shops (Kreutzmann, 2013). Nevertheless, this approach threatens the cultural heritage and lifestyle of the nomads, which is viewed by many as idyllic and sustainable.

In Tibet, which comprises 68% alpine rangeland, the Chinese invasion in the 1950s and subsequent forced collectivization left a huge resentment of the attempts to interfere with Tibetan culture, including livestock keeping practices. At its worst in the early 1960s, the Chinese authorities forcibly seized thousands of tonnes of animal products and grain in lieu of taxes. Workers' enthusiasm for animal production declined as a result, which together with forced settlement in communes resulted in widespread famine between 1968 and 1973, when a third of a million people died (in comparison, Stalin's purges of the countryside and the famines of Soviet lands are estimated to have killed approximately 11 million people). In the Tibetan occupation by China, animal grazing on mountain pastures was restricted and livestock slaughter controlled by central authorities without regard for their condition and suitability. In 1978 Deng Xiapeng started the process of decollectivization with dissolution of the people's communes (Kreutzmann, 2013). Since that disastrous period in Tibetan agriculture there has been relaxation of central planning control, with a re-emergence of pastoral no-madism in parts of Tibet. However, the settlement of large numbers of Chinese in Tibet since the 1980s has placed an enormous strain on the food resources available, threatening food security again. More recently the progression of the Chinese economy into a market-based system has produced pressure to utilize Tibet's precious land resources for the benefit of all of China.

The Second World War

In the Second World War, food supplies were once again used as a weapon of war, just as they had been in the First. Before the war, Britain imported approximately 60% of its food supply (Ministry of Information, 1945). During the war food sup-plies to the civilian population were limited because of the reduced labour avail-ability on farms (men being required on the battlefields and both men and women for the production of armaments), insufficient opportunity to transport them safely, both nationally and internationally, and increased food demands for the troops. Women were enlisted to work the farms of the warring nations, and by the end of the war 80% of workers on Soviet collective farms were women (Wasserstein, 2007). Britain replaced 98,000 men on the land with 117,000 women (Ministry of Information, 1945). Early territorial gains by Russia, in league with Germany, led to an expansion of collectivization to Poland, Belorussia and Ukraine in a pro-gramme of Russification of the newly acquired territories.

Limited food stocks led to rationing and a thriving black market. Eggs and poultry were smuggled from neutral Ireland to Britain, for example. Rampant inflation led to the devaluing of many currencies and gold or barter was often used for trade. Under a Lend-Lease agreement, food supplies continued to be exchanged between America, Britain and the Commonwealth. Tinned meat pro-duction doubled in the early war years in response to troop needs, beef and pork being the most common meat traded in this way. This trade in food supplies be-tween America and Britain, albeit under a blockade, prevented the British from facing the starvation that devastated the populations of many Central and Eastern European countries. Butter and meat were nevertheless rationed, and nutritious but new foods such as whale meat and spam[1] were introduced as substitutes for the traditional meat supplies. Mock meats were constructed with ingenuity, 'goose' from potatoes, cooking apples and cheese for example. Nevertheless, there was widespread reduction in calorific intake at the very time that extra nutrients were needed for labour. This was partly dependent on one's ethnic background; for ex-ample, in an instance of appalling Germanic racism, the allocation of staples to Jews was only 30% that of Germans.

The Russian retreat from the front with Germany in 1941 in a Soviet Union much expanded to the west not only temporarily halted collectivization, it resulted in grave loss of farm production. The 'scorched earth' policy holding sway over vast swathes of Central and Eastern Europe required farmers to drive away their cattle and destroy anything that would be of value to the advancing German army.

Not surprisingly, agricultural output declined dramatically as a result of slaughter of herds, and a shortage of both draught animals and manpower. In 1943 output was just one-half of its level of 1940 and it did not recover until the end of the war. Soviet industrial and armament production recovered rapidly, however, and this was crucially underestimated by Hitler. As the war progressed, and the eventual outcome for the German nation began to become apparent, many farm animals were again requisitioned by the Germans in their over-run territories 'for the benefit of the Reich'. Removal of cattle and horses from Polish farms, for example, rapidly reduced the population to starvation.

During the war the US/Britain-led Allies were able to use their access to food supplies to their advantage, withholding food from neutral Spain, for example, unless they limited supplies of iron ore and other strategic raw materials to Germany. Food was still in short supply, but not to the same extent as in Russia, where millions starved to death. British farmers were encouraged to increase food production by converting pasture to cropping land, and over 1.5 million ha was ploughed up for this purpose. Farmers' duty to the children of Britain was emphasized, in their quest for increased production. 'England expects...' was a common dictate to farmers of the day, a protected occupation. Although dairy cow numbers increased, numbers of beef cattle, sheep, pigs and poultry plummeted, by 400,000, 6.3 million, 2.5 million and 19.2 million, respectively. 'The dairy farmer, in addition to making his direct contribution to the granaries of this country, has now to fill his own barns, rickyards, silos and mangold claps with animal feeding stuffs grown on his own farm in order to feed his herd and thereby provide the people of this country with one of the essential and most valuable foodstuffs – milk. Life is going to be harder for him, but he can take it' (Ling and Egdell, 1941). Milk was seen as an essential food to provide nutrition in the place of meat, butter and eggs. Not everywhere did stock numbers decline – in the Scottish Highlands where lax grazing had allowed the ingress of bracken, deer were shot out on the mountains and replaced by sheep and cattle (Ministry of Information, 1945).

Wool supplies from Australia assumed a new importance for serge battledress for the troops. However, the popularity of wool was short-lived; after peaking in the 1950s the wool prices steadily declined in response to competition from artificial fibres and less need for warm, hard-wearing clothing. Wool, which had been Australia's most valuable export for much of the 19th and early 20th centuries, had had its day.

We can now reflect that the German plan for a much expanded Reich, with supplies of food sent from satellite states in the periphery of the empire to the fatherland, was only narrowly averted.

Post-war food supplies

After the war, the victorious Soviets exacted a terrible price from the territories in Eastern Europe that they had occupied in their advance to Berlin to overthrow the German army. Large numbers of people were forced to move east from Central European countries to work in the Soviet collective farms. Communist governments were introduced into these countries and in 1949 the Soviet Union

established a Council for Mutual Economic Assistance, or Comecon. Although formally bound by ideology, this group was established initially to further economic ties between the Soviet Union and the Central European states. It was established in part in response to Western European plans, through Marshall Aid, to support countries with market economies and a free currency. In 1950 the Soviet Union adopted a more autocratic role and the Comecon agreement was restricted to practical facilitation of trade within the region.

Soviet responses were partly a reaction to events in Western Europe, which was unifying at a rapid pace. One of the stimuli to unification was the growing tension in the late 1940s between the Soviet and Allied zones in Berlin, with the latter isolated in the Soviet-controlled part of Germany. Berlin itself had been divided into French, American, British and Soviet administrative sectors at the end of the Second World War. Eventually, in 1949, the Soviets blockaded the Allied sectors by severing their road and rail supply lines from the west. Food supplies in the Allied Berlin sectors ran perilously low and the Allies attempted to airlift food in. Stalin desisted from challenging them, knowing that if the planes had been attacked it would probably lead to a third world war.

The establishment of the European Economic Community in 1958 united Belgium, France, Italy, Luxembourg, the Netherlands and West Germany in free exchange of goods, workers and capital. At the same time there were several factors that led to a desire in Western Europe, and Britain in particular, to intensify animal production, a move that was facilitated by an increase in trade. First, continental Europe and Britain had been exposed yet again in the Second World War to being dependent on food imports, as it had in the First World War. Attempts to increase food from British resources started in the war itself, employing such schemes as ploughing up permanent pasture to grow more productive sown pastures or other crops, using non-traditional labour on farms and increasing the genetic potential of animals and plants utilized. Intensification was introduced in part to reduce between-animal contact by placing them in cages and hence improve the capability to reduce infectious disease and control individual feeding. Also, inactive caged animals needed less feed and rapidly became fat, an important nutrient for a human population used to hard physical work. Better control of hygiene was possible in intensive housing, but the close contact between animals was eventually to lead to an increased risk of epidemics in the animal population. At first antibiotics, which were just being introduced in the middle of the 20th century, were effectively and routinely used to control diseases, but resistance and novel diseases have since assumed a new importance.

Another factor favouring intensification was the shortage of labour on the farms, after millions were killed during the war (in all of Europe, but most in Germany and the Soviet Union). Although the intensification movement was not obviously led by either of these countries, the large collective farms in the Soviet Union had barns with long rows of individually tethered cattle where they had been pastured or in small sheds beforehand. A less recognized factor in the acceptability of intensification of animal production was the wide-scale suffering that people had witnessed or personally experienced in the war years, and the resulting failure to recognize that close confinement caused any serious degree of animal suffering in intensified systems.

By the mid-1950s poultry production had changed dramatically and was at the vanguard of the livestock industrial development. 'Since … 1935, the pattern of poultry-keeping in England and Wales has undergone great changes. Economic considerations have stimulated a very great interest in intensive methods, while specialised poultry-keeping has recovered from its war-time depression and is already exceeding in importance its pre-war standing' (MAFF, 1955).

The 1960s heralded an era of relatively rapid growth and improvement in Europe and most other developed regions of the world. The austerity of the war years and their immediate aftermath became a distant memory for many. In Britain the continued industrialization, and the absence of rationing and national service, encouraged a spirit of experimentation with new technologies, including more intensive animal management. Human life had only recently been wasted irrationally, in two World Wars, and caged animal systems which did nothing more than deny them their freedom must have seemed relatively harmless by comparison. Increased ownership of refrigerators, for example in France from 17% in 1957 to 90% in 1974 (Wasserstein, 2007, p. 378), enabled households to more safely store meat, raw and cooked, and dairy products. Self-service supermarkets were introduced, with competition from major retailers that required farmers to lower their costs of production. This led to expanding farm size, to maintain profit levels, facilitated by opportunities offered to feed the growing populations in the cities. To limit the ensuing rural depopulation, the European Commission introduced a Common Agricultural Policy, which provided support to small farmers in Europe. The support stimulated production, creating surpluses that distorted prices and frustrated countries, such as the USA and Australia, that did not support their farmers. Ultimately many of the surpluses, such as the 'milk lake', had to be controlled with quotas to avert conflict with the free trading countries. From the 1950s to the 1980s the General Agreement on Tariffs and Trade (GATT) encouraged liberalization of trade, and formed the precursor to the World Trade Organization (WTO), which was founded in 1995, with broader representation than GATT.

The push for intensification pervaded not just the pig and poultry industries, but also cattle and sheep production, which revived areas of the hills and uplands, in Britain for example. Improved pastures, with faster growing varieties of grass that responded to the application of artificial fertilizers, better access to the hills and more controlled grazing all combined to increase output of cattle and sheep.

However, as animal production intensified to meet increased demand from the growing middle classes, a social movement started that rejected the use of intensive housing systems, such as small cages for chickens and narrow pens for farrowing sows. A seminal work, *Animal Machines*, by Ruth Harrison (1964) captured and encouraged the mood of rejection by the public in 1964. Predictably it came from England, at the vanguard of animal intensification and also one of the bastions of free speech and democracy in capitalist Western Europe. It led to the formation of a technical committee to enquire into the welfare of animals kept under intensive livestock husbandry systems, headed by Roger Brambell. Their report (Brambell, 1965) stated that farm animals should have freedom 'to stand up, lie down, turn around, groom themselves and stretch their limbs'. In 1967 Britain was the first Western country to establish a body to provide independent and scientific advice to government on animal welfare, the Farm Animal Welfare Advisory Council.

Western European governments generally favoured a high level of control of agricultural systems (and other aspects of society) and subsidies/welfare payments to those in need. In much of Western Europe food was locally produced and traded, and on the continent a greater proportion of the population was engaged in agriculture than in more industrialized Britain. Maintaining people on the land was seen as a goal, in contrast to the USA and Australia, which have more readily witnessed and accepted widespread rural depopulation with the growth of industrial production in urban and suburban zones. Furthermore, given the strong culinary heritage of continental Europe, maintenance of high quality food using traditional methods of production was strongly supported, and the emergence of convenience 'fast' food of poor quality rejected. When the economics of the maintenance of a small-scale rural agriculture was questioned in Europe in the 1980s by net contributors to the European Economic Community, such as the UK, the leaders of countries like France and Germany made it clear that this was an important part of the fabric of their nations.

The Western systems of food production also attempted to embrace the philosophy that food could be produced in regions most suited to the purpose; this was one of the founding principles of the Treaty of Rome that inaugurated the European Common Market in 1960. At the same time, eating habits were changing due to less physically demanding jobs, requiring less high-energy food, and central heating in houses and offices reduced demand both for high energy food to keep warm and for woollen garments that retained heat better than their artificial counterparts. The proportion of the population engaged in agriculture continued to shrink rapidly, with increased mechanization and larger, more efficient farms. In former communist countries this trend was even more exacerbated because the state farms had been a large user of surplus labour, which was abruptly halted following collapse of the communist states. In Western Europe rural pursuits like hunting came under sustained attack from urban dwellers, who failed to understand the necessity for such blood sports. The new eco-idealism favoured the production of agricultural products without cruelty to animals and without the use of potentially noxious chemicals.

In the Comecon countries the advance of television enabled viewers to become aware of the increasingly affluent lifestyle of those in the West. One of the commodities that was most commonly in short supply was meat. Soviet leaders agreed to subsidize livestock products to keep retail prices affordable, and feed-stuffs were imported for this purpose, in particular high quality oilseed products.

Beginning in 1989, the communist apparatus was systematically and suddenly dismantled in the face of overwhelming support for capitalist enterprise. The material success in the West had encouraged a revolution in favour of a system based on individual enterprise. Enforcement of power by secret police and corrupt governing bodies added to the disillusion with communist regimes. Ironically for many, in particular the elderly, meat consumption actually declined, as imports of livestock products and feed were almost wiped out overnight. A poverty-stricken sector of the population emerged, which was widespread in the early years of the 1990s, and reverted to a staple diet of bread and potatoes.

Communism was not the only authority to crumble; the church in Western Europe saw a steady decline in influence over the last quarter of the 20th century, aided by an ultraconservative pope, John Paul II, who failed to take account of the liberalization of ideals towards homosexuality and abortion in particular. Western governments too found their power diminishing in the vanguard of campaigners for women's, homosexuals', ethnic minorities' and animals' rights. Many opted to appeal to the centre ground in an attempt to secure the democratic licence to govern. Power to the people went hand-in-hand with the liberalization of trade worldwide, creating a generation of ideologues in the name of capitalism.

The capitalist system of production was based on allowing individuals the chance to develop successful, independent enterprises, which were essentially market-led. The old monarchies of the early 20th century, with their power and opulent splendour, were mostly dismantled, or were retained only symbolically. Whereas communism had narrowed the divide between rich and poor, the loss of opportunity to advance personal wealth, the corruption at the head of communist governments, and the setting of and failure to reach unrealistic production targets combined to erode confidence in Marxist ideals. A new set of oligarchs emerged to lead large multinational companies, often with interests in food production that gave them a power that rivalled the pre-revolutionary monarchies in Europe in the early 20th century. The new McDonald's in Pushkin Square, Moscow, which opened in 1990, symbolized an avid embracing of the Western diet. Coming as it did at a time when the price of bread and milk quadrupled in 1 year, it demonstrated the enthusiasm of the former Comecon countries for fast food. The re-entry of Russian troops into Ukraine in 2014 prompted Western countries to impose sanctions, to which the Russian government responded by closing the Moscow McDonald's, ostensibly because of health concerns (Marson and Jargon, 2014). Evidently the availability of Western-style fast food in Russia had become a major political football.

After the rapid exit of communism from Europe in the early 1990s, Nestlé and Mars began to peddle their wares as avidly as the Western cigarette manufacturers. However, hunger became widespread in several of the former communist countries after the Soviet empire collapsed, mainly due to escalating food prices following economic liberation. In Romania the new government distributed salami from the private stockpiles of the secret police (Securitate) to combat the poverty. Meat shortages in the 1980s had led to the manufacturing of soya-based salami, and foreigners, or rich Romanians returning home from overseas, were heralded as those 'who did not eat soya-based salami' (Buscu and Catavencu, 2010). After a belated rescue package by the G7 nations stability returned to Romania, but the proletariat, and in particular the pensioner population, struggled with poverty for many years.

The Western European proletariat, if indeed it still existed in the relatively classless society that was emerging, was not immune to change; indeed an ability to change with public sentiment was one of the characterizing features of capitalism. Early on the society showed evidence of embracing ideals based more on ecological and libertarian values than on any allegiance to a crumbling set of morality standards established by the church. In the 1960s and 1970s students in the expanded higher education system of post-industrial Europe clashed repeatedly with their authorities to espouse a desire for freedom of expression. Into this miasma emerged a radical youth that later came to challenge the might of the major industries and, more profoundly, advocate respect for all life forms and the integrity of the planet's flora and fauna. A new philosophy was born to rival the power that Marxism had inflicted on much of the world 100 years earlier. Nowhere did the growing philosophy of respect for life and freedom to live as one wants have the power to inflict greater change than in our diet. Although meat consumption has expanded worldwide in recent years because of a growing capability of Asians to purchase meat, in some Western countries demand has diminished or stagnated due to ethical and health concerns (see Chapter 4).

Free enterprise was literally the trademark of the new Europe, facilitated by the adoption of a common currency. Nevertheless, the vast diaspora of people in the European continent and the cultural diversity made for an uneasy common market. Issues like animal welfare and environmental impact of animal production systems were more carefully controlled in some regions than others, leading to inequalities of market externalities that artificially manipulated production economics. To make matters worse animals and animal products were imported from outside the European Union (EU) because countries there were not subject to EU legislation.

The last few decades of the 20th century saw the expansion of large-scale animal production in many regions of the world, in response to changing socio-economic circumstances. Nowhere did the animal trade develop faster than in the Americas at the end of the last century, as exemplified by one of the largest companies involved, Cargill Inc. The enterprise started almost 150 years ago when a young American, William W. Cargill, bought a grain store in Iowa. The company expanded to include a wide range of food production and processing enterprises, prospering most in times of food shortage, such as the world wars of the 20th century and more recently with the diversion of grain to produce biofuels and to feed an expanding world population. Global revenue from sales is now in the region of US$120 billion per annum, with earnings of US$2.7 billion. The company is still 90% family owned and employs 130,000 people worldwide. Now with undisclosed personal fortunes estimated in the billions, the Cargill family is one of the richest in the world. In Australia the merger in 2012 with beef processing giant Teys Bros provided the expanded Australian division with the opportunity to manage the entire food chain from production of feed to processing the carcasses of 1.5 million beef cattle per year.

In recently colonized countries, the USA and Australia in particular, the strong work ethic from the pioneering days and desire for convenience led to the emergence of a fast-food culture. Food was increasingly obtained in just a few minutes from a local 'take-away', rather than being elaborately prepared at home. This allowed both partners in a family to work and enabled them to pursue their goal of ever-increasing living standards. Some British colonies, including Australia, New Zealand and Canada, had little food heritage, unlike the African nations that had been colonized by Mediterranean European countries. In the former, convenience products such as homogenized beef were enjoyed by the masses and supported by trade with Britain. Most of the European powers retained some trading connection with their former colonies, which were mostly formally relinquished in the 1960s. The ready acceptance of fast food paved the way for the development of large-scale food animal industries to mass produce the necessary animal ingredients. The USA and Australia favoured development of large enterprises; it is ingrained in their culture, which places emphasis on personal freedom to develop businesses, with limited government intervention. This has led to the development of many interest groups, which seek to lobby government on individual causes. The relevant governments have become subservient to these interests, which diminishes their ability to act in the national interest. Farming interests, by virtue of their historical importance and appearance of representing a vulnerable group of people, are strongly supported. This explains how farming activities, such as the export of livestock long distances, can be supported by government when they are apparently not supported by the majority of the population of Australia.

In contrast to this, most of Western Europe, Africa and South-east Asia have continued with small-scale agriculture, supported in Europe by government subsidies organized under the Common Agricultural Policy. However, within the last few decades this has started to change in some developing countries, supported by importation of grain or destruction of indigenous forest to support home-grown animal production. Emerging and other developing economies in Latin America and Asia are changing their diet over a period of perhaps 20–40 years, compared with the 100 years that it took in the West (Guyomard *et al.*, 2013). In the first stage the quantity of food available increases and calorie intake increases. After this there is a transition away from consumption of cereals and vegetables towards increased consumption of animals and animal products, particularly those with a high fat content, and a transition to a 'mature consumption market' (Guyomard *et al.*, 2013). These changes are driven by urbanization, economic growth and demographics, together with increased food processing and supermarket sales. At the same time livestock production has become more specialized, with advances in animal genetics, nutrition and a farm structure that is increasingly based on hired labour, borrowed capital and importation of feed and fertilizer on to farms in large quantities. However, even with rapid production growth in a few key developing countries in Latin America and Asia, especially Brazil and Thailand for poultry, developing country importation of animal products has grown far more rapidly than in developed countries. Currently approximately 80% of export trade in ruminants and poultry is in the hands of just five countries. For pigs it is less, about 20%, and imports are slightly less concentrated into a few key countries than exports (Guyomard *et al.*, 2013). This raises serious concerns about the risks that volatile markets could pose to developing countries. Under these conditions, small increases in grain prices could have catastrophic effects on affordability of the products. Growth in animal production in developing countries is logical as it is cheaper to transport grains than animals, and the developing country itself has the benefits of low labour costs and the opportunity to add value.

1.5 Conclusions

The trade in animal products is several thousand years old and since its beginnings it has consistently grown, but most rapidly in recent years with the onset of globalization in the world's commodity trading. During its growth, there have been many models followed for animal production, which have impacted on the way in which animal products are traded. In the early days feudal systems were largely self-sufficient, but with serfs yielding a portion of their production to the lord of the manor. This was followed by the beginnings of industrialization of agriculture in the 18th century, coupled with the development of an urban population with the potential and desire to consume animal products. The development of improved transport facilitated the process of rural areas supplying animals and their products to the cities. At the same time, there were proletariat revolutions in the 17th to early 21st centuries that demonstrated reluctance on the part of the peasantry to accept serfdom as a system of agricultural production. After this the world divided, with a large sector having egalitarian styled, communal land ownership imposed by government, with the rest of the world allowing entrepreneurs to develop their own animal production enterprises, with a focus on the capital growth of their businesses. Both systems facilitated major growth in animal trade within each of the two sectors. A more rapid pace of growth in living standards in the capitalist system caused the rapid collapse of most of the world's communist regimes, which then embraced the capitalist ideals. The 21st century has seen the emergence of large multinational animal trading companies. At first this was focused on the developed countries, but as trading restrictions eased with a move towards free-trading markets, the developing countries increased their animal production and now export at a rapidly growing rate. The sustainability of this growth will be tested over the coming century, as the challenges of environmental impact and concerns about the welfare of mass-produced animals escalate.

In the light of the central position of the animal trade in the transition from hunter gatherer societies to settled agriculture, it is relevant to consider the implications for animal ethics. Surely animals were put on the earth for our benefit and we can use them as we wish, or were they? Philosophers have long argued for equal consideration of interests in animals and humans, principally to maximize happiness and minimize suffering. This might seem at odds with nature, which seeks to allow some animals to exploit the interests of others, through predation or parasitism for example. However, the philosophers and anyone that has thought deeply about the subject come to the conclusion that this exploitation is ultimately detrimental to the harmony of humans and animals on the earth. In humans a failure to recognize the interests of other humans leads to racism, tyranny and war, and similarly our failure to recognize the interests of other sentient beings leads to extensive suffering on their part, and because of the intertwined nature of human and animal lives, also to humans. Even though Darwin tried to play down the impact of his discovery of natural selection for our understanding of the suffering of animals in nature, it was a fundamental change in our thinking. In his seminal essay on the origin of species Darwin (1859) wrote 'We may console ourselves with the full belief, that the war of nature is not incessant, that no fear is felt, that death is generally prompt, and that the vigorous, the healthy, and the happy survive and multiply.' His discovery of nature's harsh methods of maintaining appropriate species in a varied ecosystem had damaging impacts for about a century in justifying artificial selection of supposedly superior humans and animals. If animals exposed each other to untold cruelty in the name of natural selection, surely it was acceptable for humans to keep animals in conditions in which they suffer for the benefit of humans? It was not until the 1970s that a substantial movement towards recognizing equality of interests in humans and animals began with the writings of Peter Singer (e.g. Singer, 1975). This movement began to redress the damage caused by the integration of Darwinian principles into our moral behaviour, causing a belief that the methods of nature were acceptable for human–animal interactions. This movement had at its core the belief that the minor human benefit from farming animals for food did not justify the major impact on their welfare. While considered extreme in its infancy, it has gained more widespread support in recent years and is likely to be an accepted principle in the future (see Chapter 10).

Note

[1] Special army meat. The poor quality of the meat led to the term eventually coming to mean useless electronic messages.

Trade Policies for Animal Products

2.1 Development of Trade Policy

Trade is a natural activity for a species that is very social, highly communicative and mobile around the planet. Humans evolved as an opportunistic species, seeking out new environments to occupy. When the majority of the habitable areas of the planet had been colonized, several thousand years ago, humans naturally turned to trade to cement relations with people in occupied lands for mutual benefit. Through trade they could obtain goods that they could not produce or obtain at home, and in return they offered goods they were able to produce or could produce more easily, or economically, than those in the lands they visited. Trade also developed relations between peoples of different cultures, allowing fringe benefits to be had through the cultural exchange that ensued. Inevitably, it required a degree of trust between the traders, concerning delayed payment for example, or the benign intent of visitors. In some cases trade was a smokescreen for an attempt to take over a region, and thus great caution was required on the part of the hosts for a visiting party.

In the early stages of trade development the goods exchanged were mainly luxury items, precious stones and metals in particular, but also durable animal products, especially ivory from animal's tusks and silk from the cocoons of the silk worm. Later, as populations grew, there was a need to trade in goods of a more basic nature, which included agricultural produce as people became concentrated into towns and cities and lost their connection with the land. Only the largest political entities, such as the Soviet Union, were able to develop economies that embraced most of the needs of the people without much external trade. There was also a dependency of developing countries on developed ones by virtue of bilateral trade between these two groups of countries. The low prices that were paid for basic commodities and raw materials from developing countries, together with high prices for value-added goods and intellectual property, often protected legally by patents, enslaved the developing countries for many years. In addition, the reliance of developing countries on export of a small number of products to just a few major importers made them vulnerable to fluctuation in exchange rates and the potentially devastating effects of climatic change. These risks prevented such countries from developing at the same rate as the industrialized nations, further widening the gap and leading to unrest and corruption. This undesirable situation has been reversed in the last few decades in many developing regions, most notably Asia and South America, as they negotiated better terms for trade and used their resources wisely. In such cases the large labour forces, rather than being a drain on the economies, have become a benefit when harnessed towards efficient production of higher value goods previously only produced in developed countries.

In parallel with the growth of international trade was the emergence of major international companies that have come to rival national governments in their degree of influence on public consumption. Initially these transnational corporations focused on raw materials, with a high degree of control of the manufacturing process. More recently (in the last 30 years) this has been extended to food chains, with companies, such as Cargill that was described in Chapter 1, emerging to control production from basic feedstuffs for animals to processing and marketing of animal products. Others, such as McDonald's, have a widespread fast-food chain network, in this case 36,000 outlets in over 100 countries.

Over time policies emerged to control trade, driven largely by a desire to ensure that it makes a contribution to social well-being, as well as helping to meet consumer demand, achieve food security, manage disease and other health risks, and respond to changing demographics. Local policies, often unwritten, gave way to national policies, which eventually led to the international agreements that bind much of world trade nowadays. Such international agreements rely on the sound intent of member countries, with the threat of temporary or permanent expulsion from the group acting as the major deterrent to malpractice. Such action often results in trade restrictions and removal of the trade advantages that were outlined above. Animal trade policy generally recognizes the need to integrate policy over the entire food chain. Animal product policy has been developed and contested more than any other commodity, addressing agricultural inputs, production methods, processing and product retailing. Particular attention is given to by-products of the animal production systems, including pollutants, animal welfare and food safety issues.

Risks to food safety may be managed by the Hazard Analysis and Critical Control Point (HACCP) system. Hazards are biological, chemical or physical components that may make an animal product unsafe, and are estimated from two components, the extent and duration of the risk. The critical control points are the main places where hazard control can be applied to effectively minimize a risk to food safety. As well as identifying hazards and critical control points, the HACCP approach to food safety seeks to establish and monitor limits at each point, facilitate suitable corrective actions and ensure procedures are in place to assess and document that the system is working adequately. These principles are enshrined in international standards under the International Organization for Standardization (ISO). Increasingly this approach is applied to aspects of the food chain other than food safety – animal welfare, for example (e.g. Grandin, 2013).

Now that international trade in animals has advanced to a complex, integrated web of activity all around the world, these standards are an attempt to harmonize the requirements of importers and exporters, producers and consumers.

Trade is greatly influenced by the extent of competition, which ranges from a complete monopoly (no competition) to a perfectly competitive market. In the latter case, animal product supply meets consumer demand, and every possible firm offers the same, homogenous products, which are sold at the market price. In a monopoly the price is absolutely dictated by the seller. Despite the emergence of a few major international companies dealing with animal products, noted in Chapter 1, few monopolies exist. The liberation of trade worldwide, which has allowed developing countries to compete with traditional trading partners, has expanded the scope of animal product trading. Worldwide trade in animals is transitioning from an oligopoly, with just a few key providers selling at premium prices, to a more competitive market. This has come about partly as a result of the change in production methods, as can be seen in the example of exports from two of Britain's former colonies, Australia and New Zealand. For much of the 20th century these countries sent large quantities of livestock products to the UK, nearly all from cattle and sheep, because they had some of the best conditions to produce these at low cost from pasture-based production systems. This allowed them to elevate their standards of living for their relatively small human populations, becoming two of the first countries to depend largely on animals and their products for trading power. Sending these products from countries with low human population densities to one with high population density made good economic sense. From the UK's perspective close historical ties with these two nations facilitated the trade, but recently intensive feedlotting of cattle has emerged as a major competitor to pasture-based production systems. Beef production in feedlots is possible in a much wider range of climatic zones as the feed is bought in. The availability of cheap labour to manage the animals is one of the major factors in developing a successful enterprise. Furthermore, the intensification of livestock production is supported by investment in agricultural research and education, and the use of rapidly growing and high milk-producing livestock breeds and high-yielding grass strains that respond well to high levels of inputs (energy supplements and fertilizers, respectively) to support the high output. The original providers, in this case Australia and New Zealand, have responded to such competition by opening up new markets, mainly in Asia. Trade agreements with Asian countries, in particular China, Japan and Korea, are arranged to reduce import tariffs and ensure mutual benefits.

In the spirit of globalization, trade liberalization has been a goal for most developing and some developed countries in recent times. Although multilateral trade agreements are usually the objective of the major trade conferences, bilateral agreements have been the major tool to generate increased trade. Negotiated over long periods, the agreements are usually successful but may stall if policies of one of the governments involved change. Usually there are dispute settlement clauses, which attempt to guard against changes in policy. Governments can theoretically be sued by foreign companies if they alter their policies to adversely affect trade, although in reality this does not happen. Policy changes arising from varying environmental or public health situations are usually exempt, and it could be argued that animal welfare should be included in the light of changing public opinion and level of concern. For example, concerns emerged recently in the Australian public about the way in which Australian cattle were slaughtered in importing countries in Asia.

Many of the Australian and New Zealand trade agreements have sought to secure markets for their cattle and sheep products, and their dominance of the trade internationally derives from the natural advantages that these countries possess for these industries. In contrast, competition for other animal meat-producing sectors has intensified, with developing countries such as Thailand increasingly importing high quality grain-based feeds to produce low-cost chicken meat or, as in the case of Brazil, developing their own capacity to grow these feeds by destroying indigenous forest.

2.2 Trade Distortions, Subsidies and Security

In post-World War II Europe there were acute concerns about the extent to which farm incomes failed to keep pace with the recovery in other sectors. A shortage of manpower and desire for greater self-sufficiency led to intense industrialization, and a desire for farm income support and stabilization, as well as commodity price stabilization, drove many countries to implement trade restrictions. Supported by the European Economic Community (EEC), as it was then called, import tariffs and export subsidies distorted trade, which many would argue was to the detriment of people's welfare in the countries concerned. For example, in the early 1960s EEC levies on chicken imports led to retaliation by the USA in the form of controlled imports from the EEC in the so-called Chicken War (Ritson, 1977, p. 333). Also influential at this time was the General Agreement on Tariffs and Trade (GATT), introduced in 1947 between 23 mainly industrialized countries to liberate trade, negotiate and reduce tariffs and where necessary mandate a floor price that would guarantee minimum returns to farmers for their commodities, with government purchases being stockpiled in the event of shortages. For example, the British government introduced a guaranteed floor price for beef in a stabilization scheme towards the end of the 1960s, which removed the price troughs but not the peaks (Ritson, 1977, p. 337). This was an attempt to stabilize prices above their equilibrium price. This protection of commodity prices was subsequently argued to distort trade to the extent that, in the words of one observer at the time, 'a significant fraction of world farm output is being produced in the wrong place ... It is difficult to overestimate the dangers of current trends in agricultural protectionism to the future of trade liberalisation generally' (Johnson, 1973).

Such guaranteed prices inevitably led to the creation of surpluses, most notably the 'milk lake' of the EEC, which then required quotas to constrain production. Initially quotas were introduced on imports, and sometimes formed part of a trade agreement. For example, the British government's agreement with its former colonies, Australia and New Zealand, on sheep meat imports from these two countries was introduced to allay concerns that British imports would come mainly from the EEC to the detriment of the former colonies, which it had a moral duty to support. Of more direct pecuniary interest was the Bacon Market Sharing Understanding of the time (Ritson, 1977, p. 369), which sought to restrict imports to artificially increase the price paid to British farmers, reducing the need for government subsidies. Britain at the time was operating a deficiency payment scheme, and was the world's biggest bacon importer. The support for British production was a blatant attempt to bolster an industry that at the time was inefficient, but it encouraged modernization of the industry, with the result that many farmers adopted labour-saving intensive housing systems that were being developed at the time.

Price support was also achieved by national output controls, as in the European milk quotas, introduced into the EEC in 1984 to stabilize output, which at the time was growing rapidly because of high prices paid for milk and relatively inexpensive feed costs. They were set for most countries at 1981 levels of production +1%. Initially they were not intended to have a monetary value and quota transfer between countries was not allowed, with the result that the system perpetuated some inefficient practices. At that time Holland operated much more intensive production methods than in the rest of Europe, having the capacity through their ports to import cereals and distribute these throughout the relatively small country. From these, concentrated feeds for the cows were formulated. Nitrogen fertilizer was also imported in large quantities to be applied to the pastures. In terms of energy and nitrogen use and pollutant emissions per farm, this system was inefficient compared with systems based on traditional pastures. Quotas therefore led to a perpetuation of inefficient practices, supporting environmental pollution, in countries with historically high quotas for intensive production. They also led to welfare problems in cows fed large quantities of concentrates in the form of production-related diseases, such as acidosis and laminitis. Quotas came to be saleable within countries, sometimes tied to land, which restricted new entrants into farming and created an undesirable rigidity in the labour force. The inflexibility of the quota system and its perpetuation of inefficiencies led to growing criticism in the 21st century, resulting in their being finally abandoned in 2015. Another method of supporting prices adopted in the EEC in the latter part of the 20th century was to retire land from production, so-called set-aside schemes. Paying farmers not to produce from their land was unpopular with the public and only led to the worst quality land being removed from active cultivation.

Subsidies have also been used to offload surplus products in an attempt to support internal commodity prices. Occasionally used at home, for example the sale of cheap butter and beef to pensioners and low-income families in the EEC (Ritson, 1977, p. 379), these actually undermined home prices rather than supporting them. Subsidized beef and butter were also provided by the EEC to the Soviet Union in the 1970s. More popular at home, but desperately unpopular with farmers in recipient countries, were the dumping schemes for the EEC to offload surplus products at bargain-basement prices in developing countries. Dairy products, in particular powder from surplus milk, were subjected to dumping schemes at regular intervals during the escalating production in Europe in the 1970s. These were fiercely opposed by countries that wanted to export animal products at world price, e.g. the USA. In 1973 the EEC sold 200,000 tons of butter at 16% of the market price to Russia (Ritson, 1977, p. 378), a move that was very unpopular with European consumers. Eventually GATT approval was given for disposal of the butter mountain in 1985, and the milk production quotas that were imposed gradually diminished the surplus. Export subsidies were unpopular at home and abroad, especially when it was realized that much of the product for which subsidies were received never actually changed hands. There was the extreme case of 1300 tons of butter sent annually to the ex-EEC territory of the Vatican, which it is claimed was sufficient to support a consumption of 5 kg of butter per head per day (Beloff, 1973). However, there were, and still are, well intentioned examples of low price or free food dispersal overseas, including famine aid for situations in which food production persistently fails to keep pace with population growth or for populations without food as a result of war or natural disaster.

Eventually the extensive trade distortions at a world market level led to the establishment of a World Trade Organization (WTO) to control such policies, leading to a freer market and undoubted benefits to all. It aims to reduce trade-distorting tariffs, but has led to increased technical barriers to trade, e.g. sanitary and phytosanitary barriers to trade erected as anti-dumping measures. The WTO standards were based on GATT, which specified the requirements for trade in goods. GATT had introduced the principle of equal opportunity for member countries. Although the WTO replaced the GATT in 1995, it retained the GATT treaty as its principal instrument to control trade. The Agreement specified, in Article XI, that Export Licences should not be used to implement any prohibitions or restrictions on the export of a product. However, exemptions are possible in the case of defending public morals. In particular, discriminatory treatment of 'like products' may be enforceable if the products are substantially different because they are from systems where animal welfare is evidently different (Kahn and Varas, 2014). This would allow mandatory labelling to be introduced. The treaty also allows for the protection of animal life and health, as well as public morals, which may be necessary to develop an argument that products varying in animal welfare standards are 'different'. However, the relationship between animal health and welfare is not simple, and some products from apparently high welfare systems of animal production, e.g. rangeland systems, may involve significant health risks for the animals. Similarly, some intensive production systems that safeguard animal health through keeping the animals in sterile conditions, with diseases additionally controlled by vaccines and antibiotics, have major animal welfare problems.

Many regions of the world are members of the WTO but continue to support trade distortions. For example, the European Community continues to support its small economically-inefficient farmers. Recently, in the growing realization that small farmers used methods that were less damaging to the environment, and to a lesser extent, animal welfare, income support has switched to direct payment for using methods that supported these ideals.

Support for livestock farmers is also evident in the USA, often with the backing of the public who believe that they are part of the national heritage and history, and farmland should be protected to ensure an adequate food supply (Furuseth, 1987). However, the public also recognizes that farmland is needed for residential, commercial and industrial growth, and attitudes towards farmers are conflicted between respect for the past and what has contributed to the success of the country and a desire to move forward with industrial development. There have been limits to people's support for policies that allowed farmers to receive prices above the world market price for their products, mainly in the name of self-sufficiency. In Australia too support for farmers often receives public approval, and is focused on assisting cattle and sheep farmers when they have to cope with extreme weather conditions, in particular droughts and floods. A formal declaration of drought triggers concessional loans, as well as there being pressure on banks not to foreclose loans to cattle and sheep farmers when they are unable to make repayments because of drought conditions.

The vulnerability of many less developed countries to world animal trading policy is increasingly evident. In 2004, low human development index countries, as specified by the UN Development Programme (UNDP), had 71% of their export merchandise as primary goods, compared with just 17% for high human development countries (UNDP, 2006); manufactured goods made up 8% and 80% of the export merchandise, respectively. The Standards and Trade Development Facility is a global partnership between the Food and Agriculture Organization of the United Nations (FAO), the World Organisation for Animal Health (OIE), the World Health Organization (WHO) and the WTO that is managed by the World Bank. It assists developing countries in enhancing their capacity to analyse and implement international sanitary and phytosanitary standards to improve their human, animal and plant health situations. The WTO and the Organisation for Economic Co-operation and Development (OECD) also promote an Aid for Trade initiative, the Enhanced Integrative Framework, which is targeting least developed countries to help them integrate into world trade and use it as a driver for improvement.

Sub-Saharan African countries are particularly vulnerable to animal trade distortions because their population is increasing at over 2% per year. Many, such as Sudan and Ethiopia, rely heavily on a livestock trade with Middle East countries. However, most trade in high value primary goods, such as milk and animal products, is concentrated into a limited number of high and medium human development index countries. In the case of beef meat and veal, India, Brazil, Argentina, the USA, Australia and New Zealand dominate the export markets, while on the import side, the USA leads, then Russia, Japan and the European Union (EU). Just two countries, Brazil and the USA, account for over 70% of world exports. Pork exports are also concentrated into a few key players, with almost 90% of exports coming from the USA, the EU, Canada and Brazil (Guyomard *et al.*, 2013).

2.3 Conclusions

International trade policies in animal products have emerged in the last half century, initially focused on support of floor prices for animal-based commodities
to limit the price fluctuations in the market that make long-term planning and
finance procurement difficult. The high cost of such policies led to a gradual
shift towards output restrictions, particularly in the EEC, but this has been demonstrated to restrict entry to the marketplace and perpetuate inefficiencies. Such
measures are now being largely abandoned in favour of a free market, although
some direct support for farmers experiencing extreme weather or orienting them
towards sustainable production systems is provided in many developed countries.

Trade Wars, Sanctions and Discrimination

3

3.1   Introduction

When the British Raj in India was attacked by local tribesmen in 1897, within hours 'astute financiers were considering in what degree their action had affected the ratio between silver and gold' (Churchill, 1964). Observing this, Churchill marvelled at the 'sensitiveness of modern civilization, which thrills and quivers in every part of this vast and complex system at the slightest touch'. Since that time the world has become a much smaller place, with financial ripples in even a remote corner having an almost immediate effect on world markets. The intricate nature of the world's financial markets has opened the door to modern warfare being conducted in the stock exchanges rather than on the battlefield. Animal products, seen as essential commodities by the most developed nations at least, are often central to the sporadic warfare that has pervaded the world since the guns of the last major conflicts of the 20th century fell silent.

The recent growth of the animal trade and the delicate way in which the trade is interwoven into complex societies makes it subject to fluctuating fortunes and even collapse, albeit often temporary, in a very short period of time. Conflict in the animal trade may arise from territorial disputes, superior product quality claims, including more ethical production, or in retaliation for other trade issues. In the worst cases trade breakdown can disadvantage large numbers of consumers, but in other cases concerns about the trade appear justified from an ethical standpoint and interruptions are forced by public opinion.

3.2   Trade Disruption Because of Disease Risk

Trade disruption can be triggered quite suddenly, by a disease outbreak for example. If there are major financial interests at stake, this can quickly escalate into a full-blown trade war. Even before disease outbreak wars, the world saw traces of this with the EU/US cattle wars on growth promoters in the 1980s, but in reality this seems now just to have been a rehearsal for the major world disease wars that emerged following the outbreak of a new nervous disease in cattle in the UK in 1985. Bovine spongiform encephalopathy (BSE) emerged as a pandemic in Britain following the feeding of meat and bone-meal to cattle, which included material from sheep's brains that had been infected with a spongiform encephalopathy (SE) known as scrapie, a disease recognized in sheep at low prevalence for several centuries. Changes in the rendering process may have increased the potency of the product but, regardless of the cause, the result was the introduction of SE into a new species in sufficient numbers to cause concern that it might again jump species into humans. With the cross-species potency being confirmed in zoo ungulates that had been fed the meat- and bone-meal, evidence of transition into humans created panic in the UK when new variants of a human SE disease, Creutzfeldt-Jakob disease (CJD), emerged in the 1990s. What followed can only be seen in retrospect as a disaster on a worldwide scale that was caused by attempts to maintain a dangerous trade in cattle and associated products. The public concern was made all the worse by the potentially long incubation period of new-variant CJD, although it distinguished itself by affecting not only the elderly but also younger members of the population, with those that had eaten beef in the 1980s being chiefly at risk. What also emerged and horrified many members of the British public was the widespread nature of the use of products from cattle in a large range of products used on an everyday basis, including cosmetics, glues and a wide range of food products. Demand for beef plummeted and the British government attempted to allay concern by a range of measures to reduce risk together with widespread publicity about the continued safety of beef in the UK. Scientists were divided as to the adequacy of the measures taken but the biggest mistakes made included the continued sale of meat and bone-meal overseas. Much went to developing countries and, not surprisingly, cases of BSE began to emerge overseas. Concerned for their meat markets, governments quickly invoked bans on importation of beef from countries with infected cattle, even if only a single case had been reported. Closure of the Canada–USA trade, for example, cost the Canadian industry dearly, and a ban on imports from the USA by Japan similarly caused major fluctuations in the price of cattle. Scientists that spoke out about inadequate measures being taken by governments to control the spread of the disease were at times silenced or ridiculed.

Major lessons to be learned included the vulnerability of world trade to an outbreak of this nature, the unpreparedness of a major beef producer – Britain – for such an outbreak, and the dangers of governments ignoring scientists' recommendations in an attempt to preserve a trade that at best could be considered risky. The economic loss, including from trade restrictions, as a result of BSE was over US$1 billion worldwide (Smith *et al.*, 2005). Fortunately, some scientists' worst fears about potential human mortality were not realized – only hundreds of people died, not thousands or hundreds of thousands. Next time we may not be so lucky.

3.3 Import Bans on Cheap Chicken

The USA is one of the world's largest producers of chicken meat, mainly to supply their massive fast-food chain market. However, consumers in the USA prefer white meat, especially breasts, as this is less fatty and believed to be healthier. This leaves large numbers of chicken legs and wings available for export. There is a strong market for these in South and East Asia, where demand for meat is growing, and traditionally chicken legs have been viewed as having better taste characteristics than white meat. However, because the US exports undermine prices for the local poultry production industry, often retailing for just 40% of the price of local product, countries like India have banned import of the legs, ostensibly because of the risk of bringing in avian influenza. In response to the Indian ban, the USA appealed to the World Trade Organization (WTO) to require it to be abolished, which it did. India has appealed the verdict and awaits a decision on whether the ban will be allowed to remain (TNN, 2015). The Indian ban included poultry from the European Union (EU) even though it was free of avian influenza at the time.

Phytosanitary restrictions are a common trade measure invoked to protect against the risk of disease, and are often quite blatantly used to restrict imports of cheap meat without scientific justification (Wieck *et al.*, 2012). The USA has for some years imposed an import ban on cooked poultry meat from China because of the supposed risk of avian influenza to its poultry flocks, despite evidence that most outbreaks originate from wild birds. Furthermore, the World Organisation for Animal Health (OIE) has clearly identified that cooking deactivates the virus, recommending that trade restrictions should not apply to cooked poultry products. Transmission of the virus to poultry flocks from imported poultry products seems very unlikely as its transmission to humans in cooked products is unproven. China similarly has imposed a ban on importation of poultry from avian influenza-infected regions of the USA and levies duties to protect its industry.

3.4   Constraints on Trading in 'Iconic' Animals

3.4.1   Japanese whaling

The Japanese have been whaling for many centuries, but the last 50 years have seen major challenges to the whaling industry by non-whaling countries; mainly these were on the grounds that the populations of these demonstrably fine creatures were diminishing, sometimes to a critical level at which sustainability of the species was threatened. Japan harvests up to 1000 whales per year, ostensibly for research purposes, although meat not used for research is openly sold to the Japanese public.

The harvesting of wild animals, including whales, kangaroos and seals, inflames public opinion in a way that farm animal harvesting does not. Although farm animal production can be said to be under the full control of humans, in some circumstances, e.g. cattle ranching in extensive rangeland systems, it resembles a harvest, with contact between animal and humans just once or twice a year and little or no management of the land on which the animals live. Most humans accept farming of domestic species for food, but if we farm other species or harvest species from the wild then public concern is aroused. This may seem counterintuitive, because the welfare of many farmed animal species is much worse than that of their counterparts in the wild. The battery-caged hen, for example, has little freedom of movement and no dietary variety, access to a mate, space to move or ability to control her environment compared with the wild jungle fowl to which she is closely related. The biblical notion that certain species were put on the earth for our use pervades Western society at least.

In the case of public concern about Japanese whaling, so strong have been the feelings that American and Australian activists have taken to the southern seas and attempted to disrupt the whale slaughter with increasingly determined and dangerous moves. They have disrupted whaling activities by laying lines to foul the propellers of whaling vessels, throwing smoke and acid bombs on to the ships, preventing them from refuelling and even ramming them on a few occasions. Court cases ensued and injunctions have attempted to prevent the activists' vessels from coming close to the whalers' vessels. In response to US court directives, Sea Shepherd Conservation Society founder Paul Watson, indicating that his ultimate allegiance was to animals not humans, stated: 'We're answering to our clients, which is the whales.'

Australia started proceedings to take Japan to the International Court of Justice in 2010. The Court decided that Japanese whaling activities did not support their lofty scientific goals, confirming therefore that they were essentially to support a meat trade. There has been extreme variation in the catch between years, driven not by scientific need but political objectives. A Japanese appeal was overturned but the possibility exists that even though Japan has indicated that it will abide by the ruling, the whalers will continue their activity but readjust their scientific goals. The lesson from this prolonged trade disruption is that activists will go to extreme lengths to protect animals, especially marine mammals, and that some countries will fight hard to maintain their right to harvest wild animals, which in this case is seen as a cultural heritage.

3.4.2 The ivory trade

The apparent success of the anti-whaling activists in limiting the harvest of the world's biggest marine mammal has not, unfortunately, been mirrored by campaigns to protect the world's biggest land mammal. In the case of whaling, the demand for the product is not particularly great, particularly amongst the young, and the activity can only be undertaken by major organizations because of its relative remoteness. The Japanese government's insistence on the right to harvest an animal from the wild could be compared to the Australian government's sanctioning the harvest of kangaroos in its own territory. However, in the case of the elephant, the product, which is no more than the animal's teeth, is produced in a continent where poverty abounds and it has immense value in Asia, a continent of growing wealth, of up to US$1 million per tusk. In addition it is relatively easily harvested and traded, and the animals themselves are accused of damaging the environment through their destructive feeding habits. Enclosure of land for farming, with rapidly growing populations has also threatened the elephants' habitat. For these reasons the elephant has suffered indiscriminately in the last few decades at the hands of poachers, and it seems highly likely that it will disappear in the same way that the mammoth, its close relative, did approximately 5000 years ago.

Prized for its ability to be carved, its hardness, durability and its off-white colour, ivory has been traded for centuries. Prior to the growth in South-east Asian economies, demand was mainly in Western countries and Japan to produce piano keys (up until the 1970s), billiard balls and souvenirs. The growth of the plastics industry has produced replacements for all of these products, yet demand remains stronger than ever with the growing wealth in China fuelling a rapid increase in prices.

Attempts to control a trade that was endangering the iconic African elephant have proved ineffectual and have even hastened the demise. Illegal poaching was addressed in the 1980s by the Convention on International Trade in Endangered Species of Wild Fauna and Flora (CITES) registering the product, some of which was known to be coming from Tanzania, a country that had officially banned harvesting. Thus the CITES action provided a seal of authority that essentially legitimized trade in countries that were attempting to control poachers' activities. When this became evident there was intense lobbying for CITES to list elephants in Appendix 1 and thereby ban the trade. Eventually, despite opposition from southern African states that argued for a legalized trade, elephants were listed in CITES Appendix 1 in 1989 and ivory trading was made illegal internationally. The intense publicity surrounding this action helped to bring about a temporary collapse in the trade, stockpiles developed and poaching for a while abated.

Since the ban, southern African states persisted in their desire to pursue a regulated trade, and in 1997 ivory trading was allowed under CITES in the southern African states Botswana, Namibia and Zimbabwe. It was argued that it could be better controlled in national parks than in the rest of Africa where elephants roamed wild in the bush. South Africa followed suit in 2000. Japan was approved as the recipient. This effective lifting of the trade ban has precipitated a renewed international trade, which coupled with growing Asian wealth has led to a lucrative trade re-emerging. Despite the promises that revenue would return to conservation purposes, the use of revenue for arms purchases has further soured the reputations of the southern African states in elephant management.

Stockpiles of ivory have existed ever since CITES began regulating the trade and recently some countries have been destroying them as a demonstration to African countries that poaching elephants for their ivory will not be accepted. The USA destroyed 6 t in 2013, as did China in 2014; France destroyed 3 t in 2014 and the Philippines 5 t in 2014. Hong Kong, a major gateway into the Chinese market, is scheduled to destroy 30 t seized between 2003 and 2013.

The ivory trade has almost obliterated one of the world's most revered animals. Celebrated in legend, children's books and animal art, the elephant has a limited time left on this planet unless the trade finally can be halted. At current estimates (17,000–22,000 elephants killed illegally per year), one-fifth of Africa's elephants will be lost in the coming decade (WSJ, 2014). The attempts by CITES have been clearly inadequate, but it is likely that the battle to save the elephant can only be won by African states bringing poaching under control, which will happen if and when the demand slows. The media have already played a part in controlling poaching and could have the same role in reducing Asian demand. There is growing animal welfare awareness in Asia, but there is also an increasing disparity in wealth between the rapidly growing Asian middle class and the Africans that might be tempted away from agriculture and pastoralism into the lucrative poaching trade. As a consequence of the growing demand in Asia, the price of ivory tripled from 2006 to 2011 (WSJ, 2014). Of increasing concern is the development of Asian business interests in Africa, which might facilitate the ivory trade.

3.5   Territorial Disputes

Between 1958 and 1976 a rift between Iceland and Britain over fishing rights jeopardized the livelihood of thousands of fishermen. Britain was in decline, exhausted after its major involvement in two punishing world wars. Both had been fought at a massive cost, financial and in manpower, which necessitated economic revival if Britain was to retain even a fraction of its former power. Fishing and other primary industries were vital for this revival, but when Iceland extended its fishing exclusive zone from 4 to 12 then 50 and finally 200 miles, Britain came close to military action to preserve the economic future for its fishermen. After mediation by NATO, Britain was forced to accept the loss of its fishing rights within 200 miles of Iceland, a distance that was to become a widely accepted international standard, but this cost about 1500 British fishermen their right to fish.

3.6   Products with Moral Advantage

3.6.1   Mulesing and the Australian wool industry

In 2008 the American-based activist group People for the Ethical Treatment of Animals (PETA) persuaded wool retailers in Europe to boycott Australian wool unless the producers gave an assurance that they would phase out mulesing. This is an operation to remove skin from the hindquarters of Merino sheep, thereby eliminating the folds of skin that attract blowflies to lay their eggs. The operation is conducted on large numbers of sheep without anaesthetic. The wool industry representatives in Australia knew that this could further reduce their wool prices and responded by: (i) developing a mulesing accreditation, which would ensure that the operation was only done by skilled operators; (ii) volunteering to phase out mulesing by 2010; and (iii) funding research to develop sheep with fewer wrinkles and folds of skin on their hindquarters. The phasing out of mulesing did not happen, principally because by that time scientists had shown that the stress caused to the increased number of sheep that would become fly struck was likely to be greater or at least similar to the stress caused by mulesing. Therefore, phasing out of mulesing would not necessarily reduce suffering in the sheep, but would just exchange a relatively small amount of pain in a large number of animals (mulesing) with a large amount of pain in a smaller number of animals (fly strike). The incident serves to remind us that developing a suffering-free industry is not as simple as phasing out a single operation, but also the vulnerability of the industry to advocacy groups that are able to utilize public sensitivity and fears to put pressure on animal product processors.

3.6.2   Cosmetics testing on animals

Cosmetics are a suite of products that has traditionally been tested on animals for their potential to cause harm when used by humans. However, the superfluity of cosmetic use by humans and the major harm done to animals has encouraged trade issues that, while not yet a trade war nor even a dispute, have the potential to escalate. Action taken by the EU over more than a decade to ban trade in cosmetics that have been tested on animals is being rapidly discussed around the world by countries that either are heavily involved in the trade or that believe they can gain political advantage by introducing a ban. Since the 2013 ban by the EU on testing or sale of cosmetic products tested on animals elsewhere, the issue has become a trade concern.

Cosmetics are liberally defined, for example legally in the USA they are 'any articles intended to be rubbed, poured, sprinkled or sprayed on, introduced into or otherwise applied to the human body for cleansing, beautifying, promoting attractiveness or altering the appearance and the component parts of such an article'. As such they include a wide range of products: make-up, skincare products, soaps, shower gels, deodorants, shampoos, toothpastes and sunscreens (RSPCA, 2012). The industry has grown significantly recently, particularly in sales to young girls that enter puberty at an increasingly young age and are under pressure to emulate their elders. The major countries of manufacture are Germany, Japan, the USA, France and Italy, with the major importing countries being in Europe, especially France and Italy. The growth of the industry has been led by a small number of multinational companies, and much of the growth is in the contentious area of marketing to young girls. Two of the major manufacturers, L'Oréal and Proctor & Gamble, have annual revenues of US$28 billion and US$84 billion, respectively.

Testing has included assessment of acute and chronic toxicity, often using the notorious LD_{50} test, which challenges the animals with ever higher doses until 50% of them die. A more logical test would assess the harm of realistic maximum potential doses, but the LD_{50} test was devised when the welfare of laboratory animals counted for little, and ensuring some animals died as a result of the test was not an ethical issue at the time. Other tests include assessment of skin, respiratory tract and eye sensitivity. Eye sensitivity was measured in another notorious test, the Draize test, in which rabbits were restrained by the neck while compounds were added to their eyes. Tests are also made on animals for reproductive effects, including fetal abnormality, and carcinogenicity and mutagenicity of the product. Most of the animals used were rats and mice, although rabbits were also used. The choice of animal was more on account of its availability than its suitability as a model for humans, and the reliability of animal testing to predict effects on humans has been repeatedly challenged. Alternatives include the measurement of penetration of cosmetics into human skin that has been obtained from cosmetic surgery, a variety of other *in vitro* tests, and clinical studies using volunteers.

Testing of cosmetic products on animals was first banned in Germany in 1986 and has been banned in the EU since 2004, with EU regulations being extended in 2009 to include cosmetic ingredients. The argument made for a ban on ingredients is that there are now toxicity reports on thousands of ingredients, making it less necessary to use animal tests on cosmetic formulations than previously. Other countries that have banned cosmetic testing of animals include India, Israel and Norway. In other countries with a major stake in the cosmetics industry, e.g. the USA and China, animal testing is still used; indeed in China it is currently compulsory to test new products on animals. However, bans are being actively considered in both of these countries. In other countries, such as Australia, cosmetics tested on animals are not explicitly banned, but testing of compounds proposed to be used for cosmetic purposes is not currently undertaken. However, products that have been tested elsewhere can still legally be sold. Many national codes and laws that regulate animal use, including The Australian Code of Practice for the Use of Animals in Scientific Practices, require that scientific testing could only be undertaken if the benefits outweigh the harm to the animals involved. As the harm is significant, including irritation to skin or the eye using doses vastly greater than those used by humans, and the benefit to humans is small, it is likely that an animal ethics committee applying the relevant code of practice, or government regulator, would not sanction such research. However, the Australian federal government lacks the power to legislate on animal welfare issues; this rests with the States and Territories. Until testing bans are more widespread advocacy groups can only recommend that concerned members of the public purchase products or products with ingredients that have not been tested on animals. Policies such as these have led to many cosmetic manufacturers branding themselves as 'cruelty free'.

After the 2009 EU ban on cosmetics and cosmetics ingredients testing on animals, it was proposed that this be extended to include cosmetics supplied by trading partners in 2013. In 2011 a review of the proposed expansion by experts from the USA, Japan and the EU concluded that there were good prospects to replace sensitization and toxicokinetics testing, but that it would be more difficult to replace the complex human health effects of repeated dose toxicity, including skin sensitization and carcinogenicity, reproductive toxicity and toxicokinetics (Hartung *et al.*, 2011). L'Oréal, the major cosmetics company in France, also opposed the ban. However, it did come into force in 2013, after which time it became illegal to market any cosmetics in the EU that had been tested on animals.

The evolution of this control on cosmetic testing demonstrates a trade advantage for companies that recognized early the benefit of selling 'cruelty free' products.

Few countries have yet banned animal testing, but most have a majority of the public opposed to it. Although it may seem clear that animal testing is now obsolete, considerable difficulties face those attempting a comprehensive and meaningful ban. Some products, such as onabotulinumtoxinA (Botox®), can still be legally tested on animals because they are licensed as medicinal products, although being within the definition of cosmetics. Some lines of perfume were tested on animals many years ago, and it is unclear whether bans on imported products extend to these. To introduce a widespread ban and halt the cruel testing on animals that is still common, clear and narrow definitions of cosmetics are required that are recognized worldwide, coupled with continued public support for products produced without testing on animals.

3.6.3   Foie gras

Force-feeding geese and ducks large quantities of high-energy food enlarges their livers, which can be made into a fat-rich paté much loved by the French and some Francophone countries. The food comes with a cultural heritage, having had a strong following in France since the 18th century, and foie gras itself has been produced for thousands of years, utilizing the ability of geese to store energy in their livers prior to migration. In 2008 France passed a law claiming that foie gras was part of its cultural heritage and considered adding the method of production to the UN's World Heritage List. However, in many other parts of the world the method of production has caused serious concern for the welfare of the birds. Some countries have ceased production because of this, such as Israel in 2003.

Forced feeding of geese and ducks has many problems associated with it: pain, an urge to vomit, a scarred oesophagus, reduced mobility and a distinct avoidance of the person doing the feeding (Gille, 2011; PETA, 2014). The housing systems adopted to facilitate forced feeding are necessarily confined and also adversely affect the birds' welfare. The controversy between activist groups and the poultry industry, with its government backing, has been particularly prominent in Hungary, traditionally a strong poultry-rearing country. The end of the communist era and liberation of ideals saw the emergence of an animal rights movement championing the rights of poultry not to be force fed. Of the global output of 20,000 t/year, Hungary produces 2000, second only to France (16,000 t/year), with Spain and Bulgaria producing the remaining 2000 t/year (Gille, 2011). Several countries have banned the use of force-feeding techniques, but only one, India, has banned the importation of paté de foie gras. Much of the Hungarian output is sent to Germany and Austria. An activist group, Four Paws, negotiated with the Hungarian Ministry to have products labelled according to whether forced feeding had been used, to work towards developing a legislated code of practice, an animal welfare monitoring programme and a research programme that would render the forced feeding unnecessary (Gille, 2011). In return the group volunteered to suspend its company blacklist, to blacklist products in future not companies, to help in designing the regulation and to support the research programme, including presenting a positive image of companies adopting improved techniques. The Hungarian Ministry reasoned that improving the industry was better than banning it; if production was banned in Hungary, it would simply support production outside the EU, especially in China, which has invested in this method of feeding. However, there were concerns that the actions of the advocacy group had an ulterior motive. When they first produced their blacklist, a prominent waterfowl-producing company that supplied to Germany was missed out, leading to suspicions that they were acting on behalf of this company in their attempt to damage rival companies. In the end, the legitimacy of the advocacy group campaign has had to be assessed by the extent to which it reflects an opinion of a significant sector of the public and whether their methods reflect their beliefs. In relation to the first, Hungarian production is supported by the majority of the population, however, many also believe that the producers should have anticipated public concern and changed technology. For example, they could have used ad libitum rather than forced feeding, which gives the birds the right to refuse extra food. Such products would not be allowed to be called foie gras in France, where forced feeding is integral to the process, but could perhaps be defended in Hungary.

The geese producers argue that foie gras production is better conducted in Hungary than China, because there is at least some protection, and that the welfare of geese there is better than that of intensively reared chickens. These arguments of relative welfare advantage, however, are questionable as the legitimacy of a production method should be absolute. The relativity argument is akin to saying that bashing someone to within an inch of their life and then allowing them to go to hospital to recover is acceptable because you did not actually kill the person, or that it is acceptable where you live, because if it was done somewhere without suitable hospitals the person probably would have been killed. However, people also criticized the advocacy group for blacklisting companies, and especially those in Hungary rather than France, the biggest producer, because of the relative weakness of the farmers in Hungary. Hungarian farmers had only recently emerged from major changes to agriculture after the collapse of communism; hence they were badly organized, small and seen as vulnerable or likely to change their production methods with a little persuasion. People also thought the advocacy group had taken liberties by documenting and reporting animal abuse to the media. The advocacy group even attempted to appeal to Hungarian nationalism, saying that the farmers were enslaved to Israeli and French investors (Gille, 2011).

Another argument often levied against products like foie gras is that they are manufactured for the elite consumers, a privileged group that can afford a product that is extremely expensive. However, in both Hungary and France the public seem to be prepared to waive this argument in support of the production of traditional consumables. Recognition that this was how our forefathers lived and worked is comforting, providing a sense of stability, whereas novel food items are greeted with suspicion because they may be unhealthy or even make us ill.

The industry's defence was that force feeding is not cruel and in any case is monitored and complies with current EU regulations, and that the product is deeply rooted in folklore and culinary traditions, contributing to Hungary's reputation abroad and supporting Hungary's ailing food industry. The public were encouraged to believe that the farmers are the guardians of the national cultural identity. They criticized the members of the advocacy group as being angry young radicals from the cities, without either the realism of members of the public that have experienced the tumultuous changes that have taken place in Hungary in the last 50 years or the pastoral tranquillity that pervades the agricultural production and farmers in the country. The pro-foie gras Hungarians also invoked a victim mentality, that powerful foreign organizations are controlling their production methods, including the EU, WTO, IMF, etc.

   This not atypical case of trade issues surrounding an elite food product is symptomatic of the tensions surrounding free trade in the democratic Western world: cultural heritage, animal welfare and ethics, economics of production, and competition from other producers or products all sit juxtaposed in the battle for the hearts and minds of the consumer, or in the case of some advocates, non-consumers. Compromises often ensue: labelling of products, regulating methods of production and promises to improve production systems over long periods of time. Often the changes made do not ally with public sentiment, which can oscillate more rapidly than legislation in many cases, but in the end it is usually the consumer that is the ultimate arbiter of production methods.

3.6.4   Australia's live cattle export to Indonesia

Australia is the world's largest live exporter, sending hundreds of thousands of cattle and millions of sheep to markets in Asia and the Middle East annually, in total about 3 million animals (Livecorp, 2014). Many northern Australian producers are currently locked into live export as the only method of selling their cattle because the costs of road transport to the nearest abattoirs are prohibitive.

   In 2011 the Australian government, led by Agriculture Minister Jo Ludwig, banned the export of cattle to Indonesia for 6 weeks as a result of release of an activist's video footage showing cattle being cruelly slaughtered there. Slaughtermen were shown struggling to restrain the big Australian cattle, hacking at their necks in a laboured attempt to decapitate them. Cattle were shown shaking at the prospect of joining the line. The indirect result of the ban was that some producers were left with unmarketable cattle for far more than the 6-week period because it was followed by the wet season, when trucks cannot easily travel the northern roads. There is no doubt that the hardship experienced by northern cattle producers was real and widespread. Fortunately fodder supplies in most areas were good after a series of wet seasons, otherwise the impact on the industry would have been even greater.

   To add to their difficulties, the value of cattle properties declined substantially as a result of the loss of confidence in the industry, despite a growing market in Asia. This has opened the door to overseas property buyers from Asia, which ironically includes Indonesians.

The financial implications extended considerably beyond the producers. Transporters, employees on properties, including cattle handlers, cooks, mechanics and school teachers, workers in the service industries and even Indonesian consumers suffered when the supply of beef from Australia to Indonesia was abruptly cut off.

With the benefit of hindsight, astute producers might have predicted that there would be problems. The trade had been temporarily suspended many times before, by actions of both the Australian government and the importing countries. However, none was as damaging as the 2011 Indonesia ban because most of the Australian live export cattle travelled this route. As any good businessman will tell you, relying on marketing a single product primarily to just one country, and a developing country at that, is risky.

Most previous trade embargoes were in the Middle Eastern sheep trade, and it was generally believed that the short duration (about 7 days; Phillips, 2008) of the cattle trade to South-east Asia and the low mortality statistics of the voyages presented few, if any, problems in comparison. However, the cruelty that activist groups and Four Corners exposed shocked and disturbed the public. People instantly felt pity for the cattle (Tiplady *et al.*, 2012), but powerless to do anything about it. Some even resorted to professional support services. Afterwards, it was clear that the government and industry had known about the cruelty from a fact-finding mission they had undertaken (*Tasmania Times*, 2014).

Producers carried excessively high numbers of stock through 2011 and 2012, and then in many areas the rains failed and fodder supplies declined. One welfare problem compounded another and cattle prices plummeted, making it difficult for producers to purchase extra feed for them. Meanwhile Indonesia, having lost confidence in the Australian market and with its religious slaughter publically humiliated on an international scale, placed a quota on the numbers and size of cattle sourced from Australia. Instead they began to source beef from other, more reliable sources. This was subsequently relaxed somewhat as shortages and high prices hit the Indonesian consumers.

The Australian cattle industry sought to broaden its markets for live cattle, extending these to Russia and other Asian countries. Once again cattle welfare was compromised with the long journeys to Russia. Most significantly, the largest producing company planned and commenced the building of an abattoir near Darwin.

A change of government allowed Australia to apologize for the previous government's 'mistakes', and consideration was given to preventing activists gaining inflammatory footage in the so-called 'Ag-gag' laws. The RSPCA responded by recommending that employees on farms should be legally required to report cruelty to animals. The government pressed on with its plans to develop northern Australian agriculture, but the emphasis has switched to intensive crop production in regions with the necessary warmth, rainfall and labour sources.

Even though the exposés have been ongoing, the public appears to have got compassion fatigue. But their initial action has made us question the ethics of our live export to developing countries. The industry watches with baited breath. Will the meatworks succeed, will the new markets grow, and even more radically, is this the best use of some of the best land in northern Australia? The ban forced cattle producers to consider whether their production systems, from paddock to plate, meet the expectations of the Australian public. Any interruption to international trade damages relations between the two countries; it destroys trust and has impacts far removed from those involved in the action itself. In this case it was unfortunate that the trade was in a contentious product, a live, sentient animal sent from one of the richest to one of the poorest countries in the world.

3.7   A Trade War Driven by Political Ideology – Russia's Food War with the West

In the 1970s Russia imported large quantities of grain to sustain their livestock production, principally from the USA, which provided three-quarters of the world's feed grain exports (Paarlberg, 1980). This led to a perception of American control over Russian food supplies and ultimately to President Carter using this to punish the Union of Soviet Socialist Republics (USSR) for invading Afghanistan in 1979, with a grain export embargo imposed in 1980 (Paarlberg, 1980). The measure met with little success, because using food exports as a sanctioning tool in this way requires three conditions to be in place: (i) the government of the exporting country must be able to control its exports, which was not the case in the USA where there was no grain marketing board (but has been possible in Australia, another major grain exporter); (ii) other countries must not provide an indirect conduit to the embargoed country; and (iii) the export volume must be sufficient to damage the country. Carter's ban fell down mainly on point two, with significant imports from other countries. Eastern European countries immediately increased their imports of feed grain from the USA, which filtered through to the USSR, and other major grain producers, especially Australia and Canada, increased their exports to the USSR. Carter also had to hastily arrange for the US Department of Agriculture to buy 9 million tons of undelivered embargoed grain from the exporters to avoid a collapse in grain futures, which it then gradually filtered back into the market channels. Inevitably farm prices in the USA fell and the American Farm Bureau withdrew its support for the ban, allowing Reagan to come to power promising to terminate the ban, which he estimated had cost the American taxpayers US$1 billion. The lesson the USA had learnt, the hard way, was that tampering with feed-grain shipments was likely to disrupt both the economy and the political party in place at the time. There was one silver lining to the cloud surrounding the US grain embargo to Russia following the Afghanistan invasion. The USA established a 4 million ton grain reserve to meet the needs of the world's poorest countries, however, unsurprisingly the negotiations to establish a global reserve were blocked by the USSR.

In 2014 the tables were turned, with Russia imposing a 1 year ban on food imports from Western countries, including the USA. This time the major products affected in relation to the USA were poultry meat, nuts, soybeans and cattle. Imports from the EU alone exceeded US$1 billion for some commodities, most notably cheese and pork. Inevitably, although Russian producers were told to increase production, food prices in Russia increased and in exporting countries they decreased. The reason for this action was that Russian involvement in Ukrainian separatist movements had inflamed tensions in the West, which resulted in sanctions being placed by the EU, the USA and Canada on Russian and pro-Russian Ukrainian politicians and businessmen to freeze their overseas bank accounts and limit their access to Western countries. Other countries quickly followed suit that were sympathetic to Western interests. Russia and its allies responded with their own similar sanctions, but there were fewer Westerners with interests in Russia than vice versa. Hence in April Russia imposed a food import ban, effectively banning the importation of products from specified countries that it considered could be produced at home or were of little value to Russian consumers. Imports of dairy products from Baltic state countries were particularly badly hit. The estimated value of dairy imports from the EU was US$12 billion, with another US$1 billion worth from the USA. Some plans were made for importation from other countries, such as animal products from Brazil and Chile. Following the ban the price of these goods rose sharply in Russia, and the Russian consumer had to either pay the increased price or switch to similar goods.

This example shows how food imports were used to escalate tension in an already dangerous situation, in this case to the detriment of both consumers in Russia and producers in the EU, mainly. Curiously lamb was left out of the sanctions, but some exporters took unilateral action themselves. Hence both governments and individuals can use the animal trade to harm others. Trade links take years to establish, as trust and networks grow, and even if the sanctions were to be lifted suddenly there would be a long-term effect on all parties involved.

3.8 Conclusions

Trade in animal products can bring substantial benefit in terms of reduced cost to consumers, support for rural industries and reduction in environmental cost, but it relies on trust and goodwill on the part of both trading partners. Too often trade wars have involved animal products because embargoing these has an immediate and significant impact. Long-term storage may be difficult and alternative markets hard to find; hence disruption to the animal trade is a powerful tool if used in support of political ideals. On many other occasions, disruption to the trade has derived from activist groups' ideological opposition to products that involve harming animals, killing them unnecessarily or taking them from their natural habitat. Such disruption tends to accelerate government action to control such practices if they have sufficient public support.

Although trade restrictions have damaging effects on both the exporting and importing countries, the rest of the world often benefits as prices decline due to enhanced supply (Wieck *et al.*, 2012). Models can be used to predict and analyse the impact of trade restrictions (Wieck *et al.*, 2012). If the restrictions are in place between major exporters and importers, there is considerable trade flow restructuring after the ban. This may include enhanced trade between countries operating a ban.

Trade in Meat

4

4.1 Introduction

Humans are not anatomically or physiologically designed to eat raw meat. The absence of elongated canine teeth makes tearing through raw meat difficult and the relatively high pH in our stomachs renders us susceptible to food poisoning if the flesh is at all contaminated. For our ancestors the infrequency of successful hunts would have made contamination of stored meat likely. However, their ability to master fire provided a method of processing meat to make it more easily consumed and less likely to be contaminated. Hence for as long as prehistoric records are available, meat consumption has been a part of the human diet. Our ancestors' advanced ability to communicate facilitated complex hunting methods, luring animals into traps for example. Cave paintings suggest that there were ritual gatherings before the hunt, perhaps even with music and hallucinogenic drugs, which bonded the males together to improve their performance in the hunt.

Hunting for meat provided an alternative to the long process of gathering nutrients from plant life, which varied with climate and season and often required a nomadic lifestyle to follow the geographic availability of suitable plants. The nutrient demands for hunting, gathering and nomadism were considerable, and meat was able to provide the highly digestible food needed. Nevertheless, the risks involved and uncertainty in finding food meant that life was short, typically 25–40 years. With the coming of agriculture, and the development of improved plants, principally cereals, with higher seed yields, a settled way of life became possible and it was no longer necessary to hunt animals for meat. However, in colder parts of the world, particularly the northern parts of the northern hemisphere, meat consumption remained necessary because it could provide the nutrients needed, and in these regions crop growth was limited. Over the last 1000 years people from these regions came to colonize most of the rest of the world and the colonizers took their meat-eating habits with them. For example, the British colonies covered one-third of the world at the beginning of the 20th century, Russia extended its influence southwards and westwards in the Soviet era, and lesser colonizers such as Holland and Germany also had significant influence. Amongst the Mediterranean countries, Spain and France also had considerable colonies overseas, but it was the high rate of meat consumption in countries like the UK and in its colonies in North America and Australia/New Zealand that set a trend overseas that has extended its influence beyond the initial colonies. The increasing meat consumption worldwide that was begun by the European colonizers is now having major adverse effects on the environment, people's health and the availability of food for poor people. The adverse effect on human health stems largely from the impact of meat consumption on obesity. The USA, the UK, Australia, New Zealand and Canada are all high in the world's obesity ratings (ranking 1, 3, 6, 7 and 11, with 14–31% of the population classified as obese; Nationmaster, 2013). Here increased disposable incomes have made it possible to increase meat consumption and nutrient intake at the same time as sedentary jobs and recreational interests have reduced nutrient demands. Although there has been considerable controversy surrounding the relationship between meat consumption and obesity, particularly in the USA, a relationship between the two is clear (Wang and Beydoun, 2009). In Wang and Beydoun's study, an individual's meat consumption was directly related to his or her body mass index, waist circumference and obesity, with survey respondent's data controlled for age, sex, ethnicity, physical activity and socio-economic status. People in the top quintile for meat consumption were approximately 27% more likely to be obese than those in the bottom quintile.

At the same time industrial-scale meat production has reduced its cost, relative to income. Thus the growth in meat consumption has been facilitated by intensification of animal production worldwide. Many food animals are now reared in buildings, where they can be fed, watered and harvested easily. Their diets are rich in nutrients to make them grow rapidly, to reach a suitable slaughter weight quickly and enable the next batch of animals to be introduced quickly. Food produced from animals that are fed nutrient-rich diets in intensive housing where opportunities for activity are limited have higher saturated fat contents (30–50% of total fat content), compared with the same animals in the wild (Fine and Davidson, 2008). Generally the higher the fat content in an animal's body the lower the proportion of fat that is polyunsaturated (Siri-Tarino *et al.*, 2010). Consumption of saturated fat in meats appears to be related to an increased risk of the major non-communicable diseases (NCDs), i.e. obesity, diabetes and coronary heart disease (Vang *et al.*, 2008; Siri-Tarino *et al.*, 2010), and public health nutritionists advocate reducing saturated fat to avoid NCDs like diabetes and cardiovascular disease (Browning and Jebb, 2006; Everitt *et al.*, 2006). It is suspected that red meat consumption in particular increases insulin resistance, oxidative stress and inflammation. The latter two were proposed by a major European study of 27,548 residents from Potsdam, Germany (Montonen *et al.*, 2012), the results of which suggested a specific involvement of high levels of meat consumption in diabetes, colorectal cancers and cardiovascular disease. Careful analysis of such data is crucial, because increased red meat consumption is associated with lower levels of exercise, reduced consumption of wholegrain bread and vegetables and increased alcohol consumption (Montonen *et al.*, 2012).

Case study: restricting high fat meat imports into Ghana

Occasional attempts have been made to limit intake of fatty meat to reduce the risk of NCDs. These are most needed in countries where either the people are particularly susceptible to obesity, e.g. Pacific islanders, or countries where poverty forces the people to buy poor quality meat with high fat content. In the case of the former, trading standards have largely resisted attempts to implement restrictions on importation of high fat livestock products. The latter has been put to the test by the government of Ghana (Thow *et al.*, 2014), which specified in the 1990s that cuts and carcasses of pork and beef could contain no more than 25% fat, poultry 15% and lamb 30%, although these were later relaxed for pork to 42%. Regular tests were introduced on both imported and locally produced meat to check compliance, and continue to this day. The regulations were in response to declining home production and increasing imports of low quality, high fat meat, especially high fat turkey tails in the 1990s and, later, chicken legs, as a result of increased trade liberalization. This appeared to be related to growing prevalence of NCDs in the human population of Ghana. Meat importation continued to increase, with poultry imports from Brazil escalating rapidly in recent years. Periodic increases in low-quality meat importations, e.g. low-grade chicken legs from the USA, are countered by media exposures and warnings about the health risks of low-quality, high-fat meat. The impact of cheap imports on home meat production is undoubtedly severe, reducing demand and undercutting the home products, which are necessarily expensive because of high cereal costs.

This approach to meat fat restriction provides an interesting lesson in effective trade management. The restriction was imposed on both home-produced and imported meat, and it was not product specific, rather it was generic to any cuts from a particular species. Thus discrimination against products from particular regions could not be demonstrated. Second, the restriction was in response to a human health concern, which is permissible under WTO regulations. The policy has the broad support of the public and may be extended to neighbouring countries in the region of West Africa. However, the restrictions only control trade in high fat products; an equivalent risk of NCD could occur with high intakes of moderate fat livestock products.

Regardless of its health effects, meat is now a food that humans eat in vast quantities. In an average British person's lifetime they will eat their way through 550 chickens, 36 pigs, 36 sheep and 8 cattle (Anon., 2008). In Australia, a typical developed country of major meat eaters, people consume most beef (39 kg/capita/year) and poultry (38 kg/capita/year), with less consumption of pig and sheep/goat meat (22 and 12 kg/capita/year, respectively). Over the 15 years to 2009, Australians' poultry consumption increased most, by 0.71 kg/capita/year, followed by pig meat, which increased by 0.35 kg/capita/year. Beef consumption showed no change and sheep and goat meat consumption declined by 0.45 kg/capita/year (FAOSTAT, 2014). Poultry meat is the least elastic in response to price change, i.e. when price increases there is less reduction in consumption of poultry meat compared with other meat types.

4.2 The Scale of the World's Meat Production and Consumption

There was rapid growth in livestock consumption starting soon after the Second World War in developed countries. World meat output is now dominated by fish (wild caught and aquaculture in almost equal proportions, 160 million t/year), then pig (109 million t/year) and poultry (106 million t/year) meat, with a smaller contribution from beef and veal (63 million t/year) and finally sheep meat, a much smaller sector (8.5 million t/year) (FAOSTAT, 2014).

Since the early 1960s meat production has been growing at an ever increasing rate (Fig. 4.1), particularly since the year 2000. There was an overall world growth of meat production of 2.6% per year from 2000 to 2010, made up of 4.3% in the poultry sector and about 2% in the other three sectors. The biggest growth is in developing countries in response to rising incomes and growing urbanization, with over 50% of the world's population now living in cities (Narrod *et al.*, 2011). Between 1962 and 2009 per capita income grew annually by 6% in East Asia and the Pacific and by 4% in India, compared with just 2% in high income countries in the OECD.

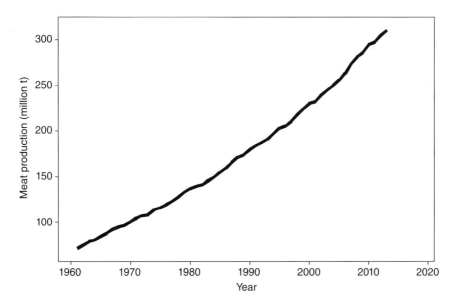

Fig. 4.1. Growth in annual world meat production between 1961 and 2013 (FAOSTAT, 2015).

The growth has not been uniform across the different animals used for meat production. The biggest growth in land animals has been in the poultry sector, with stocks now growing at a steady 3% per year (FAOSTAT, 2013). Stocks of cattle are now growing at less than 1% per year, compared to 2% in the 1960s; pig growth has also declined, from 4% to 0.8% over the same period. Egg production grew over this period at about 2.5%.

The growth in the poultry meat sector, and in particular the intensive poultry industry that is reliant on cereal grain, provides the most efficient increase in meat production per unit of grain, due to the inherent efficiency of poultry meat production compared with ruminant livestock. This leads to lower prices, relative to beef, which is one driving force for the change. In contrast to this growth, the collapse of marine fish stocks has reduced the market for this product dramatically in the last decade; however, this is offset by growth in the farmed fish sector and a 7% growth in world fish production between 2000 and 2010, even though this is reduced from 10% growth for the 20 years prior to this (FAOSTAT, 2014). The major producers of Atlantic salmon are Norway, Chile, Scotland and Canada, with the first two providing over 61% of global output (FAO, 2008).

An increasing number of women in fulltime employment have directed families towards meats that favour quick preparation and fast food choices (Haley, 2001). Consumers are preferring meats with less saturated animal fats and lower cholesterol levels, which chicken has compared to beef and sheep. One reason that growth in the ruminant sector has been less than in other livestock sectors is because in small ruminants, sheep and goats, there are difficulties in intensifying production. In the Mediterranean, North Africa and West Asia these animals are kept for their ability to survive in harsh, dry rangeland conditions. Annual growth in goat and sheep populations in North Africa and West Asia was just 1% over the last 50 years (Aw-Hassan *et al.*, 2010). Growth in production and consumption was about 2% over this period. It grew faster between 1970 and 1990 than more recently because of strong government support, including better export infrastructure, animal health care and increased and subsidized use of crops and crop residues, especially in times of drought. However, some of the countries with the lowest GDP that are most reliant on small ruminants, such as Afghanistan, Mauritania and Ethiopia, grew very little, with war additionally causing considerable fluctuation in production. Other countries in this region that have rapid population growth, urbanization and income are experiencing rapid growth in demand. Therefore in the next 15 years the deficit in sheep and goat production in North Africa and West Asia is expected to grow rapidly, in one analysis from 35,000 t/year to 375,000 t/year (Aw-Hassan *et al.*, 2010). It is expected that much of the deficit will be imported from countries outside the region, in particular Australia and New Zealand and Hungary, Romania and Bulgaria, which are better able to provide and transport healthy stock into the region, particularly the Persian Gulf. In addition, it has been widely observed that increased stocking densities of small ruminants in the North African and West Asian regions have degraded rangelands, coupled with the breakdown of tribal allocations of land.

Recently growth in consumption by developed countries has declined. Although growth in production has been most rapid in developing countries (Narrod *et al.*, 2011), prospects to export to developed countries are often restricted by stringent health standards in the latter. This has encouraged some developing countries to adopt highly intensive systems of meat production, in which the quality, quantity and health status of the animals can be assured for a Western market. In Brazil major trades in frozen poultry and beef have emerged to service the growing demand for meat worldwide (Fig. 4.1). The development of these industries has been accompanied by rainforest destruction to produce land for animal feed production, principally soybeans for poultry and cattle and grazing for cattle. Globally, greenhouse gas emissions from burning rainforest to create grazing for cattle and land for soybeans are significant, producing approximately 15–25% of total world human-induced emissions (Kremen *et al.*, 2000; Santilli *et al.*, 2008). World soya trade has been growing at a staggering 7% per annum in recent years, most being Brazilian exports to Europe and China (Galloway *et al.*, 2007). The deforestation in Brazil is assisted by uncertain land tenure and poor law enforcement that encourage illegal occupation. Converting cropping or grazing land to production of biofuel, which is subsidized in the USA, has been adding to the destruction, as it increases agricultural commodity prices.

Many other developing countries currently aspire to be major meat producers. For example, President of Kazakhstan, N.A. Nazarbayev, recently said 'We have to become the country that exports meat. For this purpose we have all conditions, there is enough pastures', and underexploited forests of the world, such as in Borneo and the Brazilian rainforest, are under constant threat. Admittedly in the central Asian grasslands or steppes there does exist the possibility to rear more livestock for meat production, if the climatic limitations can be overcome. Currently the lack of infrastructure and reliance on semi-nomadic livestock-keeping hinders the development of a livestock industry that could export or at least contribute more to self-sufficiency. Attempts to introduce more settled livestock-keeping have met with difficulties. Problems such as livestock theft, overgrazing around centres of habitation, absence of computerized livestock- records and reliance on unproductive breeds all limit the potential for trade in livestock.

For much of the 20th century meat and egg consumption was very low in the developing world, just 8 kg/capita/year in China in 1952 for example. The late 20th and early 21st centuries have brought continued rapid development in Asian economies. This, together with rural reform, is increasing consumption of meat in rapidly developing Asian countries. Annual per capita consumption of meat in rural areas of China increased from 9 to 18 kg between 1981 and 2002 (Wang *et al.*, 2005). Egg consumption increased from 1.3 to 4.7 kg/capita over this period. Traditionally meat consumption is higher in urban areas than in rural areas, mainly as a result of greater affluence in the urban population, but the increase in Chinese urban areas in meat consumption over this period was not as great as in rural areas, from 20 to 33 kg/capita and in egg consumption from 5 to 11 kg. The urban data may be underestimates due to food consumed away from home not being included, but the underlying trend is still clear – rapidly increasing consumption of animal products. Predicting future growth is difficult. Clearly income growth has been a major driving factor, but future growth will be determined primarily by the income elasticities of demand for meat products. Estimates of these are variable and depend on income level and whether the consumer resides in a rural zone, where food grains predominate, or the city, where meat consumption predominates. Foreign travel and new cooking methods are also impacting on consumption trends.

Changes in food consumption are evident in another rapidly developing district in East Asia, Taiwan (Huang and Show, 2011). Demand for rice has declined and that for meat has grown from 54 to 74 kg/year between 1985 and 2009. Most is pork (50%), fish (28%) and chicken (10%). When Taiwan joined the World Trade Organization (WTO) in 2002 it had to allow meat imports in, and beef and chicken entered in large quantities, with pork and fish requirements being largely met from domestic production. The demand for domestically produced pork and beef is more price sensitive than that of imported pork and beef, which has demand principally dependent on quality. Imported and home-produced meats do not substitute for each other well, although any imports have some negative impact on home prices.

4.3   Trade in Meat

As well as the increased production and demand for animal products, the volume of trade has been increasing even more rapidly. The value of global food exports doubled between 2000 and 2010, from US$400 billion to just over US$800 billion (FAOSTAT, 2013). World meat exports increased from 24 to 40 million t between 2000 and 2010, a 62% increase. By comparison, for milk the increase was from 73 to 104 million t, a 43% increase. Over a longer time scale, world meat exports grew from approximately 16 million t in 1992 to 39 million t in 2009, a 144% increase (Fig. 4.2) (FAOSTAT, 2014). The two major exporting regions during this period were Europe and the Americas, accounting for 45% and 36% of total meat exports, respectively. The USA was the single biggest exporter, followed by Brazil, the Netherlands, France and Australia. The major importing regions were Europe, Asia and the Americas, accounting for 52, 27 and 17% of total meat imports, respectively. The top importer was Japan, followed by the Russian Federation, Germany, China and the USA.

The number of food animals exported annually has varied between species groups. Over the last 50 years it increased from 2.6 to 36.5 million pigs, 6.5 to 15.2 million sheep, 4.9 to 10.4 million cattle, and 0.8 to 1.4 million chickens (FAOSTAT, 2014). It has been a much more rapid growth for chickens than beef in developing countries, such as Brazil (Fig. 4.3). The economic value of exported livestock worldwide has been growing rapidly, for example at about 4% per year for ruminants (Phillips, 2008). These increases in trade are due to two main factors: the increase

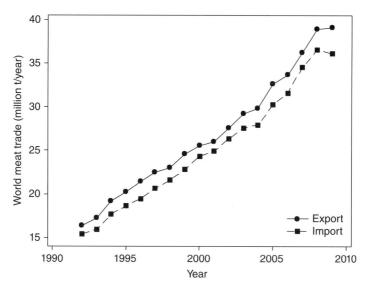

Fig. 4.2. Growth in world meat imports and exports between 1992 and 2009 (FAOSTAT, 2014).

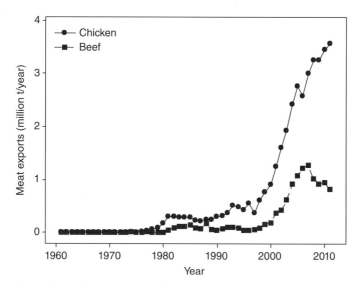

Fig. 4.3. Growth in chicken meat and beef exports from Brazil (FAOSTAT, 2014).

in meat consumption per capita, which grew globally at about 1.2% per year over the last 50 years (FAOSTAT, 2013), and the increase in global population, which grew at about 1.5% per year over this same period (WBG, 2015), and in developing countries at 1.7% per year from 1975 to 2010 (Narrod *et al.*, 2011).

International trade in livestock has increasingly focused on fish, pig, poultry and beef meat, rather than sheep meat. A total of 37% of fish harvested are traded internationally. The change in meat consumption per capita is largely because many people in developing countries are changing their diet from a roots, tuber and coarse grain base to one with meat, milk, rice and sugar.

4.4   Future Changes in the Meat Trade

Recent predictions have estimated that world meat production must increase very substantially and perhaps by as much as 135% from 2005 to 2050 to meet rising demand (Bruinsma, 2003; Elam, 2006). Based on a continuation of recent trends, this is derived from a combination of both predicted increased world population by 34% but also increased affluence, particularly in developing countries in Asia. The premise for this alarming prediction is that meat demand has increased by over 75% in the last 20 years, mainly as a result of increased affluence and population. Along with this scenario of increasing demand, the market is changing rapidly to one based on an international trade. This internationalization has progressed beyond a simple sale of meat products by one country to another. Grain may be grown in one country, exported to another where it is used to feed animals, which are then exported for processing and the meat products in turn are exported for consumption. Animals exported alive to one country may even be re-exported for processing to another country. Recent expansion of meat production in developing countries has only been possible with widespread imports of feed grain. The widespread importation of grain for livestock production probably started with Russian imports from the USA in the 1970s, which were challenged in the 1980s by a US-imposed ban (see Chapter 3).

4.4.1   The real cost of meat production

The true cost of trading in animal products must take into account the externalities, such as water and nitrogen use and emissions, which are not accounted for in the cost of the imported goods. As well as fertilizer nitrogen, there may be loss of phosphorus and potassium fertilizers to the environment, and conversion of scarce ecological resources to intensive cropping for livestock feed. A model of the externalities associated with the meat trade (Fig. 4.4) demonstrates that relative to the internal market, in one of the top two exporters of pig and poultry meat in the world, the USA, external flows of a potential source of pollution, nitrogen, are very significant. In this case they are mainly to China, Japan and the EU. Home-produced animal feed production contributes to significant pollution, even though the feed is not ultimately used to provide food for the nation's people. Although countries such as Japan can effectively expand their land base by up to 50% by importing animal products, the developing countries will be responsible for most of the anticipated increase. Globally the use of fertilizer nitrogen on feed crops

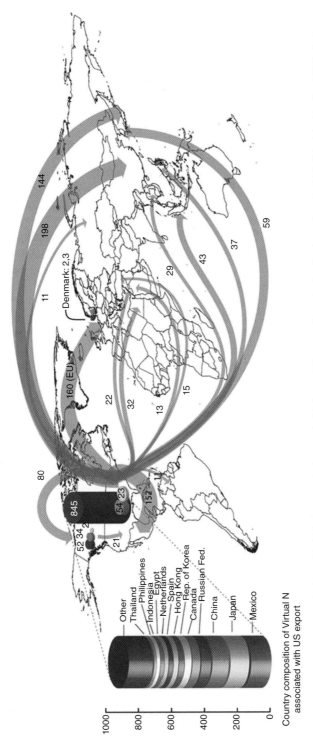

Fig. 4.4. Nitrogen association with US export of pigs and chickens. The small central cylinder refers to N left behind in the USA during different stages of production. Arrows represent total transfer of N embedded in traded products. The large cylinder on the left displays the countries to which exports are going. Data are in thousands of metric tonnes. (Springer, *Environmental Modelling and Assessment*, 14, 2009, p. 187, A Global Model Tracking Water, Nitrogen, and Land Inputs and Virtual Transfers from Industrialized Meat Production and Trade, Burke *et al.*, figure 4. With kind permission from Springer Science and Business Media.)

represents about 40% of total nitrogen use (Steinfeld *et al.*, 2006). In addition much of the N not taken up by the crop is lost to the surrounding water and atmosphere.

Trade in livestock products supports greenhouse gas production if countries buy from intensive producers that emit large quantities of gaseous pollutants. In addition to the direct global warming contribution of CO_2 associated with fertilizer production, there are significant contributions of methane and nitrous oxide. An estimated 32 million t of CO_2 equivalence from these two gases were emitted annually in association with the international trade in meat between 1990 and 2010, and over this period emissions grew by 19% (Caro *et al.*, 2014). The failure of exporting developed countries to pay the full cost of potential pollution is a serious concern. Countries such as Mexico, Malaysia, the Philippines and many in the Near East are net importers of livestock, and are therefore contributing to the overall pollution effect by encouraging production, although probably unaware of the fact. On the other hand, the importation of New Zealand lamb, or cheese, into Europe may be justified from an environmental perspective, because the production in New Zealand reduces use of fertilizer, which is used in large quantities for grazing land in Europe. The warmer climate in New Zealand favours use of legumes in the swards, which provide a source of nitrogen that is largely provided by nitrogen fertilizer in Europe. The fertilizer manufacturing process is associated with considerable output of CO_2, methane and nitrous oxide, in declining order of global warming impact.

Intensive animal production also uses large amounts of water to irrigate crops for feed production. In the USA it has been calculated that 20 km^3 of water are used to grow feed for livestock to export annually (Galloway *et al.*, 2007). In the intensive maize-growing regions the water is largely drawn from the Ogallala reservoir, the largest underground water resource in the USA, which has recently been depleted by 4 m by extensive use for irrigation. As it is also required to provide drinking water, some regulation of its use will be necessary as current patterns of use are clearly unsustainable. The under-pricing of irrigation water will prove one of the greatest political hurdles to cross in the next few decades, since the consumer will be required to bear the additional cost.

Thus the development of the trade in livestock and livestock products has allowed both the pollution of the atmosphere, groundwater and the land to accelerate until it is on a scale that causes serious concern, which was not the case when the livestock were produced in simple, extensive systems for local consumption.

The impact of rapidly increasing trade in animal products on the environment is hard to quantify. The direct impact of the transport can be quantified, but a major factor is that there is an opportunity cost to land and other resources utilized for animal production in any country, which could bring positive benefits in environmental management, or at least less negative impact. For example, the land could be used for timber production, or kept as natural forest, with positive environmental benefits. Thus the increasing meat chicken production in Brazil is at the expense of a forest sink for CO_2, whereas if those same chickens were produced in Europe the necessary feedstuffs may derive from existing agricultural land.

At the same time that the environment is affected by animal trade, the trade itself is influenced by environmental quality. While there is a push for animal products produced under conditions of minimal environmental contamination, there is also a growing awareness that it is necessary to have a screening process to detect animal products with high levels of microbial toxins (including fungal), toxic elements (especially heavy metals), antibiotics, pesticides, nitrates, nitrites, nitrosamines, dioxins and dioxin-like compounds, polycyclic hydrocarbons and radio-nuclides.

4.5 Animal Slaughter for Trade

The scale of livestock transport to abattoirs is vast. More than 100 million pigs are transported to processing plants annually in the USA alone. As many as 0.2% may be dead on arrival and a further 0.3% unable to walk but alive, with especially high levels at extreme ambient temperatures.

Auction markets played a major part in livestock trading until recently, an interim process on the way to the abattoir. Britain had approximately 800 in the 1970s, not all for finished stock, but store cattle and sheep too, with about 65% of cattle and sheep and 20% of pigs passing through the auctions (Edwards and Rogers, 1974). Selling is by the live weight. The rest of the stock, and nearly all poultry, are sold on contract direct to abattoirs. These can be sold on dead weight, live weight or increasingly by dead weight and grade.

Male dairy calves are transported to abattoirs at a young age in many countries because the cost of rearing them for beef exceeds the returns. Their carcass conformation is not well suited to providing large quantities of high price cuts of beef, in the loins in particular. Transporting the calves, which may be only 1 week old, to the abattoir potentially causes them to experience serious hunger, as well as the stress of a new environment without the protection of their mothers.

The demand for specific types of meat can determine the way that they are slaughtered. However, economic considerations may also determine whether meat or animals are transported. Animals may be traded internationally alive rather than as meat:

- If it is cheaper for them to move themselves on to and off of transport vessels than to be moved mechanically as carcasses, even though the weight of the live animal is about twice that of the carcasses.
- If it means that refrigerated vessels are not required.
- If there are religious and cultural preferences for live animals that are slaughtered by specific methods. For example, at the end of Ramadan in the secular Islamic nation of Turkey, cattle and sheep, and occasionally goats, are slaughtered for the festival of Eid. Each family aims to support one of three festivals by an animal slaughter each year. Meat is divided one part for the slaughterer

and seven parts for poor. If people are not aware of how to donate to the poor, it can be done through a central agency.

- If fresh meat is preferred to tenderized and frozen meat. In Western cultures meat is usually hung in chillers for several days to allow tenderization by the breakdown of collagen fibres within the meat by naturally occurring enzymes, and also to enhance the taste, by the evaporation of moisture from the flesh.

The Muslim religion specifies the conditions under which adherents to the faith can eat meat (Malaysian Standard, 2004; Masri, 2007), which include:

- Not eating diseased animals.
- Providing for the welfare of animals.
- Not eating pigs, pig products, dogs and other carnivores, pest animals, amphibious animals, diseased animals, carrion, animal exudates, such as blood, pus, etc.
- The slaughterers must be Muslims and they must invoke the name of Allah during the act (thereby recognizing that only God can sanction the act of killing).
- The animal must die by a single cut by a sharp knife across the front of the neck, which severs oesophagus, trachea, jugular veins and carotid arteries.
- Stunning animals pre-slaughter is generally not recommended (but see below).
- Meat produced under such conditions is declared lawful or halal.

In most Western countries halal slaughter includes stunning, but some abattoirs still slaughter without stunning, which is usually allowed under religious exemptions from national laws. Stunning is acceptable if it is reversible, as in an electrical stun applied to the head. However, a non-penetrating percussive bolt is commonly used for cattle as the electric stun only lasts for 30–40 s, potentially allowing recovery before the thoracic stick becomes effective (Shaw *et al.*, 1990). In cattle, temporarily halting blood supply to the brain may be difficult if this is maintained by an alternative blood supply via the vertebral arteries (Robins *et al.*, 2014).

Most Islamic countries do not support stunning of cattle, such as in Malaysia where there are currently no facilities to stun cattle (K. Blaszak, personal communication). Following revelations about cruel slaughter of cattle in Indonesia, stunning was introduced into several slaughterhouses there in support of an Australian exporting agreement. However, Indonesian religious leaders then issued a fatwa against stunning. The government has expressed the intention to produce more home-grown beef from its extensive native forest lands that could be clear felled to provide grazing land for cattle, as has happened in extensive areas of Brazil.

Case study: Bhutan – growing demand for meat but reluctance to slaughter cattle.

The idyllic image that we have of animal life in Bhutan – small groups of animals happily co-existing with their human carers, no intensive animal production systems, animals not slaughtered but dying a natural death – is rapidly vanishing as the government seeks to use funds from aid agencies and commercial interests to increase meat consumption. Traditionally the Buddhist population thought it sinful to slaughter their animals, which were often released into the forest after their productive life. Meat sales are still banned for periods of the year to encourage abstinence, even if people do stockpile beforehand. People buy good karma by purchasing animals from the slaughterhouse and releasing them to the forest, both out of compassion for animals but also a fear of not being favoured in a future life. However, since the democratization of Bhutan in 2008 aid monies have flooded in from the European Union, ostensibly to reduce the extent of malnutrition in the country. These are being spent on establishing relatively large animal farms of for example 500–800 cows on the small amount of flat land available. Although the concept of animal welfare is widely recognized, for example in the countrywide ban on battery cages for chickens, this development of new large-scale production facilities is contrary to Buddhist ideals but sufficiently far removed from the main population bases to be tolerated. To try to capitalize on the unfulfilled meat demand in Bhutan, India has developed slaughterhouses on the Bhutanese border to supply meat, especially beef from their own cattle herd, the largest in the world. Is it better to organize meat production within the nation state, using large farms that are likely to have welfare problems for their cattle, or buy cattle from India that has too many cattle but concerns about killing them for her own people to consume? The result either way is that meat consumption has been increasing rapidly since democratization, but there is a distinct tension between the Buddhist beliefs of the people and the government action to facilitate increased meat consumption. At a time when people in the West are beginning to realize the dangers of a heavily meat-based diet, perhaps education of the people to live by their Buddhist virtues would be best.

4.6 Conclusions

The world meat trade is growing rapidly. The growth is stimulated by growing affluence and increasing population and is focused on the developing Asian region. In Western countries we now know that high levels of meat consumption are detrimental to human health, contributing to several NCDs. Worldwide there is concern that the growth in animal production to support the meat trade is having a negative impact on the environment, both locally and globally. A particular problem is caused by the contribution to greenhouse gases from the ruminant livestock sector, but the growth in intensive cropping to support the intensive poultry sector, often at the expense of native forest, is an increasing concern. The much greater growth in the intensive poultry industry than other meat sectors is having the effect of increasing systems of production with inherent welfare problems. Finally, the largest meat sector, fish, is transitioning from a wild-caught modus operandi to aquaculture. This too has many environmental and animal welfare concerns, but is largely exempt from the human health issues that pervade the terrestrial farm animal products.

Trade in Some Key Animal Products: Dairy, Wool and Fur

5

5.1 Introduction

The primary purpose of keeping agricultural animals has been for the production of meat. However, two key commodities, milk and wool, were highly instrumental in the development of the farming of animals because they did not require the animal to be destroyed. Both were involved in the original domestication of sheep and cattle and have remained of major significance to this day. A third commodity, fur, developed because of the need for people to keep warm, and the use of animal skins for this purpose dates back to before domestication, when hunters in cooler climes had no alternatives to keep warm other than the use of animal skins. In contrast to milk and wool, which can be obtained without animal slaughter, the terminal consequences of obtaining an animal's skin and, nowadays, limited need to use fur to keep warm because of the many alternatives available, has given users of fur the image of decadence and cruelty as a result of the trapping and farming methods used.

5.2 Dairy Products

The supply of milk and dairy products was originally in close proximity to the major centre of population. Dairy products, cheese in particular, were useful to extend the keeping life of milk. Improved transport networks brought the opportunities to produce milk and dairy products away from the cities, largely in the 19th century. The form of traded dairy products has altered much in the last 100 years. Originally focused on butter, this now makes up only a small minority of dairy exports and has been replaced by cheese, condensed milk and cream.

The expansion of European milk production in the 1980s led to the establishment of quotas (Chapter 2) that concentrated production in countries that were high producers at that time, necessarily the most efficient places to produce milk. With the abolition of quotas in 2015 within Europe, there are concerns that a north European intensive milk production belt will emerge (Astley, 2014). This belt seems likely to embrace the maritime regions of Ireland, south-west Britain, northern parts of France, Germany and Poland, Denmark, southern Sweden and Finland and the Baltic States. Intensive cereal production, which will support the intensive dairying, is forecast to dominate in areas south of this region.

Recently (1995–2011) world annual growth rate in animal product exports has been between 1.5 and 3%. However, for dairy products the growth has been greater than this, up to 5–7% (FAO, 2014). Prices have been very volatile over the last 10 years, with three major peaks (2008, 2011 and 2014). In between the peaks the low prices have opened up new markets, including in Africa, especially Algeria, Egypt and Ghana. Milk production also exhibits major fluctuation, dependent on markets. For example the recent growth of dairy production in Brazil, which is increasing self-sufficiency, has been displacing imports.

A total of 65% of the export trade is supplied by New Zealand, the European Union (EU) and the USA. The growth in milk product trade has not been even across commodities; it was exponential between 1961 and 2011 for cheese, but for skimmed milk powder, the major by-product that is traded as calf milk replacer, there was an increase in world trade from 1961 to the mid-1980s (Fig. 5.1). After this the volume traded was constant. The leading trading region is the EU, and it was in the mid-1980s that milk quotas were introduced to control the growing surplus of milk powder.

Much of the recent growth in milk production has been to satisfy the growing demand in Asia. China in particular has greatly increased importation of dairy products, especially whole and skimmed milk powder, mozzarella cheese for pizzas and other cheeses for hamburgers. Almost 0.5 million t of milk powder were imported

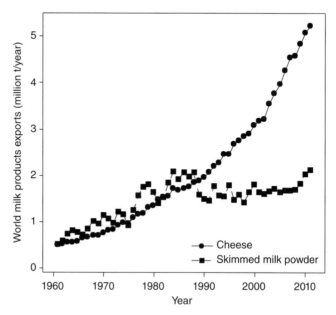

Fig. 5.1. Growth in world milk products exports between 1961 and 2011 (FAOSTAT, 2014).

to China from New Zealand in 2012, this constituting 85% of the imports of that product into China, with the remainder mainly coming from Australia and the USA (Beijing Shennong Kexin Agribusiness Consulting, 2013). Cheese is especially attractive to the young urban members of Chinese society, the older members still finding the product unpleasant.

Whole milk powder is widely used in processing, with about 2.7 million t exported annually, principally by New Zealand, Argentina, the EU and Australia (FAO, 2014). There is slightly less skimmed milk powder – about 2 million t exported annually – with similar major exporters to whole milk powder but with the addition of India in 2013 as a major exporter. Russian Federation imports have declined substantially with their sanctions introduced to retaliate against those imposed by Western nations, especially the EU (but not including New Zealand).

World butter exports are now just under 1 million t, with China a major and increasing importer, second only to the Russian Federation. New Zealand is by far the major exporter, with the focus on producing milk for the dairy product market allowing farmers to operate a spring calving system for their cows, with few cows milking over the mid- to late winter period.

With supermarkets chasing down prices for home-grown liquid milk and dairy products, New Zealand and Australian dairy farmers have increasingly connected to the Asian markets. This is not just for dairy products (yogurt, skimmed milk powder and cheese especially); liquid milk can now be sent by air and be on the shelves within 2 days. With the cost of milk per litre in China recently being approximately seven to eight times the cost in Australia and New Zealand, this high-cost trade is economically justifiable. The price incentive has existed in China in the last few years, but oversupply of imported dairy heifers drastically reduced milk price in China in 2015, leading to business collapse in some heavily indebted Chinese dairy farms. The Chinese dairy industry will undoubtedly reduce their imports in response to this oversupply. This illustrates the fickle nature of rapidly growing markets and the dramatic impact that this can have on production systems.

The increase in demand for milk and dairy products in Asia over the last 30 years has contributed to 60% of the total increase in world consumption (Moran and Doyle, 2015). Consumption is expected to continue increasing, with net imports doubling between 2000 and 2020 (Delgardo *et al.*, 2003). Most East and South-east Asian countries have policies to actively increase self-sufficiency but they are critically short of fodder for cattle. High-producing cows are often imported but rarely are the environment, nutrition and infrastructure adequate to support high outputs per cow. Dairy heifers are sent in increasing numbers from New Zealand and Australia to China, Indonesia, Malaysia, Pakistan, Sri Lanka and Vietnam (Moran and Doyle, 2015). Small herds of approximately five cows were traditionally the suppliers of local milk, but new units of several hundred cows are emerging, copying the large production systems in the USA and Europe. As well, in India, Pakistan, Nepal and China buffalo play a significant role in producing milk and dairy products, but do not produce the high yields expected of modern dairy cows.

In central Asia milk is more likely to be produced by horses, camels and yaks, with cattle used less because of their lack of adaptation to the harsh climatic environment. There is a strong and growing demand for koumiss, a fermented milk product from Kazakhstan, both at home and in China and surrounding central Asian countries.

Although New Zealand and Australia only produce 4% of the world market in milk, their exports constitute almost half of the internationally traded dairy products. Exports are mainly dependent on currency trading value and demand in the Asia-Pacific region. The other major trading group is the EU, but much of the trade is internal (but international). The New Zealand and Australian trade to Asia has been facilitated by protectionist policies to milk imports in the USA and the EU. The containment of European surpluses in milk production, which were previously turned into skimmed milk powder, has allowed Australia and New Zealand to enter into this market.

Cheese export has for some time been led by the EU and to a lesser extent the USA. Specialist cheeses have an international market, especially mozzarella, increasingly needed for pizza production, edam and feta exported from Italy, Denmark, the Netherlands and Bulgaria. The USA, China and the Republic of Korea are the major importers. Almost 2.5 million t are imported internationally every year. Cheese export has benefited from continued efforts to liberate the world trade in dairy products.

Strong trade fosters intensification, with the consequent increased risk of runoff of nitrogenous and phosphate compounds to pollute groundwater. Traditional production systems in temperate regions, such as New Zealand, rely on grass and clover pastures that can be highly stocked without use of large quantities of fertilizers. Clovers have nitrogen-fixing bacteria around their root nodules that naturally provide nitrogen to grass and clover instead of having to supply fertilizer nitrogen, which uses much energy to produce with consequences for greenhouse gas production. Hence, per litre of milk, New Zealand grass and clover pasture systems have less global warming potential than highly fertilized grass pastures that predominate in European systems, especially in the Netherlands, where the high stocking of pastures means that their global warming contribution per unit of area is more than less intensively stocked systems in Sweden (Table 5.1). For eutrophication,

Table 5.1. Environmental efficiency of dairy production systems in New Zealand, Sweden and the Netherlands, in terms of global warming potential (GWP), contribution to eutrophication and acidification and energy use (from Basset-Mens et al., 2009).

Country	GWP (kg CO_2-eq.)		Eutrophication (kg PO_4-eq.)		Acidification (kg SO_2-eq.)		Energy use (MJ)	
	per kg milk	per m²	per g milk	per ha	per g milk	per ha	per kg milk	per m²
New Zealand	0.86	0.8	2.7	25.5	7.5	70.8	1.39	13
Sweden	1.10	0.6	6.1	31.4	18.0	93.5	3.55	18
The Netherlands	1.41	1.1	11.0	85.9	9.5	74.2	5.00	39

the contribution of the New Zealand system is less than a semi-intensive Swedish production system and much less than an intensive Dutch system. For acidification, the New Zealand system contributes less than the Swedish system and per unit of milk produces less than the Swedish or Dutch systems, but per hectare it approaches the Dutch system. Energy use is much less in the New Zealand system either per unit of milk produced or per unit area. We can conclude that the less intensive production in New Zealand produces fewer pollutants, which may justify an export trade to countries where the milk would have to be produced in intensive, heavily polluting systems.

5.3   Wool

Wool, unlike the other animal trading products considered in this book, is not a staple commodity when traded. Its 'consumers' are those with sufficient funds to purchase the commodity and who need its insulating properties to keep warm. This is generally not those in developing countries, but those in the cooler climes of the northern hemisphere, especially Europe. Wool has had an important role to play in the development of several major economies. In north-western Europe, England, Flanders and Germany all grew significantly in the Middle Ages by virtue of their capacity to produce and process wool.

Half a millennium later in the late 19th and early 20th centuries, Australia grew rapidly from its ability to produce wool, which it sent mostly to northern Europe and in particular Britain. Australia had, and still has, much marginal land, dry and weathered, on which sheep can be kept but with limited capacity to grow and fatten lambs. Most of this land is in the south, there being many environmental and disease constraints to sheep-keeping in the north of the country. Merino sheep were introduced to produce the ultrafine wool fibres required to produce the best products, woollens and worsteds, in contrast to the coarse wools that were used largely for carpets, filling mattresses and upholstery and now may also be used for house insulation. In Europe fine wool was processed to meet the growing demand from the expanding middle class following the Industrial Revolution. Thus, unlike milk, wool was an easily traded commodity, it just had to be washed (scoured) and compressed into large bales and shipped around the world. By the middle of the 20th century wool made up two-thirds of the total value of Australian exports (Wadham *et al.*, 1964, p. 97). Over the course of the 20th century the export market for Australian wool switched to Asia, initially to Japan in the 1950s and more recently to China, where low-cost processing industries developed. In North America there was less demand than might be expected, due mainly to widespread availability and popularity of cotton and synthetic fibres and common use of central heating of houses where necessary. Wool production by the top five producers (Australia, New Zealand, South Africa, Argentina and Uruguay) has declined by about 35% from its peak in 1989 and is back at the production levels of 1961. Worldwide, the decline from the late 1980s has been even more dramatic, with current production levels well below those of the early 1960s (Fig. 5.2).

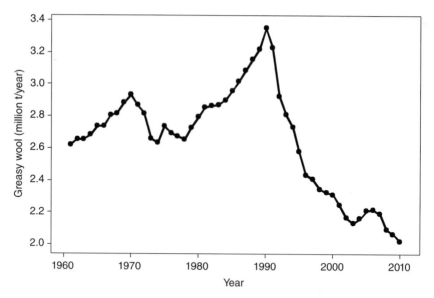

Fig. 5.2. World greasy wool production from 1961 to 2010 (FAOSTAT, 2015).

This decline is principally due to lower wool prices as a result of competition from alternative fibres and more attractive alternative land uses, in particular for cattle. For example, many wool producers in Australia are now converting to producing lambs for meat or cattle.

Over the course of the 20th century the importance of wool in the world market for textiles has therefore diminished, being substituted largely by artificial fibres. These were principally of two types, those derived from cellulose and protein, of which rayon is the most common, and those derived from fossil fuels, especially nylon and Terylene. Although these did not have the heat-retaining properties of wool, increasing prosperity and more people working indoors in the Western world diminished demand for warm clothing. The artificial fibres became popular, both as blends with wool and alone, due to their advantages of being quick drying, slow to crease, inexpensive and strong. Indeed it was the high price of wool in the mid-20th century that encouraged the search for alternatives, the competition from which has eventually diminished demand for wool. On a per person basis, world wool use per person halved between 1987 and 2007.

5.4 Fur

The fur trade has a history going back at least 1000 years, when trading in Siberia used the rivers to establish trading posts for furs such as sable and marten. However, it was not until the 16th and 17th centuries that Russian furs began to command high prices because the European forests had been cleared of these animals, an early example of overexploitation of wildlife. Such fur resources also enabled Russia to trade with Turkey for spices, silks and dried fruit. A rival trade developed in North America, and this helped to drive the colonization of this land by Europeans, particularly the Dutch, but later French and English. Beaver-wool felt hats became a fashion accessory in Europe, which was experiencing a mini ice age, being prized for their warmth and also unobtainable locally as European beavers had largely disappeared. In the late 17th century English and French explorers explored the Canadian outback and eventually the Hudson Bay Company was formed, which sent mainly beavers' pelts to London for hat making and fine furs to the Netherlands and Germany.

More recently the fur trade has been challenged by animal welfare and rights protesters, both because of concerns about trapping and farming methods. Production declined from the 1980s to the 1990s as the welfare concerns were having an impact and wearing fur was generally unpopular, but since then rising demand and production in Eurasia, and in particular China, has returned production to 1980 levels, e.g. world mink production was 42, 20 and 56 million pelts in 1988, 1993 and 2007, respectively (Fur Commission USA, 2010). The increase in disposable income in Russia has also increased demand.

The major species used for fur production are beavers, chinchillas, foxes, mink, sables and rabbits. Most (85%) come from fur farms, the rest from captured wild animals (Peterson, 2010). The most common wild-caught animals for fur are beaver, coyote, ermine and fox, mostly from Canada, Russia and the USA (Peterson, 2010). Seals are also harvested in Canada, but a number of countries, including the EU, have banned importation of products from this cull. A significant number of non-target animals are also caught, reputed by animal protection groups to be from three to ten times the number of target animals (Peterson, 2010). About 60% of the farmed fur comes from European farms, especially Denmark. China, the Netherlands, Finland, Sweden and Poland are also top fur producers. There is also a very significant trade in cat and dog fur, but numbers are not able to be verified.

As well as the trade in furs, which has been volatile lately, there is extensive trading in animal skins or hides. Mostly these are a by-product of cattle and sheep production, and are used for shoes and clothing. However, some leathers, such as from alligators and crocodiles, are the major products from the animals, with the meat being a by-product for pet food or niche markets. The skins from these reptiles are produced from animals grown to a specific size for the desired product, with the animals kept often in isolation to avoid potential blemishes that might result from fighting. The market is focused on fashion accessories, in particular handbags, in the haute couture world of the major European cities.

5.5 Conclusions

Animal products are subject to major fluctuation in price and volume sold. While the dairy product trade has grown very significantly recently, that of wool has declined.

Fur production has suffered under criticism from animal welfare and rights groups but now there is resurgence in fur's popularity because of growing affordability in China and Russia. These trends emphasize the fickle nature of the market for animal products, with diversification being necessary to ensure long-term survival of a farming system.

Trade in Live Farm Animals

6

6.1 Introduction

Trade in live farm animals spans a wide range of cultures and societies, from a local level to the big bilateral export trades that exist around the world. The local trade has a long history. Livestock have been used as dowry for thousands of years, and are still used in Africa and by primitive tribes in Asia (Anon., 2010). However, the live animal trade usually refers to live export and import, i.e. animals that are traded across national borders, but many livestock are also traded within a country, particularly if it is large, such as the USA, Australia or Brazil. Nowadays, with intensification of the livestock industries, the availability of fast transport and growing demand for animals and their products in many parts of the world, the live animal trade is rapidly increasing.

Demand for trade in live food animals is principally dependent on the size of the human population, their demand for animal products and the feasibility of them being traded alive, rather than as a processed product. The trade most obviously follows a migration of animals from the southern to the northern hemisphere, with regions such as Australia/New Zealand, southern Africa and South America in the southern hemisphere producing large numbers of livestock that are transported to the more densely populated regions of the northern hemisphere, both as live animals and as animal products. This is not just because there is more land available to grow grass and arable crops to feed the animals in the southern hemisphere; in South America and southern Africa at least the labour costs are significantly less than in the densely populated European and North American consumer regions.

As the human population grows and becomes more urbanized, it becomes more difficult to transport live animals to the point of consumption and more likely that processed animals will be traded. The transportation of animals as live or dead stock is determined by several factors. In some developing countries that import food animals, tradition and lack of refrigeration capacity in the home, during transport and retailing mean that live export is preferred to export of carcasses. As these countries develop, more refrigerators are becoming available (e.g. 60% of Indonesian households were reported to own at least one refrigerator in 2011;

WSPA, 2013), and the growing urbanization means that supermarket sales are taking over from the 'wet markets' in which recently killed animals are offered for sale. Wet markets are less hygienic, with many opportunities for disease to contaminate carcasses, aided by flies and human handling, although this traditional method of purchasing meat remains favoured by older people in these regions. Wet markets allow purchasers to buy meat that has been very recently slaughtered rather than being tenderized by hanging as is preferred in Western diets. They also guarantee that animals have been slaughtered locally using the appropriate methods prescribed for specific religions, in particular the Islamic and Jewish faiths. These factors favouring live export, together with the avoidance of refrigerated transport costs, mean that higher prices per kilogram of meat are often achieved than for carcasses. However, live export has the disadvantage for the exporting country that the jobs of killing the animals and processing the carcasses into meat are exported along with the animals.

High prices for exported livestock encourage farmers to look after their animals well on the farm, for example rangeland livestock will be provided with supplementary feeds during feed shortages. However, an export trade based on carcasses offers a wider choice of markets worldwide and reduces the risk of disease transfer. Governments of countries engaging in live animal trade often support it financially in the belief that they are supporting rural industry, which is important in times of rural depopulation in many countries. However, in the long term the potential market security and diversification possibilities mean that a carcass trade could be more profitable. For example, two of Australia's biggest export markets, for cattle and sheep, are Indonesia and Saudi Arabia, respectively. Live cattle and sheep trades to Muslim countries have experienced major fluctuations in volume in recent years, mainly as a result of political interference.

Trade between highly developed livestock-producing nations and importers in underdeveloped countries must be managed delicately to avoid accusations of exploitation. The Muslim faith places a high importance on imported animals being in perfect health, and sometimes shipments are rejected because of diseased animals in the consignment. In reality this is hard to avoid because of the stress of the long, arduous journey, which reduces animals' natural immunity. In such situations, to avoid the prolongation of journeys while exporters find alternative markets for the animals, Australia as one of the major exporting nations has contingency plans for each shipment, to offload a rejected shipment to an alternative, predetermined country.

Direct government subsidies for the live trade in farm animals are offered in some countries, e.g. in Bahrain, and in some countries feed, land and water supplies to the trade are subsidized. In Australia, federal government provides financial support for live export promotion and research, as well as supporting cattle producers in difficult times, usually during drought or flood.

This chapter starts with a brief description of the different types of travel involved in live export of farm animals, followed by an outline of the cattle and sheep trades. A detailed analysis of the live export process follows, after which the relevant legislation is discussed. In the next chapter the risks of disease transfer and loss of biodiversity by live export of farm animals are considered.

6.2 Types of Transport

The chosen means of transporting animals depends on the distance to be travelled, the time available, the availability of infrastructure for road, ship and air travel and the relative costs of each. Most animals are transported the long distances between continents by the relatively inexpensive method of shipping. Air transport, although relatively expensive, has also grown.

Rail travel for intercontinental travel was used more extensively in the 20th century than the 21st century, especially where good rail networks were in place, e.g. the USA. Rail offers some benefits for livestock transported over long distances, because motion forces are primarily in one direction only, forwards, and acceleration and deceleration are relatively gradual. Transporting stock along winding roads in rural districts can be stressful due to the constant movement that requires the stock to constantly move to maintain their balance. However, the number of livestock moved by rail has declined, due in part to the pressure to transport other commodities, such as coal, on the limited number of lines available, and in part because of a better road infrastructure to transport livestock in trucks. With rail travel there is still a need to load the animals on to trucks before and after rail travel, whereas for commodities such as coal the fact that there is a point source, rather than diverse sources as occurs for livestock, and the large volumes involved make it economical to run rail lines to transport it direct from source to ship without involving trucks.

For centuries stock have been droved along roads for short distances (see Chapter 1), but the difficulties of moving stock on busy roads, the long time and expense of managing droving and the stress on the animals has led to a major reduction in this form of travel. Australia still maintains specialized stock routes, which are sometimes up to 1 km wide, traversing the vast country to enable cattle to reach abattoirs from the remote outback regions. A fringe benefit has been the habitat reservoir that the routes provide, even though few are used for droving today.

The stress that animals evidently experience during long-distance transport is a major public concern, and this depends on the type and species of animal being transported. Young animals, e.g. bobby calves, are often assumed to be particularly susceptible to the stress and are most likely to be protected by law. However, old animals may also have heightened reactivity to stressful transport situations by virtue of their limited adaptability to novel stimuli. Farm animals that have been used for production of offspring or milk and have reached the end of their usefulness to the farm as economic producers are particularly vulnerable: dairy cows, broken-mouthed sheep and old, 'spent' hens and sows, in particular, because less care is often taken due to the low value of the animals. Usually they are not of sufficient value for the export market, but are more likely to be used for low-quality meat products, in particular pet food.

6.2.1 Transport by ship

Shipping offers the potential to move animals long distances in an environment in which they are fed and watered, which is different from most trucking that is used for shorter distances and without feed or water. There are currently about 40,000 large merchant ships that offer an ergonomically efficient mean of transport for most of the world's growing international commodity trade (Langewiesche, 2010). This growth is occurring as a result of relaxation of import/export restrictions, fostered by the World Trade Organization (WTO), as well as a reasonable period of relative stability in international relations.

The steel cargo transporters are largely unregulated, due to the international nature of their operations. Most fly under 'flags of convenience', traditionally those of Panama or Liberia, but now any number of minor world powers offer limited or no regulatory control for the precious registration fee. Crew for livestock ships are frequently sourced by offshore management companies, mostly from developing countries, especially Pakistan and the Philippines. The wages are low, by international standards, but high by standards of their country, and rather than the luxurious leave in exotic destinations that used to lure men to the ships, the crew work non-stop, 12 months of the year, with refitting mostly taking place en route to save berthing fees in ports.

A degree of acceptability of the trade has been provided by maritime standards that operate under the auspices of the International Maritime Organization, a UN agency, but there is little will or power to enforce these at sea. Maritime activities remain essentially lawless, as they have done for centuries. 'The ocean looks tight in print.... The entire structure is something of a fantasy floating free of the realities at sea. Worse, from the point of view of increasingly disillusioned regulators, the documents that demonstrate compliance are used as a façade behind which groups of companies can do whatever they please' (Langewiesche, 2010). Australian federal government authorities have more control than most livestock-exporting countries, since they have the power to rescind export licences, but their regulatory control of animals at sea has been regularly questioned. Vets on board have 'jumped ship' and revealed attempts to make them cover up problems on board, including falsifying mortality statistics (Anon., 2013). As with other animal management scenarios, it is difficult to regulate good management. When a ship berths after 10 days at sea and the captain should be supervising unloading but instead heads off to town, there are no regulations that prohibit this. When the decision is taken to plough through the middle of a storm, rather than take the more cautious course around the edge which would add an expensive day to the journey, there are no regulations that can enforce action to support the welfare of the animals on board. When the captain keeps the ship in port, unloading slowly at temperatures of 40°C with animals suffering from heat stress rather than leaving port and seeking the offshore breezes that will ease the suffering but delay offloading, this cannot be easily controlled.

6.2.2 Transport by truck

Transport of livestock by truck is favoured for short-distance and some long-distance travel because of the high cost of handling livestock and the dispersed nature of cattle and sheep farms. It has been supported by the major growth of road networks in the latter part of the 20th century. Markets are the traditional way to aggregate livestock before sale and to pass the ownership from the farmer to the transporter, via a livestock trader. However, the process involves additional stress to the livestock, which is often visible to the public since traditional markets that were established at town boundaries are now often well within the confines of the town or city, following their expansion. Increasingly livestock are marketed online and collected direct from farms, reducing stress levels and potential loss of value.

Transport by truck in the more remote parts of the world, especially Australia, North America and Argentina, utilizes large 'road trains' able to move up to 200 head of cattle in from two to four interlinked trailers, each with two decks, that are pulled by a single tractor unit. Developed in the latter half of the 20th century, road trains specialize in collecting cattle from remote stations in the north of Australia, where there are no suitable rail lines, to take them to ports, from where they are shipped to Asia. The quality of the journey depends on whether the road is metalled or dirt and if the latter, whether it is corrugated or smooth. On dirt roads, stock in the rear trailers inevitably experience more stress from dust and trailer movement than those in the front trailer.

6.2.3 Air travel

Air travel is fast but its high cost means it is used only for niche markets, for example goats from Australia to Malaysia or Wagyu cross Friesian bobby calves from Australia to Japan. Therefore only a very small proportion of conventional livestock travel by air, for example just 1% of cattle and 2% of sheep in exports from Australia (MLA, 2013). However, within a sector air travel can be significant, with 98% of goats sent from Australia to Asia travelling by air, most to Malaysia. This form of travel limits the stress to livestock, even though it may be intense over a short time, hence it guarantees better health and low morbidity in animals such as goats that have had high levels of mortality on ships.

Animals are increasingly transported in containers for air travel, which can be moved mechanically and provide a secure environment for livestock. The transport container was an unlikely outcome of the Second World War, and the light versions are now making air transport of live animals more feasible (Reiter, 2010). Day-old chicks, racehorses, exotic pets and caged birds are all beginning to be transported in significant numbers in aircraft containers. Containers are flown with thousands of day-old chicks, and up to four horses can be accommodated in one for their travel to race meetings. Their sealed nature guarantees security for transported animals but can make adequate disinfection difficult (Reiter, 2010).

6.2.4   Travelling on foot and in small vehicles

In developing countries livestock are often driven on foot for sale, for example to market, potentially causing stress to the animals. Vehicles, mopeds or bicycles that were not designed for transporting livestock are also used. Small ruminants may be tied on to roof racks, placed in the boot of cars, or held on a motorbike or bicycle, resulting in trauma to the animal. Droving was the traditional method used to convey cattle to market, and still is in some more extensive production systems, such as in Africa and less developed parts of South America. In Brazil cattle sometimes travel on foot for 60 days to finishing farms, a journey of 700 km. It may be difficult for livestock to consume sufficient feed while being droved on foot, and reservoirs of feed at the night stop are important. During prolonged droving hooves may suffer considerable damage. In Australia, vehicle transport has largely superseded droving, but the drovers' routes have in many places been preserved as 'long paddocks', which are wider than normal routes as they also function to provide grazing for cattle. To prevent these being overexploited cattle are required to travel at least 6 miles (10 km) per day. Regular watering points are provided. These stock routes can also provide a reserve of feed in times of drought. Droving long distances causes significant stress to the animals and weight loss and lameness are common, depending on whether animals are given sufficient time to graze as well as rest.

6.3   The Live Cattle Trade

6.3.1   Introduction

Worldwide approximately 10.4 million cattle were exported alive in 2011, an increase of almost 10% over the previous 5 years (FAOSTAT, 2015). Almost half of these (4.7 million) were in the EU, entailing relatively short journeys to growing facilities, for example from France to Belgium. Similarly Canadian cattle are sent into northern states in the USA for growing out. Such journeys are in essence no different from those within a large country. The biggest long-distance trade route is probably for live beef cattle exported from Australia, mainly to South and East Asia, but also to Europe and the Middle East. There are exports of cattle that are largely unrecorded and therefore cannot be compared with existing recorded trades. One of these is cattle and buffalo sent from India to Bangladesh. Cattle are sacred in the Hindu religion that predominates in India, so they cannot be slaughtered by Hindus or indeed by anyone in many Indian states. However, they are not sacred in the Muslim religion that predominates in Bangladesh. Therefore, even though the trade is illegal because Hindi leaders in India will not sanction export of live animals for slaughter, large numbers of cattle and buffalo are smuggled across the 4000 km border between the two countries. According to one estimate 10 million animals are smuggled in this way each year (Ghosh, 2014), which would make it the biggest export industry in the world and equivalent to the rest of the world combined. The cattle are sourced from farmers in the north-east of India, many of them by rustling. Even if they are sourced legally, the trade is rife with bribes, corruption and murders of rival smuggling gang members.

The export trade is dynamic and tending to increase in exports from developing countries and decrease from developed countries, reflecting the changes in livestock production numbers. For example, in the 5 years prior to 2011 the exports from Mexico and Brazil increased and those from Canada decreased (Fig. 6.1).

The choice between live export and export as carcasses for long-distance transport is dependent on infrastructure and economics. For example, cattle reared in the tropical regions of northern Australia are only able to be exported by ship from northern ports such as Darwin as distances are too great (almost 2000 km) to economically transport the animals to the nearest towns with abattoirs, Geraldton in the west and Townsville in the east. The numbers of cattle exported alive from Australia built up steadily in the 1990s and since then between one-half and a million cattle have been exported annually. It was the strong economic performance of live-cattle exporting that caused the abattoirs in the north of Australia to close about 20 years ago, but after recent public concern about the welfare impact on the animals a new abattoir near Darwin is being constructed. The Australian long-distance trade has been mainly to South Asian countries, especially Indonesia, and the Middle East, but is characterized by extreme volatility as a result of occasional intervention by the Australian government, importing countries' restrictions and fluctuating currency values. The volatility is shown for two of Australia's major export markets, Indonesia and Egypt, in Fig. 6.2.

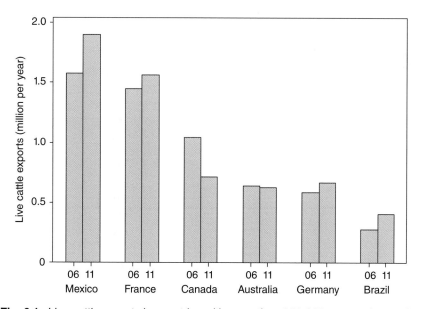

Fig. 6.1. Live cattle exports in countries with more than 250,000 exported annually (FAOSTAT, 2015). Data from 2006 and 2011.

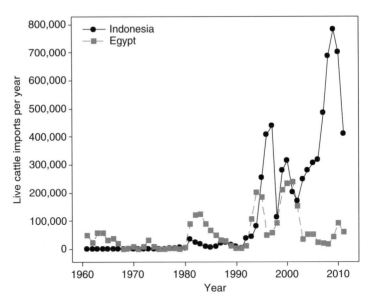

Fig. 6.2. Live cattle imports to Indonesia and Egypt between 1961 and 2011 (FAOSTAT, 2014).

6.3.2   The Australia–Indonesia cattle trade

The Australia–Indonesia trade in live cattle is one of the world's largest long-distance trades, with an average of approximately 450,000 cattle sent from Australia to Indonesia annually over the last 10 years (MLA, 2013; FAOSTAT, 2014), coming mainly from the large extensive properties in the north of Australia. Health standards are strict for the cattle because they are processed into halal meat. Castration or damage to, for example, an animal's ears is enough for the animal to be considered haram, or unclean. The breeds of cattle used for this trade are mainly Brahman or Brahman crosses, because they are resistant to both heat stress and tropical diseases. These animals do not produce the highest quality meat, but this is not of major concern for the Indonesian cuisine, in which the meat is cooked for a long time with spices to aid tenderization.

On arrival cattle are transported by truck to feedlots, where they are held for several months to fatten. Slaughtermen buy cattle from the feedlots and slaughter them in small facilities in the towns before offering the meat for sale at local 'wet markets'. Consumers prefer to purchase their meat fresh in these wet markets because of tradition and a desire to purchase meat from recently slaughtered animals, even though the quality and price are similar to supermarket meats. Most town-dwellers have access to frozen meat, but in villages access is limited and refrigerators are not always available to store it, so many villagers travel to the daily markets in towns to buy their meat.

Large numbers of cattle are imported for Eid al Adha, or Feast of the Sacrifice, the festival that commemorates Abraham's exemption by God from sacrificing his son and his use of a ram instead. Cattle arrive some months before the festival, and each animal is purchased by a group of about seven families. Every person in this group is required to share his portion with the poor, officially donating two-thirds to worthy recipients. If this proves difficult there are processes in place to allow the meat to be canned and sent to remote islands in the archipelago. City dwellers are likely to eat beef during the festival, whereas villagers prefer sheep and goats because of their smaller size.

In 2011 the trade in cattle exported to Indonesia was suspended as a result of the release of footage by the activist group Animals Australia showing cattle being cruelly treated at slaughter plants there. It included cattle being repeatedly kicked and beaten, made to slip and fall on wet concrete, with repeated, fumbling attempts to cut the throats of standing, conscious cattle. There was evidence of continued consciousness of animals with their throats cut, such as thrashing about and vocalizing. This exposé has been followed by regular video releases showing Australian cattle being cruelly treated overseas.

It is important to know why such violence is perpetrated in order to try to control it. In some of the videos, abattoir workers were shown to engage in gratuitous violence, apparently enjoying causing pain and suffering in livestock. Other motivation for the violence to animals may be to control them, in retaliation for aggression or violence by the animal, as an outlet for their own aggression, or to impress and amuse others.

These videos have caused serious concern in the Australian public, particularly amongst women, who felt pity for the cattle, sadness, anger and admiration for the investigators, but they also felt powerless to do anything about the problem (Tiplady *et al.*, 2012). The video footage has revealed how naive many in today's urbanized society are in relation to farming practices. In the USA some state governments have sought to make video-filming of farm animals illegal, the so-called 'Ag-gag' laws, but with little success. Filming of illegal actions without the animal or property owner's permission is accepted in court prosecutions in some countries but not in others. For example, the national rules for criminal proceedings of only seven of the European Union member states admit evidence in violation of basic human rights, such as the respect for human rights; the rest do not (Anon., 2011b). Issues that are considered in relation to intrusion on to property are: whether an intrusion is capable of producing the desired outcome; whether the least intrusion is used that is capable of delivering the outcome; and whether the intrusion is proportionate to the benefit derived from the measure.

Animals in overseas trade feature strongly in video releases by activist groups because the public empathize with the stress involved in transport and are suspicious of how other nationals treat their animals. Slaughter facilities are also a focus of attention. Mandatory installation of CCTV in abattoirs is being considered, at least in the UK, but it raises the question of who will watch all the footage generated. The use of undercover footage may not always be accepted in courts, but the Food Standards Agency of the UK has used it to suspend slaughtermen.

This agency also publishes a list of abattoirs that give 'cause for concern' in relation to both public/animal health and welfare of animals slaughtered within (Anon., n.d.).

Illegal filming of animal cruelty has its risks for activists as it may result in them being prosecuted rather than, or as well as, the animal manager. However, this is unlikely as it brings publicity for the cause. Online journalists' reporting of such filming is officially bound by codes of ethics. These usually stipulate that the journalists should not broadcast footage that breaches confidence or was obtained by dishonest or unfair means, unless there is an over-riding public interest. Most activists would nevertheless claim an over-riding public interest and it is, in any event, questionable whether journalists adhere to the code.

The standards for filming in animal slaughter facilities need careful consideration. A key issue is the moral or legal responsibility of the activist to maintain confidentiality of people appearing in the film, and in this respect whether distortion or alteration of video footage is required to disguise the identity of the alleged animal abusers. Activists have been accused of payment for services and mocking up cruelty events, so the validity and representativeness of the video material must be considered. If video filming becomes illegal, third-party reports of events witnessed may take its place. The intentions of those hired to work in animal facilities may be relevant in considering the value and even legality of both video and reports of events witnessed. Did they seek employment in order to expose cruelty or did they discover this and feel compelled to report it? It must also be considered how those alleged to be causing cruelty are affected, including their legal rights, but this should not stop cruelty being exposed wherever it occurs.

The exposés of animals being cruelly treated overseas highlight the difficulties in exporting animals from a highly developed country, such as Australia, with high welfare standards expected by the majority of its population, to a developing country. Indonesian slaughtermen work in small, poorly equipped abattoirs, and they are often denied the possibility to stun the cattle before cutting their throats because of religious dictates. If stunning is allowed at all it is often by a hammer blow to the back of the head or driving a spike between the back of the skull and neck.

These difficulties in the Australian exports to developing countries have caused major importing countries to look to other sources of supply, such as Brazil for cattle and the Horn of Africa for both cattle and sheep. Some major Australian cattle suppliers are transferring to a carcass trade, with a new abattoir being built in the north of Australia, the first since the last one closed in the 1990s. This would help to overcome the volatile nature of the trade, which undoubtedly has adverse consequences for animal welfare in Australia. After the Indonesian trade was banned, cattle were left unable to be sold, with no live export opportunities, no abattoirs in the north and the costs of transporting cattle up to 4000 km to the nearest southern abattoirs so high that sale of the cattle became unprofitable. The price of cattle dropped rapidly and graziers were unwilling and often unable

Case study: Control of cruelty in the live export trade by mandatory reporting.

Our tour of the various animal trades clearly demonstrates that many of the most pressing animal ethics issues, especially those relating to animal welfare, occur in association with the trade. Transport, slaughter and handling are integral to the animal trade and it is during these events that most welfare issues occur. Staff handling animals at these times do not necessarily perceive a long-term duty of care for the animals in the same way as staff on farms, at zoos or in shelters. Reliance on a strong human–animal bond cannot be guaranteed with the large numbers of animals being processed. Animals are placed under stressful conditions, some react well, others do not. Hence many codes of practice are focused on this time in an animal's life. These are usually mandated in some form of legislation, which aims to protect the animals against cruelty. Cruelty, as normally defined, involves doing or omitting to do something that causes unnecessary harm to animals. Many animal practices come within the realm of 'necessary' harm, i.e. necessary to maintain the production system in an economically viable form. However, legally protecting animals from cruelty is often not enough, people turn a blind eye to cruelty and the perpetrators escape without punishment. Minor cruelty is relatively widespread. Kicking animals forcefully to make them move or hitting them hard with a stick both come under the definition of unnecessary harm. Many people may think that cruelty only relates to the horrific videos that are released by advocacy groups, showing things like shearers putting their fingers into the eyes of sheep or twisting their necks until they break, whereas the legal definition includes a much reduced use of force. Often cruelty, such as castration without anaesthetic or analgesic, is considered necessary because it is commonplace in certain jurisdictions, and use of anaesthetic or analgesic might make an economic enterprise uneconomical. Thus decisions on necessity are firmly anchored in the status quo, which may be quite different in the various regions in which such animals are kept. Relating welfare to current systems, without allowing new ones to evolve that are better for animal welfare, is not progressive.

One solution to the need to improve welfare during the live animal trade is to mandate reporting of cruelty that has been witnessed or recorded on video. This is already mandated in many jurisdictions for those in the health profession that witness cruelty to children. However, it is not entirely clear why this is not extended to workers in a range of other professions where malpractice may result in significant harm to humans. There are many sectors of society with high risk of cruelty, but mandated reporting is limited to just a few.

Mandatory reporting of animal abuse, such as has been revealed in the live animal trade, has been proposed by some animal advocacy organizations, linked to the many releases of footage of animal abuse in previous years and attempts to suppress these in the so-called 'Ag-gag' laws. A release of video footage of abuse of sheep during shearing by People for the Ethical Treatment of Animals (PETA) added to the debate, with PETA withholding the footage for about 1 year before publically releasing it. Confirming cruelty takes a considerable amount of time, but in the meantime many more animals may be cruelly treated by the perpetrators.

Continued

Case study. Continued.

Mandatory reporting of cruelty to animals by industry professionals could, however, make reporting by the public more acceptable, engendering society with a better sense of responsibility to animals. It would come at a significant cost, with the risk that resources formerly devoted to helping animals in need would be diverted towards dealing with reported suspected abuse.

A major issue is why we need such legislation now when society has accepted up to now that people should use their own personal morals in their decision on whether to report abuse. Laws are universal and applicable to the whole community, it is argued, but animal abuse is only covered by an individual's ethics. A lack of ethical accountability has forced society to regulate to achieve its ideals, but in this case the practicality is seriously questionable. Defining what is cruelty and what is simply minor harm is not easy, with one veterinarian for example testifying that transported livestock should not be allowed to lose weight and another believing that it is acceptable because it could be quickly replenished on arrival at the destination. In a society with mandatory reporting of cruelty the number of reported cases would be multiplied many times, if experience in the human health industry is indicative. Investigation of reports would place a significant burden on the relevant authorities.

Protection of reporters from retribution could be difficult, as would levying penalties for failure to notify the authorities. Policing cruelty would depend on what is classified as unnecessary harm, and with animal welfare being managed mainly by the animal industries themselves, it is difficult to see how their classification could be considered impartial. Precedent cases might ease the congestion, but the most effective method would be to appoint an independent body to determine objectively what constitutes cruelty.

The accused may suffer significant psychological damage while proof is obtained and verified. Some might even commit suicide, as has been known in the health care industry following incorrect accusations. At all costs it would be important to avoid the pernicious atmosphere that pervaded much of Eastern Europe when secret police relied on informers to get information on offences against the state. No-one could be trusted, which pitted brother against brother and parent against child. Society should regain its direction with strong moral leadership, supported by teachers, parents and the church. If we fail in that we will drift inexorably into the 'nanny state' that will make life much less attractive for all of us.

to buy food for them. This particular crisis in the live export trade occurred soon after the global financial crisis, which resulted in banks being reluctant to lend finance, especially to a volatile trade such as the cattle export market. This further triggered a significant fall in the value of grazing land, allowing some overseas buyers from Asian economies that were not affected as badly as those in Australia to buy land and make the necessary investments for a profitable cattle trade again. While the overseas investment is to be welcomed for its capacity to provide better conditions for the animals, the manner of its introduction, at the expense of cattle and cattlemen in Australia, was at the very least unfortunate.

6.3.3 The breeding cattle trade

With increasing demand for dairy products, especially liquid milk, in developing countries in Asia in particular, the dairy industries in these countries are expanding. Low yields are a persistent problem and the high yields of cows from developed countries are encouraging governments to support the importation of breeder cattle from nearby countries with advanced dairy industries. Well-developed dairy farms often have a surplus of heifers that can be sent overseas, as only about two-thirds of the female calves born are needed for replacements in the herd. New Zealand, Australia and Chile all have well-developed dairy industries and are sending breeding heifers to China, Russia, Malaysia, the Philippines, Pakistan, Indonesia, Thailand and Vietnam. In China, the cattle are kept in large-scale industrial units, with no access to pasture for grazing and year-round housing. In 2013 there were over 40 new units being constructed, which accommodated about 10,000 cows each. The growing affluence of many Chinese has encouraged growth in dairy consumption, whereas previously they relied on a largely meat- and milk-free diet. The development of the new large dairies has been accelerated by lack of confidence in Chinese consumers for milk produced by traditional smallholders, following melamine contamination of milk in 2008, which resulted in widespread sickness and some deaths of infants. Stricter regulations and a ready supply of potentially high-yielding cows from overseas have encouraged the growth of industrial production. Average yields from the imported cows are about 8000 l/cow/year, much higher than from the 14 million local cows. Imports of dairy cows to China from Australia increased from just 15,000 in 2008 to 62,000 in 2013 (MLA, 2013), principally from the southern states because of concerns about bluetongue virus infection of cattle in the north. Breeder cows are exempt from Australia's Exporter Supply Chain Assurance Scheme (described below), hence there is no control of welfare standards once they reach their country of destination. Recently the growth of the dairy industry in New Zealand has encouraged retention of replacement heifers, leading to China sourcing cows from South America as well.

Imported cows have usually come from farms using pasture grass as the main feed for their animals, whereas the Chinese base their diets on stored forages and grain in intensive indoor feeding systems. The transition is difficult for the cows and health problems, together with lower-than-expected milk yields and reproductive rates, are common. Sea transport is most common but it takes 15–20 days. Shipments are of about 2000 animals at a time. Air transport takes less than 1 day but each aircraft can only take about 200 cows and per animal is four times as expensive as ship transport. Pregnant cows are sometimes transported, although this is outside the Australian industry code, and may give birth during the journey, creating significant stress to cow and calf.

Cows entering tropical countries, such as Indonesia, face severe heat stress, feed shortages and little or no veterinary care. Cows are often kept crowded in a small shed with limited ventilation, a low roof and poor hygiene, or they are taken to roadsides to obtain forage. Milk yields are low, typically 8 l/cow/day, and calf mortality rates are high (often exceeding 15–20%) (Moran, 2012). Most of the cows are Holstein Friesian breed, but some are of the Australian Friesian Sahiwal breed, which is better able to cope with heat stress, tropical diseases and limited feed stocks. The Australian government has been developing standards and guidelines for overseas purchasers of Australian cattle (SCA, 2013), but there is little ability to enforce these.

Apart from China, other Asian countries are expanding their dairy industry by buying breeder cattle. India already has the largest number of dairy cows of any country in the world, but its neighbour Pakistan has been buying significant numbers of dairy cows from Australia since 2007. The human population has been growing rapidly and the milk supply deficit is acute. Apart from China, most Asian developing countries still keep dairy cows predominantly in subsistence agricultural systems. Milk production is substantially less than in industrial dairies, typically 500–2000 l/cow/year. Poor nutrition is a major constraint and there has been evidence that the cows imported into Pakistan are underfed, with yields not reaching expectation, cows having difficulty conceiving and generally poor welfare. Dairy cows have also been sent from Pakistan to central Asian states via Afghanistan, a trade that has been illegal for the most part, but almost impossible to curb.

6.3.4   The calf trade

Dairy farms produce surplus calves as a by-product of cow milk production. These may be sold for slaughter or to grow into beef or dairy cattle. Transporting young calves is highly contentious as it often follows soon after other major stresses, in particular the birth process, removal from the mother and weaning off her milk if the calf was allowed to suckle. Hence the calf's welfare may be already precarious due to compounded stresses. In the USA, for example, many calves are weaned and then transported about 500 km to feedlots within 1–2 days, with the transport lasting about 6–12 h. The stress of transport contributes to increased disease susceptibility, especially bovine respiratory disease. Several factors compound the risk: low ambient temperatures; travelling longer distances; mixing with other groups of calves; and castration of male calves (Cernicchiaro et al., 2012). Ventilation rate is a critical factor, especially in hot weather when overstocking the trucks leads to ventilation ports becoming blocked by cattle.

Calves that are a by-product of intensive dairy industries are termed bobby calves, which are usually male and deemed unsuitable for growing to a suitable weight for slaughter for beef. They are killed at a very young age, typically 5–10 days. Most countries with intensive dairy industries use cows of the Holstein Friesian breed. The calves of these cows do not grow well into beef cattle, with less subcutaneous fat than beef breeds. Beef breeds have been developed that are able to cope with the range of conditions specific to a region. For example, *Bos indicus* cattle used in the north of Australia cope better with the heat and disease challenges than dairy breeds. Dairy breeds were developed in temperate conditions, and the dairy traits do not support the growth of animals with large amounts of muscle in their hindquarters, which are the high-priced cuts that earn the most money for farmers. Thus male calves born into the dairy industry in countries with intensive dairying systems have little value. In times of low prices farmers receive less for their bobby calves than the cost of the transport.

Semen sexing offers the promise of at least 75% of calves born being female, if the initial artificial insemination is with sexed semen and subsequent insemination with unsexed semen or a bull. However, the increased number of females will probably be in excess of those required to replace dairy cows culled from the herd, and alternative markets will have to be found. This may include the overseas markets in countries that are building up their dairy industries or unable to guarantee sufficient female calves of the right dairy genetics, such as in China.

The trade in surplus male calves, sometimes when they are just a few days of age, has caused much concern about their transport to abattoirs to be killed. These young calves have not yet developed a herding instinct and can be difficult to move in groups. Strict control of how handlers get the calves to move is necessary. In recent times the number of abattoirs that can meet the increasingly exacting hygiene standards has declined, forcing calves to be trucked long distances. Calves are picked up from several farms before eventual delivery to an abattoir, with the journey taking up to 24 h. By this time the calves, having been loaded and unloaded several times, are tired from constantly having to balance themselves in a moving truck, hungry and thirsty from not having milk, stressed by the absence of their mothers and in novel surroundings. They would naturally suckle about five times per day and hunger sets in after about 9–15 h without milk. Even after arriving at the abattoir, usually late in the evening, the calves usually have to wait until the next day for slaughter. Some calves are slaughtered on the farm directly and their carcasses disposed of. Blunt trauma, hitting calves on the head with a hammer, is used to stun them before slaughter, but it is difficult and tiring to do effectively and inadequate stuns are common. Slaughterers too suffer distress when required to kill calves in this way, recognizing the cruelty in the process.

The meat of bobby calves may be sold as veal, often of such variable quality that it is used for pet food. Their young hides are used for handbag leather, and pharmaceutical products are also obtained from their carcasses. These include, depending on demand: hormones from their pituitary bodies, trypsin and insulin from their pancreas and the adrenal gland, gall bladder and bile for various products. When demand for veal is good, some cattle farmers keep their calves on milk and concentrates for about 16 weeks before slaughter.

In many countries less intensive, integrated dairy and beef systems ensure that calves are kept for at least 1 year before slaughter for beef. Although the beef from extreme dairy types of animals is less marketable than that from specially selected beef breeds, as it is mostly ground into mince the origin has little consequence.

A beef breed that imparts high fat content to the meat, Wagyu, is particularly favoured as a delicacy, in Japan for example. Some entrepreneurial international producers are air freighting dairy cow × Wagyu calves to Japan for finishing.

6.4   The Sheep and Goat Trade

Demand for sheep and goat imports is focused on the Middle East, principally Bahrain, Kuwait, Israel, Jordan, Saudi Arabia, Oman, Qatar, Turkey and the United Arab Emirates. Meat imports in the Middle East have been growing over the last 15 years at a rate of about 3% per year (Davey, 2013). About one-half of this comes from Australia. Mutton, lamb, kid and goat have been the major meat animals in the Middle East since ancient times, but population growth and limited small-ruminant production potential have created a demand for imported animals. Sheep slaughter is traditional during religious festivals, providing freshly cooked meat. The large Muslim population in the Middle East especially requires sheep at the end of Ramadan, the month of fasting in the Muslim calendar, when cattle and sheep, and occasionally goats, are slaughtered for the festival of Eid. Traditions vary between the Muslim regions, but usually each family tries to have one religious slaughter per year. In Turkey, for example, the meat is divided into one part for the family organizing the slaughter and seven parts for the poor. The increased meat demand in the main centres of population in western Turkey at this time of year is met by imports not only from Australia but also by trucking live animals from the east of the country. Most animals enter a live market before going to the abattoir.

Significant numbers of sheep are exported to the Middle East from the Horn of Africa, many originating in the Sudan, to Saudi Arabia, and from Eastern Europe. Using a broad interpretation, the Horn of Africa comprises Djibouti, Ethiopia, Somalia, Eritrea, Kenya, Uganda and the Sudan. About 2.5 million livestock, mainly sheep and goats, pass through this region to Saudi Arabia for the Haj festival, which represents 42% of the 6 million animals required. The remainder come from Australia (43%) and Eastern Europe (16%) (Abbas *et al.*, 2014). Historically the trade from the Horn to the Middle East was largely unregulated, but recently there has been better recognition of the disease risks following a Rift Valley fever outbreak in 2001/02, which terminated the trade to Saudi Arabia until the Saudis finally allowed it to resume in 2009 (Abbas *et al.*, 2014). In the meantime better quarantine facilities had been installed, and with regular monitoring. Many animals have come from distant pastoral land, being trekked the long distances to the ports, utilizing watering points and grazing or browsing opportunities en route. These animals usually arrive in the best condition, due largely to the skill of the drovers. Others that are less fortunate are trucked in. In the trucks they are often overcrowded, sustaining injuries and frequently heat stressed. A survey of just over 1000 quarantined animals in the Djibouti livestock facility that receives about 1.4 million animals per year, mainly from Ethiopia and Somalia for export across the Gulf, found widespread disease in the animals on arrival (Abbas *et al.*, 2014). A total of 8% of consignments were rejected, mostly camels with pox. Pneumonia is the biggest cause of mortality, particularly in animals that have suffered stress during transport to the facility. After crossing the Gulf of Aden the animals are taken into Saudi Arabia. The crossing in a ship is another major source of stress to the animals as the ships are just general transporters, not designed for carrying livestock. Camels have to be tied down on board and often arrive with bruises, fractures, myositis and pneumonia.

Worldwide, Australia is the largest exporter of sheep, sending about 2 million animals per year overseas, with 98% going to the Middle East. In the first decade of the 21st century Australian live sheep exports declined by about 6% per year, mainly as a result of low profitability in the sheep industry. This derived from regular droughts, low wool prices and the high value of the Australian currency, making exports expensive to overseas customers. The Australian export trade in sheep has suffered from extreme volatility, similar to live cattle exports. Shipments to Saudi Arabia have been rejected because of disease problems, especially scabby mouth (pustular dermatitis), which may exceed the 5% infection rate allowed by Muslim nations. The Gulf Wars also caused suspension of the trade to the Middle East in 1990, and repeated issues with disease caused the trade with Saudi Arabia to cease between 1991 and 2000, 2003 and 2005 and most recently 2012–2013. At its peak in 2007 Australia was exporting almost half a million sheep to Saudi Arabia annually. Australian activist groups have regularly released footage of sheep being cruelly treated in the Middle East, especially by loading into the boots of cars or tied down on roof racks. There has also been evidence of World Organisation for Animal Health (OIE) standards having been broken, e.g. shackling and hoisting sheep before cutting their throats.

Goats are rounded up from remote regions of northern and Western Australia and shipped or flown to South-east Asian countries, especially Malaysia. Animals of feral origin such as these tend to have more welfare problems than domesticated animals, but the practice is condoned in Australia as feral animals are seen as pests and sending them overseas not only provides meat to developing countries, it rids the Australian bushland of a pest animal.

6.5   Trade in Germplasm and Blood

Major developments in molecular genetic techniques have enabled ever more rapid genetic modification of domestic animal genotypes, mainly with the objective of increasing animal productivity. Animal genetic material is increasingly traded, mainly between Europe/the USA and countries seeking to rapidly develop their livestock industries. This has the effect of standardizing the genotype towards that used in the developed countries, with indigenous genotypes becoming rare. The benefits of the novel genotypes to developing countries are increased animal output, for example milk yield in cattle, growth rate and reproductive rate in pigs. The disadvantages are primarily an increased risk of disease spread, together with a lack of adaptability of the genotype in the event of future challenges. The disease risk is enhanced not just by concentration of the genotype but also expansion of the industry.

The trade is managed by multinational companies based in northern Europe and the USA and is of considerable significance commercially. Major recipients include the Russian Federation, Ukraine and China. Trade in live cattle and pigs for breeding, day-old chicks and bovine semen in 2008 was worth US$2.5 billion, compared with just US$151 million in 1988 (Narrod *et al.*, 2011). The biggest growth has been in baby chicks, increased from less than US$25 million in 1988 to over US$1 billion worth in 2009. In addition franchises have been established in developing countries to supply the improved breeding stock to farmers. As described above, the breeding cattle trade has also increased, though rather less spectacularly, with Germany, Belgium, France, Austria and Australia providing over 70% of exports and the Russian Federation, China, Morocco, Venezuela and Italy taking almost two-thirds of the imports. Similarly the sales of bovine semen have expanded rapidly, to be now worth almost US$0.5 billion in 2008, with Brazil and Mexico amongst the biggest importers.

Blood is not traded internationally, therefore the risk of transmission of diseases, such as the H5N1 virus in poultry, through this means is negligible (Beato and Capua, 2011). In many countries, even those with limited food production relative to population such as Ghana, consumption of blood is taboo.

6.6 The Live Export Process

The live export process is often criticized for its adverse effect on animal welfare, particularly if the journeys are long and the stresses on the animals are many. Often it is the totality of the stresses that represents the serious welfare concern rather than individual components. Movements of cattle between countries in northern Europe, for example from France to Belgium, or Eire to Northern Ireland, or from Mexico into the USA are also technically live export. Public concern cannot necessarily be predicted from the length of the journey, with the short sea journey from England to continental Europe raising some concerns for the welfare of stock taking this route.

The most serious concerns must be focused on the longest journeys, usually from extensive rangelands in the southern hemisphere to highly populated countries in the northern hemisphere. The process starts with mustering the animals from rangelands into yards, usually by stockpeople on motorbikes, horses or in vehicles and aided by helicopter and aeroplane to flush them out of wooded areas. This typically takes 0.5–1 day, after which they are held in the yards for 0.5–1 day before trucking them to an assembly depot, which typically takes 1–2 days. The animals are held in the depot for 1–7 days, then they are trucked to the port, usually a short journey of about 1 h, where they await entry to the ship, perhaps for 0.5–1 day in total. Ships are designed to take large numbers of stock, up to 100,000 sheep or several thousand cattle. The loading process requires careful synchronization of trucks arriving and offloading on to the ship to avoid the animals remaining in the trucks for long periods on the wharf. Some ports have facilities that allow up to five trucks to be offloading at once. After arriving on board, the animals are allowed to settle and are not usually fed until a few hours later to avoid fighting. The ship voyage is approximately 7–25 days long, but the animals may wait half a day before offloading, after which they are usually taken to a feedlot by truck. There they remain for 10–50 days, recovering from the journey and gaining weight before being taken to the abattoir, usually a short journey. The entire process takes many weeks and opportunities for recovery are few until they get to the feedlot. Good handling procedures need to be used right from the beginning, with the collection of the animals from the paddocks. Ten major points for good handling of animals during transport and slaughter, derived from the OIE standards for the transport and slaughter of livestock, are simplified in Box 6.1.

6.6.1 Mortality and morbidity

Mortality statistics are rarely collated for the live export trade. However, the contention surrounding the Australian export trade has resulted in the exporters being required to report self-monitored mortality to the Australian government for all shipments, which initiates an investigation if a shipment returns high mortality figures. Average reported levels of mortality are 0.14% of cattle and 1% of sheep in shipments from Australia to the Middle East and Asia. Surveys have suggested that most sheep mortality occurs on board ship and to a lesser extent at the discharge port (Norris, 2005), with inappetence and to a lesser extent salmonellosis from *Salmonella typhimurium* and *Salmonella bovismorbificans* being the major causes of death (Richards *et al.*, 1989). The mortality of goats on shipments from Australia to the Middle East has averaged 1.4%, with the greatest risk being to adult animals (AHAW, 2011).

Box 6.1. Ten key points for the transport and slaughter of livestock (OIE Standards: http://www.animalwelfarestandards.org).

1. Prepare animals well, with suitable feed and handling.
2. Do not load sick or injured animals.
3. Load livestock carefully and calmly into suitable vehicles.
4. Do not kick, hit or otherwise hurt animals during transport or slaughter.
5. Do not overcrowd vehicles with too many animals.
6. Rest animals during and after long journeys, providing feed and water and somewhere to lie down.
7. Do not throw, drag or drop animals, such as calves.
8. Restrain animals humanely for slaughter, without breaking legs or cutting tendons.
9. When stunning animals, do so carefully and effectively.
10. Slaughter and bleed cattle as rapidly as possible.

6.6.2   Causes of stress to live export animals

Some short ship journeys are undertaken without offloading livestock into pens on the ship from the truck in which they were transported to the wharf, e.g. between England and continental Europe and between the islands of Scotland and Australia and the mainland (Phillips and Santurtun, 2013). Although such journeys are short, cattle have been recorded to lose weight, about 7%, as a result of restricted nutrition, immune responses have indicated stress and blood samples have suggested bruising and injury (Earley and Murray, 2010; Earley et al., 2011, 2012). The latter could be due to pre-transport mixing of animals and fighting during their preparation for the voyage. In similar short sheep journeys it has been suggested that the ship journey was less stressful than subsequent onward road travel (Hall et al., 1999), however, longer ferry journeys (26 h) from the south to central Chile have provided evidence of stress and under-nutrition in sheep by the end of the journey (Tadich et al., 2009).

These ship journeys are usually necessary to reach the destination. Travel by truck is used wherever feasible. On ship journeys of more than 1 day, livestock are usually offloaded on to the ship and held in pens for the duration of the voyage. There they should receive food, water and the necessary ventilation and bedding to provide for a comfortable voyage. Inadequate access to food and water are a regular problem in ship journeys in developing countries, for example between Indonesian islands described below, or from South African ports, principally Durban, to Mauritius, a journey of 7–10 days (Menczer, 2008). On arrival, synchronizing the availability of offloading vehicles with the entry of the ship to the port is extremely important in avoiding stress to the animals. Offloading several thousand animals, and in the case of major export routes from Australia to the Middle East, up to 80,000 sheep, requires considerable infrastructure to be available within a reasonable period of time.

Movement of the livestock container

The movements of a ship are different to those of a truck, exposing animals to different stresses. Trucks exert forces primarily in two directions, in a ship's motion there are up to six forces at any one time in three directions (Fig. 6.3). In a ship the most stress is caused by a heave motion, when the ship rises and falls in high seas, and is likely to result in motion sickness (Santurtun and Phillips, 2015). However, the rolling movement can also cause significant discomfort to animals because this affects balance. Unless the animals can predict the movement and sway to maintain their balance, they must make regular adjustments to their stance. In high seas roll can be as much as 20°, enough to cause the animals to crowd together and struggle to maintain their standing position.

Ship movements tend to be more repetitive than those in trucks, particularly out on the open sea, aiding adjustment movements by the animals. However, in heavy seas, vessels sometimes experience 'slamming', when waves hit the broadside of a ship without warning, causing it to judder and shake. The movements can also be unpredictable when entering a port and meeting waves that have reflected from the harbour or other solid objects, or during complex wave patterns at sea.

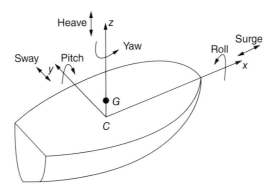

Fig. 6.3. Motion forces in a ship (Ibrahim and Grace, 2010). C, centre of gravity; G, metacentre.

Ship movements, particularly the heave and slamming experienced during high seas, stress livestock (Santurtun *et al.*, 2013, 2015). It is therefore not surprising that, anecdotally at least, mortality also increases in high seas.

The two main truck movements are a surge forwards and backwards during sudden acceleration and braking, respectively, and sway during cornering. Sheep counteract these movements by splaying their feet, providing there is sufficient space, not by leaning on their penmates, which could potentially induce random movements from which both would suffer loss of balance (Jones *et al.*, 2010). Although less predictable than most ship movements, both forms of transport present significant challenges to livestock that determine the stress levels. Thus in ships the motion is often complex but the wave motion at sea can produce rhythms that are less stressful, whereas in trucks the motion is simple, in two planes, but it is rarely predictable. The animals' responses are equally complex, with monitoring by the eyes, muscles, skin and joints, all coordinated by the central nervous system (Fig. 6.4). Orientation can help to minimize the impact of motion and livestock can be observed to orient themselves in a synchronized manner in relation to the direction of travel. The orientation is dependent on the type of journey and probably also dependent on the animal's previous experiences, but is clearly designed to minimize loss of balance. Cattle and sheep probably cope better with surge than sway movements of a similar force because of the shape of their cloven hoof and musculature of the limbs, which is designed primarily for forward movement, not sideways. Hence standing parallel to, and facing, the direction of travel would be expected to resist the surge forces well, but it could also risk their head hitting objects if there is a sudden braking movement. Some research suggests that standing perpendicular to the direction of travel is most popular amongst cattle at least, which may be to protect their heads (Tarrant *et al.*, 1992).

Sea transport is one of the most common precursors of motion sickness, which can occur in a range of species, but road, rail and air transport can also induce the same response (Santurtun and Phillips, 2015). Experts disagree on the major cause of motion sickness, either prolonged postural instability or conflict between sensory information sent to the brain. Since motion sickness clearly has a negative

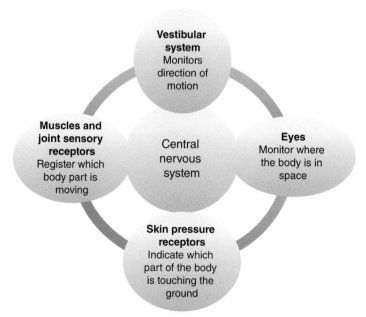

Fig. 6.4. Animal physiological responses to movement (Santurtun and Phillips, 2015).

influence on an animal's fitness, due to postural instability, the physiological response is believed to be invoked to provide an aversive stimulus that encourages those experiencing the sickness to take steps to avoid it. It includes vomiting, defecation, pica, nausea and hypersalivation. The only livestock species definitely confirmed to vomit during transport is pigs (Randall and Bradshaw, 1998), but dogs, cats, fish, some reptiles, amphibians and birds have also been demonstrated to experience motion sickness. Because it is impossible for ruminant animals to empty the rumen by vomiting because of its large capacity, this is hardly ever observed in ruminant livestock; however, an internal vomit from the abomasum to the rumen is possible (Santurtun and Phillips, 2015).

Rail transport creates largely surge forces, with occasion roll during cornering, but of a less extreme nature than in trucks. Driving style is probably even more influential than stocking density in determining the comfort levels of livestock transported by truck (Cockram *et al.*, 2004), with heavy braking, fast cornering and rough roads being major problems for livestock.

Heat stress

Cattle are more susceptible to heat stress than sheep, particularly on long voyages. Heat stress is the biggest cause of mortality in cattle. The mortality on voyages of cattle from Australia to the Middle East is about four times higher than on voyages to South-east Asia, which take about one-third of the time. The type of animal must be taken into consideration when determining heat stress susceptibility.

Large or overweight *Bos taurus* cattle, especially bulls, are at high risk, and to a lesser extent rams also are susceptible. Sourcing cattle from northern ports in the Australian winter, when cold-adapted cattle in southern parts would be readily stressed on entry to Middle Eastern waters, can reduce mortality resulting from heat stress.

Physiological measures to counteract heat stress are panting in sheep and sweating and panting in cattle. Visible evidence of cattle experiencing heat stress is exhibited by high respiration rate, panting with their mouths open and tongue hanging out, and drooling from their mouth.

Wetting cattle, but not sheep, with sea water can temporarily alleviate heat stress, for perhaps a few hours, in an emergency, although care must be taken that the increase in humidity that eventuates does not further exacerbate the stress. Wet bedding must be removed quickly. High-pressure hoses should not be turned directly on the animals or they will become stressed, and sprinklers or low-pressure hoses should be used.

Typical journeys from Australia involve an increase in wet bulb temperature from 23 to 29°C and dry bulb temperature from 26 to 35°C (Pines and Phillips, 2011). Extreme wet bulb temperatures of 30°C (Pines and Phillips, 2011) to 34°C (Beatty *et al.*, 2006, 2007) are also relatively common on the journey to the Middle East. Crucially, the cattle have no opportunity to cool down at night as there is little circadian variation in temperature, especially in the closed decks. At the higher end of these temperatures almost all cattle will be panting to help them lose heat (Phillips *et al.*, 2010). Laboratory simulations of temperatures experienced by cattle and sheep during journeys to the Middle East suggest that both cattle and sheep experience severe heat stress on a regular basis. High humidity and stocking density exacerbate the problems of inadequate ventilation. High stocking densities increase heat output from the livestock and limit the possibility that they can move to a better ventilated area when experiencing heat stress.

In cattle that are experiencing heat stress, core body temperature fluctuates widely, water intake increases, creating wet bedding and high humidity that further increase the stress levels to the cattle. Respiratory rates of cattle may increase from 50 to 120 beats per minute (bpm), and in sheep they may increase up to 300 bpm (Caulfield *et al.*, 2013). This predisposes livestock to alkalosis, for which provision of electrolytes may be beneficial (Beatty *et al.*, 2007). Increased water loss, with the associated loss of salts in urine and sweat can cause sodium and potassium deficiencies (Beatty *et al.*, 2006). Feed intake declines rapidly during heat stress, which reduces the heat load associated with digestion of the feed. It usually recovers quickly when normal temperatures resume.

In sheep, core body temperature has been observed to increase by 1.5°C during temperatures similar to those experienced by sheep travelling from Australia to the Middle East, as well as reduced feed intake (Stockman *et al.*, 2011). As with cattle, sheep show evidence of respiratory alkalosis and renal dysfunction.

The ship's course and ambient conditions at sea will impact on the welfare of livestock. It is, for example, within the power of the ship's captain to take the ship out of a port if heat stress is excessive, to catch offshore breezes and cool the animals, or to avoid high seas that, anecdotally at least, result in significant mortality of sheep. However, both cost time and extra fuel. Not offloading during the hottest part of the day may be prudent. Most livestock ships are offloading in developing countries and the level of infrastructure to support the offloading can be inadequate.

Adequate monitoring of deck temperatures is very important but rarely achieved. Although ambient temperature is reported by exporters, the siting of thermometers may not be the most appropriate to monitor what the livestock are exposed to (Pines and Phillips, 2011). Several sites should be recorded on multiple decks for an accurate assessment of temperature.

Aerial contamination

VENTILATION   The atmosphere of ships and vehicles can become polluted with dust, ammonia and pathogens, potentially creating pulmonary challenges for the animals. The ventilation rate is critical in removing aerial contamination. Ship decks, containing up to 10,000 sheep each, may have forced ventilation, natural ventilation or a mixture of the two. On closed decks forced ventilation should provide 20–30 air changes per hour and an air speed of 0.5 m/s to limit ammonia accumulation (Pines and Phillips, 2011). Even modern high-quality vessels do not always achieve this (Earley and Murray, 2010; Pines and Phillips, 2011) and there are many old, poorly ventilated vessels operating in the live animal trade. Hence ventilation is one of the major issues for livestock on board ship, but it is not as simple as just increasing ventilation capacity. The air flow should be even around the pens, otherwise there are pockets of excessive ventilation with associated risk of respiratory disease, especially pneumonia, and still air, with the associated problems of ammonia accumulation and heat stress. Naturally ventilated decks are subject to the greatest variation in air flow rate, dependent on the prevailing wind speed.

Pneumonia in animals sited near the ventilation shafts was a major cause of mortality in shipments from New Zealand to Asia in the 1980s (Black et al., 1991) and still is a problem in some ships. Sheep do not move around the pens much during the voyage, which will challenge those in places with very little or excessive ventilation (Pines and Phillips, 2013).

In the most advanced livestock ships pelleted feed is conveyed to the animal pens through a series of pipes, drawn through by forced air. Unless the feed is carefully manufactured it will tend to fragment during this process, leading to high levels of dust in the air circulating in the atmosphere. This increases the risk of respiratory disease, as well as eye infection and conjunctivitis. In trucks dust is common on unsealed roads, particularly in the rear compartments of the truck. Long-distance trucking of livestock in Australia and the Americas often uses road trains for carrying livestock, which have two to four connected trailers. Livestock in the rear trailers experience much greater dust and movement than those in the semi-trailer behind the cab.

AMMONIA   Those involved with the live export industry have rated ammonia accumulation on livestock decks as one of the top five welfare problems of sea transport of livestock (Pines et al., 2007). Ammonia concentrations well in excess of the recommended 30 ppm have been recorded in sheep voyages from

Australia to the Middle East, and these routes use some of the best ships in the trade. Levels up to 59 ppm were recorded in one voyage (Pines and Phillips, 2011) and 187 ppm on another (Early *et al.*, 2011). High concentrations are most likely in parts of the deck that are poorly ventilated, highly stocked and with high temperature and/or humidity, such as close to the engine room. Closed decks most often provide the conditions necessary for high ammonia accumulation. The ammonia is produced by urease activity that breaks down the urea in urine, faeces and bedding. It converts into the corrosive alkali ammonium hydroxide when it comes into contact with moist surfaces. Above 30 ppm the mucosal tissues which come into contact with the ammonia, including the lungs, eyes and mouth, become irritated and feed intake declines. Affected animals sneeze, cry and cough, and conjunctivitis, or eye inflammation, develops (Pines and Phillips, 2013). Immune responses in the lungs of cattle and sheep during simulated live export suggest that ammonia causes lung infections (Phillips *et al.*, 2010). Workers with the animals appear to experience similar symptoms and limit their time in the most highly contaminated areas of the ship. If given the chance, livestock avoid even quite low concentrations and it is likely that the irritation of the mucosal surfaces is profoundly unpleasant for them (Phillips *et al.*, 2012b). However, effective monitoring of ammonia on board is difficult, especially fresh air calibration of the measuring device and the stability of the reagents involved in measurements. Sampling methods need careful consideration as well, since there can be small transient pockets of high ammonia concentration in some parts of the ships (Pines and Phillips, 2011).

Ammonia can be reduced by controlling the crude protein concentration of the animal feed, which then limits nitrogen in the excreta. A maximum of 120 g crude protein/kg feed dry matter is advisable. Alternatively adsorbent compounds such as zeolites (microporous, aluminosilicate minerals) can be included in the diet or added to bedding to reduce the volatilization of ammonia.

Stocking density and pen conditions

The high cost of a vessel or vehicle for transporting livestock encourages exporters to load as many animals as possible. This creates a need to deal with waste products. If standards exist, which is rare, they are usually based on avoiding excessive mortality, thereby maximizing financial return to the exporters. However, from an ethical perspective, standards should be based on animals at least being able to turn around, lie down and eat with ease (Petherick and Phillips, 2009). Ideally, similar outcomes for different species and classes of stock would be achieved with suitable standards. Stocking density in transport vehicles can be governed by the animal's live weight, but the type of animal also needs to be taken into account. Because of the risk of fighting, horned animals need more space than polled animals, and mature males more than females. Also large animals need proportionately less horizontal space than small animals because they also occupy more vertical space, hence stocking density is related to weight to a power less than one, and a universal value for minimum space allowance per animal (m^2) of 0.033 W$^{0.66}$ (where W = livestock weight in kilograms) has been proposed (Petherick and Phillips, 2009).

SHIPS   Official standards, where they exist, for stocking density are slightly more relaxed than those for trucks, but animals may be on the ship for several weeks, whereas trucks are rarely used to transport animals for more than a day or two without resting them off the truck. Shipboard allowances are less than allowances in feedlots or sale yards (Caulfield *et al.*, 2013). Sheep typically travel at about 0.33 m² each, which is little more than the physical space that they occupy, and cattle 1.2–1.3 m² for a 300 kg animal, again little more than their physical size. In ships travelling long distances through several climatic zones, the risk of heat stress in tropical or equatorial regions is high and may determine the maximum stocking density. As noted above, cattle are more prone to heat stress than sheep, mainly because of their large body mass to surface area ratio (Caulfield *et al.*, 2013).

Stocking density is one of the major factors governing the risk of heat stress and subsequent mortality. The Australian industry has developed a heat stress risk management model that is used pre-embarkation, which attempts to predict the wet bulb temperature to which livestock will be subjected during their impending sea voyage and uses this to predict the risk of unacceptably high mortality, specifically a 2% chance of at least 5% mortality. Input data include ventilation rate, predicted ambient temperature, acclimatization of the stock and stocking density. The latter is reduced in the event of a predicted high rate of mortality. Although the validity and transparency of the model have been criticized (Caulfield *et al.*, 2013), it is a useful attempt to obviate the significant risk of heat stress impact on live export shipments from Australia.

When determining stocking density, the mixing of horned and polled cattle or sheep is unwise, since aggression is more likely than if all the cattle are of one type. Shearing sheep before transport will enable more to be loaded but also increases their susceptibility to temperature extremes. When the ship collects animals from, or distributes them to, a number of ports, there is the opportunity to reduce the stocking density at the beginning and end of the voyage when animals are being loaded from or discharged to multiple ports. For a journey from Australia to the Middle East this may be useful at the beginning to help the animals become used to the environment, and at the end it may help reduce heat stress.

Much can be done to manage sheep to reduce adverse effects of high stocking rates. Gathering sheep into groups of similar weight and size and penning these together helps to reduce stress and aggression between animals. Each deck should have hospital pens, into which animals can be placed that are diseased or have a pronounced hollow at the site of their rumen, which should make the crew suspect that they are not eating. Vigilance to detect these animals is one of the major jobs for the crew.

Suitable bedding should be provided, at least for cattle which produce more liquid faeces than sheep. For sheep the high ventilation rate turns their excreta into a dry friable powder, which after a few days becomes the bedding. However, at times of high humidity the faecal pad, up to 5 cm thick, can degenerate into slurry. This makes it uncomfortable for sheep to lie and can even lead to mortality.

TRUCKS   At high stocking densities on trucks the welfare of livestock is reduced for the following reasons:

1. They are more susceptible to heat stress.

2. They are unable to lie down or it is unwise to do so as other animals may crowd over them.

3. The risk of loss of balance is increased due to unpredictable movements by their neighbours potentially coinciding with vehicle movements.

4. Sheep against the side of a vehicle can get their legs or head stuck in the sides of the vehicle, which are naturally part open for ventilation, potentially causing injury when the sheep are offloaded.

5. Bruising is more common (e.g. Tarrant *et al.*, 1988, 1992), although the increase is not always linearly related to stocking density (e.g. Elridge and Winfield, 1988).

Many in the livestock industry claim that high stocking densities are necessary to allow animals to provide support for each other and thereby avoid loss of balance during vehicle movement. This may be true if the stocking is so tight that livestock are physically unable to lie down because they are packed against each other. In such circumstances it is likely that a slight relaxation would allow them to fall to the floor. This would be detrimental since when animals fall down at high stocking densities other animals may close over them and prevent them from getting up. They can even die in such conditions. Under more relaxed stocking, extra space gives animals the opportunity to avoid being hit by other animals, and they try to avoid contact with others. Each animal reacts differently to movement and there is no scientific evidence for the 'mutual support' theory that is often used to defend high stocking densities. Careful handling with minimal and preferably no use of sticks to help offload the animals will pay dividends in terms of making the animals easier to move and producing better quality meat products if they are destined for the slaughterhouse.

Misadventure

A chronology of live export events in the Australian trade demonstrates that catastrophes are regular and this results in the death of large numbers or cattle and sheep (Table 6.1). It may be presumed that widespread suffering occurs on many more voyages. The lack of control of the outcome for the sheep is largely due to rejection by importing countries and misadventure at sea, such as ventilation breakdowns. New Zealand was developing a trade but in May 1990 almost 10,000 sheep died en route from New Zealand to the Middle East due to inadequate ventilation, causing heat stroke, pneumonia, other diseases and failure to eat. New Zealand subsequently banned export of livestock for meat, although a trade in breeding animals persists.

Incursion of water on to open decks in high seas can drown sheep. Decks near sea level are most at risk, but these may have erectable sides that can keep water out during storms if these are anticipated and the necessary action taken.

Both cattle and sheep are likely to be stressed during loading and unloading. This makes them prone to make sudden, unpredictable movements. Injuries are common at these times, for instance cattle getting their legs trapped under railings, sheep trampling over each other. A well-designed set of races and ramps, and calm handling, is the only way to avoid this.

Table 6.1. Major accidents and events in the live export industry from Australia, 1980–2014 (Bidda Jones, RSPCA Australia, personal communication).

2014	February: 1495 Australian sheep and 162 Australian cattle died on route to the Middle East while aboard the *MV Ocean Drover*. Mechanical issues and a change of feed were allegedly the cause of the high mortality rate.
	April: Accusations of fraudulent documentation being used by a leading exporter in a 2012 export of Australian sheep.
2013	6 May: Livestock exports to Egypt suspended following release of footage showing animal cruelty during slaughter.
2012	5 November: ABC *Four Corners* programme aired about the killing of 22,000 rejected sheep in Pakistan.
	September: Shipment of sheep rejected by Bahrain, delivered to Pakistan where 22,000 were inhumanely killed in a feedlot.
2010	June: 913 dead sheep (2.5%) due to heat stress and enteritis/salmonellosis on voyage from Portland/Fremantle to the Middle East.
	July: 1914 sheep (3.7%) die as a result of heat stress and/or enteritis/salmonellosis on a voyage from Portland to the Middle East, and a further 527 sheep dead (2.1%) from a consignment from Adelaide to the Middle East (part of the same shipment).
	August: 1407 sheep (2.0%) die as a result of heat stress during the last week of a voyage to the Persian Gulf from Fremantle.
2009	August: 756 sheep (2.2%) dead on one voyage as a result of heat stress and/or enteritis/salmonellosis.
	November: 138 sheep (7.4%) died during a live export aeroplane flight to Malaysia. Inadequate ventilation and resulting high temperature, humidity and ammonia in the hold of the plane were the cause.
2008	Attempted changes to stocking densities on ships were met with legal action brought by live export companies, and no increased space allowances were introduced.
2007	During the northern hemisphere summer a number of sheep shipments exceeded the reportable mortality level of 2% for sheep:
	May: 622 sheep (4.2%) from one consignment and 349 (2.3%) from a second consignment on a single shipment to Oman;
	June: 593 sheep (2.2%) on the way to the Middle East;
	July: 653 sheep (2.5%) on the way to the Middle East;
	August: 1923 sheep (2.5%) on the way to the Middle East;
	August: 1251 sheep (2.1%) on the way to the Middle East; and
	October: 1142 sheep (2.1%) on the way to Saudi Arabia.
2006	February: Live export to Egypt suspended after investigators released footage of cattle having tendons slashed and eyes stabbed in Bassateen Abattoir.
	December: Investigators reveal further cruelty in Cairo markets.
2005	The *MV Maysora* was delayed fully laden with 80,000 sheep in Fremantle harbour when engine problems occurred. No animal welfare authorities were alerted.
	May: Australian Minister Truss announced the signing of a Memorandum of Understanding (MoU) with Saudi Arabia and advised that the ban on shipment to Saudi would be lifted. The MoU included an agreement to offload sheep into a quarantine feedlot near Jeddah if a dispute occurred.

Continued

Table 6.1. Continued.

2003   August: Saudi Arabia refused to offload the 57,000 sheep on board the
        MV Cormo Express (allegedly on disease grounds). For 6 weeks no
        other country would take the sheep.
        October: Eritrea agreed to offload sheep but mortality had reached 10%, or
        around 6000 sheep. Australia suspended all live export to Saudi Arabia.

2002   Maiden voyage of the *MV Becrux*, with 60,000 sheep and 1995 cattle
        from Portland Victoria to Saudi Arabia, experienced high temperatures
        (45°C) and humidity in the Arabian Gulf resulting in death of 1400
        sheep and 880 cattle.
        July/August: four shipments of sheep recorded high death rates during
        export to the Middle East, with a total of 15,156 sheep dead during
        the voyage and discharge phases: *Cormo Express*, 1064; *Corriedale
        Express*, 6119; *Al Shuwaikh*, 5800; and *Al Messilah*, 2173. One ship,
        the *Al Shuwaikh*, that continued transporting sheep had a further incident
        in which 2304 (3%) sheep died, while enquiries were being undertaken.

2001   At least three shipments where mortality figures were under-reported to
        Saudi authorities.

2000   Trade to Saudi Arabia resumes.

1997   Australian Livestock Exporters' Council (ALEC) introduced a Quality
        Assurance programme, the Live Export Accreditation Program.

1996   67,488 sheep died when fire broke out on board the *Uniceb*; 8 days
        elapsed before any rescue attempt was made.

1992   Published figures show increased on-board death rates, rising to almost
        3%, this being attributed mainly due to a large number of ships
        unloading at multiple Middle East ports.

1991   Approximately 30,000 sheep died from heat stroke and dehydration due
        to poor infrastructure and feedlot facilities in Kuwait.
        January 17: suspension of the trade to Saudi Arabia.

1990   Livestock on board the *Mawashi Al Gasseem* were not allowed to offload
        at destination, then forced to stay on board for 16 weeks before any
        country would accept its remaining sheep.
        April: After acceptance of several shipments, the *Arwa* with 18,000 sheep
        on board was rejected by Saudi authorities (alleged scabby mouth).
        April: The *Uniceb*, with 30,000 sheep on board, was rejected (alleged
        scabby mouth).
        April: The other countries of the Gulf Co-operation Council (UAE, Oman,
        Qatar, Kuwait, Bahrain) refused to allow the unloading in their ports of
        any sheep previously rejected by Saudi Arabia.
        May: The *Mawashi Al Tabouk*, with more than 68,000 sheep, was rejected
        (alleged scabby mouth).
        May: The *Corriedale Express* with 56,000 sheep rejected, alleged to be
        too old.
        August: Iraqi invasion of Kuwait led to the suspension of the trade.
        November: The *Mawashi Al Gasseem*, with 86,000 sheep, was rejected by
        Saudi Arabia, later unloaded 54,000 in the UAE, but the remaining sheep
        (26,000) were not unloaded until accepted by Jordan on 16 February 1991.

Continued

Table 6.1. Continued.

1989	Several Australian shipments rejected by Saudi Arabian authorities due to alleged high incidences of diseases. Death rates on board increased to an average of 6% as sheep waited on the ships either outside the ports or en route to alternative ports.
	July: 72,000 sheep rejected – alleged bluetongue.
	July: Further shipment rejected at Dammam – alleged bluetongue.
	August: 33,500 sheep on the *El Cordero* rejected – alleged sheep pox.
	August 15: Temporary halt to the trade, Australian delegation visits Saudi Arabia.
	August: A fourth ship was rejected (alleged sheep pox) as the delegation arrived. Sheep were unloaded in Abu Dhabi for 1 week, then reloaded on to the *El Cordero* and were reported to be subsequently refused by both Jordan and Egypt, even as a gift.
	August: The Australian Meat and Livestock Corporation (AMLC) formally suspended trade to Saudi Arabia.
	September: Two shipments that had already set sail from Australia were rejected.
1985	15,000 sheep died of heat stress on board the *Fernanda F*.
1984	Ventilation breakdown in the *Mukairish Althaleth* caused the death of 70 sheep/day.
1983	15,000 sheep died from exposure in Portland feedlots while awaiting loading.
1981	635 sheep died while being transferred from the *Kahleej Express* to the *A1 Shuuwaikh*.
	8764 sheep perished on-board *The Persia* from ventilation breakdown.
1980	The total cargo (40,605 sheep) of the *Farid Fares* perish in a fire aboard.
	Disease outbreak caused the death of 2713 sheep on the *Kahleej Express*.

Crowding is a risk for sheep entering pens but is unlikely when they have settled down after a few days. During the panic of crowding events, animals die from suffocation as they are pressed against each other and lose their ability to breathe normally. Coupled with often severe heat stress the accumulated stress makes the conditions unbearable for the animals. Such events occasionally happen in crowds of humans, in sports stadia, for example, and the notorious Black Hole of Calcutta. From survivors' accounts it is clear that death by suffocation in a panic situation follows stress that is so severe that death seems like a merciful delivery. In the case of the Black Hole, in which 146 prisoners were held in a cell at approximately $6/m^2$, death came from a combination of suffocation and heat stress, exacerbated by panic, for a few within minutes of entry, but for most over a period of several hours of agony and distress (Barber, 1965). Heat stress and hyperventilation resulted in rapid dehydration and a raging thirst. However, a fear of collapsing to the ground and being trampled upon gave them their will to live, just as it seems to be a focus of attention for livestock experiencing high stocking densities during transport. The desire to remain upright is all pervasive, as no hope can be had after collapse to the ground. In the Black Hole those 22 men and one woman that survived the single night of incarceration were mostly the fortunate or strongest ones that could secure access to the small amount of ventilation available. Just as in ships and trucks when crowding events occur, those that were near the ventilation ports fared best. But for livestock exported around the world, the stress of transport, crowding and suffocation endure for much longer than a single night. And another difference, livestock are undoubtedly more prone to such panic in such events, being unable to fully comprehend the situation, indeed exhortations for those in the Black Hole to keep calm apparently assisted some to survive.

Neophobia

Changes in social structure of sheep in particular can lead to aggression between animals and other deleterious behaviours. Rams are most at risk because dominant animals will chase and mount subordinates to the point at which they become exhausted and may have to be removed from the pen. Detection of animals' suffering in this way, or those that become emaciated as a result of inanition, is often the job of the crew. Leadership in these tasks is usually provided by a veterinarian, if present, or qualified stockperson. In Australian shipments, which have a veterinarian only aboard all long-distance cattle shipments, he or she provides a daily report to the captain of the ship detailing any problems with the livestock such as diseases, evidence of heat stress, etc.

Inappetence

Sheep are particularly prone to inappetence when on board ship, despite the fact that food is available all day. This seems to arise from the multiple stresses that they experience. A high stocking density and a change in social conditions are partly responsible, but often they are not well adapted to pelleted food if they have come off rangeland where no supplements are fed. In rangeland conditions sheep learn as lambs to recognize which grasses and forbs to eat. In their natural, mountainous conditions survival can depend on it. It is therefore expected that some sheep refuse to eat pellets when they are stressed and apparently decide to wait, in the hope that they will be returned to pastureland. Sadly, such an event does not usually happen. Sometimes chaff and clay minerals, bentonite, are fed in addition to pellets on board ship, or they can be added just to the diet of inappetent sheep if they are drafted into the hospital pens (Round, 1986; McDonald *et al.*, 1988).

Overfat sheep are most reluctant to eat, probably because they can survive several days just by utilizing their body fat. All sheep, but particularly the overconditioned ones, should be adapted to pellets during the time that they spend in the pre-loading assembly depot, typically 5–7 days. The high ammonia concentration experienced by sheep on sea voyages also reduces feed intake (Phillips *et al.*, 2012a; Pines and Phillips, 2013).

Goats too are at risk, particularly if they are rounded up from rangelands and are still essentially feral. Together with salmonellosis, inappetence is the greatest cause of mortality in sheep and goats.

Handling and slaughter

At any point in the movement of livestock, rough handling causes stress and potentially baulking by the cattle. Techniques to get cattle and sheep moving rapidly without excessive force or by frightening them have received much publicity in recent years. Use of electric goads, hitting of animals, kicking them or otherwise abusing them are all unlikely to achieve the desired goal, the arrival of the stock at their destination rapidly and unstressed.

Developing countries often employ means of moving livestock that appear cruel when compared with the mechanized systems used in the West. For example, in Indonesia when cattle are shipped between the islands, to go for slaughter for example, the means of getting them on and off the ships can appear inhumane by Western standards. The main goal is to get the animals alive to their destination. In the early days of colonial occupation of the islands by the Dutch, animals were hoisted on to ships with the aid of a body harness (Fig. 6.5; WSPA, 2013). Nowadays, with larger numbers of animals being transported it is quite common for ropes to be placed around a number of animals' necks and they are then hoisted en masse on to the ship (Fig. 6.6). Heart failure has been recorded in response to this process and cattle have been observed to be unable to raise their head properly after a neck hoist (WSPA, 2013). The use of ramps is rare, in part because purpose-built loading/unloading docks are not available. Ships are not purpose built and indeed may not only be used for livestock transport.

Most cattle travel from the more remote eastern islands to heavily populated western islands, in particular Jakarta. A typical journey, from Timor to market in Jakarta usually takes about 15 days, including initial transport to a local market (1 day),

Fig. 6.5. Dutch loading of a cow in Lombok, Indonesia, 1924 (WSPA, 2013). (Nationaal Museum van Wereldculturen. Coll. no. TM-60014403, the Netherlands.) This figure is licensed under the Creative Commons Attribution-Share Alike 3.0 Unported license.

Fig. 6.6. Hoisting cattle on to ships at Port Perak, Surabaya, Indonesia. (Source: World Animal Protection.)

holding in a trader's compound (1 day to 2 weeks), quarantine (2–4 days, but could be up to 4 weeks), loading on to the ship, ship journey (4 days), unloading and holding in a depot (1–8 days) and finally truck to Jakarta (36 h) (ACIAR, 2011). Stocking densities on ship are reported to be very high in some instances (WSPA, 2013), leading to excessive ammonia accumulation. Mortality rates are reported at about 1%, which is much higher than the longer cattle journeys out of Australia (0.1–0.2%). Injury rate during hoisting on and off ships is also reported to be high (0.3%), often broken legs. Weight loss of about 10–12% during the journey indicates a severe shortage of food and water, or stocking constraints preventing access to these resources. There is no forced ventilation in the hot environment, adding to the ammonia problem. There is neither veterinary care nor provision for extended journeys due to poor weather. The latter can occasionally cause very high mortality of 35–70% due to extreme events such as losses overboard.

Slaughtering livestock is a particularly difficult task because they quite naturally resist. In developing countries cattle are often slaughtered by poorly paid workers in buildings that lack the usual restraining and processing facilities that abattoirs have in the West. The cattle, from Australia at least, coming off rangeland are unused to human handling. This often leads to considerable difficulty in restraining the cattle to cut their throats, and in Muslim countries the slaughterer usually does not have the luxury of stunning apparatus before the knife cut is administered.

Traditional facilities include the use of a halter and manual handling to cast the animal before the knife cut. Some abattoir workers also use eye gouging or hoisting the animal off the floor to help them. Others tie them to a post or rail and the head is then lowered to the floor, after which pressure can be exerted on the animal's loins, causing it to fall. The floor may be deliberately wet to make it slippery. Restraining boxes were developed in Australia and donated to killing facilities in South-east Asia. These relied on the operator tying the legs of the cattle, using a foot-catching device or mechanically lifting the animal off the floor before casting it to the floor, a very stressful procedure for the animals. After casting and loosening any ropes around the neck that would restrict blood flow, the knife cut is applied, preferably in a single swift action.

There may be problems with relatively large, wild cattle coming off rangeland being stressed by the long export process, as well as changes in climate and diet, before being slaughtered. For example, Australian cattle are much larger than Indonesian cattle. The traditional method of restraining the cattle in Indonesia is to tie them to a pole in the centre of the building and gradually tighten the rope until they can be manhandled to the ground.

In other countries animals are cast before slaughter by cutting the Achilles' tendons of their rear legs to prevent them running away (Sidhom, 2003). They are usually restrained in a crate, which is inverted to make the knife cut easier because it is made downwards. Inversion causes severe distress to cattle because of pressure on internal organs, inhalation of digesta and blood due to the fact that the rumen contains large quantities (up to 100 l) of fluid and partially digested food which are able to enter the lungs during inversion. The practice also contravenes OIE standards (2013), which state that:

> Animals should be handled in such a way as to avoid harm, distress or injury. Under no circumstances should animal handlers resort to violent acts to move animals, such as crushing or breaking tails of animals, grasping their eyes or pulling them by the ears. Animal handlers should never apply an injurious object or irritant substance to animals and especially not to sensitive areas such as eyes, mouth, ears, anogenital region or belly. The throwing or dropping of animals, or their lifting or dragging by body parts such as their tail, head, horns, ears, limbs, wool, hair or feathers, should not be permitted.

The OIE standards do not specifically outlaw inversion boxes, but their use contravenes the principles of the standards. Specifically, the standards accept that the method causes 'inversion stress; stress of resisting restraint, prolonged restraint, inhalation of blood and ingesta'. At the same time, users are advised to 'Keep restraint as brief as possible'. OIE Standards also state that (Item 4a, i) necessary provisions for animal welfare include 'avoidance of excessive pressure applied by restraining equipment that causes struggling or vocalization in animals' and (Item 4, b) 'Methods of restraint causing avoidable suffering should not be used in conscious animals because they cause severe pain and stress'. It is evident that: (i) an inversion technique will cause struggling; and (ii) the method causes avoidable suffering, because the neck cut is effectively applied to standing animals in many other circumstances.

One remedy for handling problems is effective training. Often truck drivers are required to undertake a handling course, but stockpeople and animal handlers on board ship also need training. Veterinary inspectors need training in recognizing animals that are not fit to travel, for example if they are too fat or thin. Handlers in recipient countries need training in dealing with animals that have become sick or injured during the journey and in disease recognition. They must learn that rough handling and transport, such as dragging of sheep by the horns or front legs or taking them in the boot or on the roof of cars, is unacceptable. Particularly careful handling is required for pregnant cattle or sheep, although in the case of the latter the pregnancy is often not detected until a lamb has been delivered. Treatment of the offspring requires care, and disposal at sea or by other means is also not ethically acceptable. Similarly the disposal of animal waste and casualties at sea by ships is increasingly coming under scrutiny for its environmental impact. Handling method will impact on disease susceptibility, for example when cattle that have been stressed over a long period of road transport before ship transport develop bovine respiratory disease.

6.6.3 Relevant laws, standards and guidelines for live export regulatory control

Transport guidelines and standards

There are no internationally regulated standards for the carriage of livestock by sea (Schultz-Altmann, 2008), but standards for the development of national standards for the welfare of livestock transported by sea, land and air were developed by the OIE in 2003–2004 (OIE, 2012). These are less stringent than many national animal transport and slaughter standards, permitting for example slaughter without stunning, whereas in most developed countries this is required for livestock. These OIE standards are contained in a Terrestrial Animal Health Code, with the aim of providing guidance to attain a required level of animal welfare and health during the pre-journey, loading, journey, unloading and post-journey handling stages of sea, land and air transport (OIE, 2012). The collection of standards had to be agreed to by the very large number of countries (180) that are signatories to the OIE, and as such may be seen as a lowest common denominator for international standards.

The standards contain a mixture of aspirational statements, such as 'Animal handlers should be experienced' and enforceable requirements, such as 'Animals that are unfit to load, including those blind in both eyes, shall not be loaded onto a vessel' and requirements that could be enforceable if detail were available, e.g. 'Providing an adequate number of animal handlers to load the animals with minimum stress and injury' (OIE, 2014b). They have been distilled down to key aspirational messages by the Animal Welfare Standards network (AWS, 2015) (Box 6.1). From these, standards need to be developed that are enforceable by first incorporation into national statutes and second reliably audited in a repeatable manner.

The OIE acknowledges that 'the OIE mandate does not include policing the implementation of adopted standards ... for animal welfare' (Kahn and Varas, 2014). They accede that implementation of the standards is even more problematic than establishing them (Kahn and Varas, 2014). The value of the OIE standards in future needs exploration. One possibility is that they become a framework for member countries to develop their own national regulations. In many cases this would be more stringent than OIE standards, in others the OIE standards would be adopted without variation, but in both situations compliance would be the job of the relevant country. However, with increased trade in animals, and both importing and exporting nations wishing to control the welfare of animals to satisfy public demand for high standards, it would be more desirable to improve the standards to a common and high level, with enforceability worldwide. Some aspects of the standards are hard to enforce and currently have little scientific validation. The argument can be made that the standards are necessarily general and not prescriptive because of the large number of countries, developing and developed, signing up to the organization. Much work will be required if these standards are to play their part in improving the welfare of animal internationally.

Regardless of their scientific validity, the value of the OIE standards will depend on an individual country's willingness and ability to adopt, develop and enforce them nationally. Key questions for enforcers in individual countries are whether they are evidence-based and whether they safeguard welfare to adequate standards. Individual countries may like to introduce cultural and historic constraints on the content of the standards, but this is likely to lead to a lack of scientific validity and comparability, most importantly with trading partners.

There are alternatives to OIE standards that may come to be more widely recognized for their part in establishing international standards. Private standards and specifications for animal welfare are increasingly established by global companies. Although these may address major public concerns, the public rarely understand the major welfare problems suffered by transported animals. The Australian government has in the past favoured a model of co-regulation, in which the standards are contained within 'an industry-owned quality assurance programme that also includes independent third-party audit as a basis for accreditation of industry members in the scheme' (Paradice and Thornber, 2014). However, the main problem with government distancing itself from the programme is that auditors that are managed and paid by industry have a conflict of interest that may influence their judgement on observed breaches of the quality assurance programme. Similarly, if industry manages and pays for the research that supports the programme, the researchers have a conflict of interest that may influence their judgement on the acceptability of welfare practices and standards. It can be argued that it is the researcher's job to do the research and that the decision on whether a practice unacceptably compromises the animals' welfare should be taken by a much more broadly representative group of people: lawyers, religious leaders, consumer groups, members of the public and stakeholders in the industry who, with the aid of the researchers to interpret results, will come to an agreed position.

Exporter supply chain assurance scheme

The OIE ship transport standards are also referenced in an Australian scheme to govern standards for exported livestock. In the wake of outrage by the public at video footage aired in 2011 and 2012 of animals being slaughtered in abattoirs used by exporters handling Australian animals, the Australian federal government introduced an Exporter Supply Chain Assurance Scheme (ESCAS) in 2012. The main principles of the assurance scheme are as follows:

1. Animals will be handled and processed at the internationally accepted standards for animal welfare established by the OIE or better.
2. Exporters have control of the movement of animals within their supply chain.
3. Exporters can trace or account for animals through the supply chain.
4. Exporters conduct independent verification and performance audits of their supply chains against these new requirements.

Because the Australian government has no power to monitor or enforce these standards overseas, the exporters must provide evidence of independent monitoring. If this is inadequate the only power that the Australian government has is to restrict the issue of subsequent export licences to the offending exporter. Another potential problem with the scheme is the potential to contravene WTO goals, which focus on trade liberalization. Usually nations attempt to apply restrictions at the level of imports, rather than exports, but restricting live export in the way that ESCAS potentially do could be seen as a contravention of WTO standards. At very least the restrictions should be universally applied, rather than to just one country, Indonesia, as was initially the case.

Maritime orders

Ship design for the carriage of livestock is specified in some countries. For example, Australian Maritime Safety Authority Marine Orders (Part 43) specify that the maximum pen sizes are 21.0 m^2 and 40.5 m^2 for cattle and sheep, respectively. Adherence to these maximum sizes will help to avoid crowding and crushing injuries. Deck loading capacity, rail strength and spacing (to avoid losing animals overboard on open decks; Waghorn *et al.*, 1995), passageway width and ceiling height are also specified. Stocking densities are specified in many standards, but there is no empirical evidence for these (Petherick and Phillips, 2009). The Australian live export industry and the Australian taxpayer have invested probably more than any other nation on research addressing livestock welfare on ships, but still there is no research published on the economically sensitive issue of stocking density from this investment.

Few exporting countries have standards or guidelines for the treatment of livestock on the vessels. The live export of cattle and sheep can only be legally challenged in terms of compliance with the animal cruelty statutes of a jurisdiction if the animals are within national territory. For Australian exports this usually means within the first 24 h of the journey, but a potentially precedential case, in Western Australia in 2003, was rejected because of disparity between State and Commonwealth law. In international waters the animals are not subject to such regulatory control. Further difficulties may arise because the ownership of the animals usually transfers to the importer on loading, or if the vessels carrying the animals are registered overseas, as they usually are. Transport in the exporting country itself and the destination country may be covered by national regulations. Australia, as one of the world's largest live exporters, has one of the only set of standards for live export that is monitored. The Live Export Accreditation Programme was introduced in Australia in 1997 by the Australian Live Export Council. More stringent and mandatory standards were introduced for Australian exports in the form of the Australian Standards for the Export of Livestock in 2005. For example, mortality figures are reported by the captain of the vessel to government, who releases the figures for high mortality shipments (>2% for sheep and goats and 1% for cattle travelling for more than 10 days). Welfare indicators for animals on ships travelling from Australia are therefore primarily based on mortality, and this has declined for shipments of sheep from Australia to the Middle East in recent years. This may be due to the transport of younger sheep or it may indicate a greater awareness of livestock needs. Other indicators that could be used are the ammonia concentrations on deck, space allowances and temperature on deck. The impact of the considerable noise and vibration from the ship's engines, dust from feed that is blown around the ship, and other stressors, such as the social changes, are not known or incorporated into standards.

Food and Agriculture Organization and other international and national guidelines

The Food and Agriculture Organization (FAO) has issued Guidelines for Humane Handling, Transport and Slaughter of Livestock. Like the OIE guidelines, these are both descriptive of the procedures but also offer advice on how to best manage livestock during these events. They have no legal authority. They describe best practice, for example in relation to handling, and occasionally recommend that certain practices should be outlawed, for example the use of the puntilla, or sharp knife, which severs the spinal cord of cattle and renders them immobile before slaughter.

The EU has the strictest standards for transported animals (Council Regulation, 2005). These cover people's responsibilities (including a certificate of competency for drivers), the types of transporters that can be used, journey times for different classes of stock, inspection protocols, fitness of animals for transport, rest periods etc. Difficulties in monitoring journey times have led to attempts to develop on-board satellite navigation systems for vehicles. The European Commission has also issued guidance on import and transit rules for live animals and animal products from third countries that are within the OIE (European Commission, 2010).

In developing countries and some developed countries laws are often generic and hard to implement, with few welfare indicators that can be monitored. Even though penalties are listed for non-compliance, without welfare assessment these are rarely if ever used. Establishing these laws is sometimes done to convince trading nations that welfare is adequately safeguarded and in order to protect their markets. For example, Indonesia has issued Law no.18 year 2009 on Animal Husbandry and Animal Health and the Government Regulation (PP) 95 year 2012 on Veterinary Public Health and Animal Welfare (WSPA, 2013). This focuses on the physical and mental state of animals, with reference to their natural behaviour. There is no attempt to assess compliance. Reference is made to the 'good way' of transporting and handling animals, with limited definition (WSPA, 2013). Another Indonesian law (82/2000) relating to animal quarantine refers to 'prevention of animal forced action, stress and disturbance of its welfare', again hard to enforce. There are more detailed voluntary standards available (Indonesian National Standard, Voluntary, 10–4665–1998), which specify recommended standards for provision of shelter, food and water requirements and trough provision, stocking densities (1.8 m² for cattle or buffalo animals, regardless of size) and stockman:livestock ratios (1:50). The level of provision at which the shipping agents are operating can be gauged from suggestions that feeding and drinking containers should be strong and not leaking, that there should be gangways, etc. Recommendations for feed provision (3% of body weight daily) in this voluntary standard are more precise than in the Australian standards, which require livestock to be provided with 'suitable feed to satisfy their energy requirements' (ASEL, 2011). In other countries standards may be high for religious reasons, for example, India has some of the strictest animal welfare legislation but this is rarely able to be enforced.

Private standards

The difficulties surrounding government standards have led private organizations to establish their own, developed under the auspices of retailers, farmers or supermarkets. These standards may embrace environmental, human health and animal welfare concerns, and may take the banner of organic or biodynamic standards. The Global GAP framework is a network that was established in 1997 as a retailer group working in conjunction with supermarkets in Britain. Since its inception, it has spread to Europe and is now international, as its name suggests. Certified livestock producers must use certified hauliers, using the standards that have been created by the network.

6.7 Conclusions

The international trade in live cattle and sheep has grown significantly in recent years. Some of this is just between neighbouring countries and represents no greater challenge to animal welfare than transport within a country. However, a substantial trade in livestock by ship has grown up over the last 30 years that takes animals to far distant countries for slaughter and to a lesser extent to form the basis of breeding herds of dairy cows. This has been supported by trade liberalization measures. However, there are substantial animal welfare concerns about this long-distance trade. In response to concerns about travel by truck and ship, animal welfare standards have been developed that attempt to control the practices sufficiently to guarantee good welfare standards. Most are established by governments, but international standards have also been developed and private organizations have also developed quality assurance schemes that include animal welfare. Unless greater pressure is brought to bear on governments to control the live export trade, it is likely to further expand to meet the growing demand for animal products worldwide.

Disease Transmission and Biodiversity Loss Through the Trade in Farm Animals

7.1 Introduction

As well as the risks to the environment and to human health from non-communicable diseases (NCDs) discussed in Chapter 4, there are significant risks to humans and other animals from transmission of infectious diseases, as well as major risk to biodiversity of farm animals as a result of trade.

About 60% of pathogens that cause human disease are of animal origin, and the proportion of emerging infectious diseases that are of animal origin is even higher, 75% (OIE, 2013). Severe acute respiratory syndrome (SARS), avian influenza, Nipah virus, West Nile virus, Rift valley fever, brucellosis and echinococcosis are just a few examples of zoonoses that have had severe impacts on human health.

At the 81st General Session of the Assembly of World Organisation for Animal Health (OIE) delegates in Paris in 2013, Princess Haya of Jordan, Goodwill Ambassador to the OIE, said in her opening address:

> As a population, we need to be able to harness the products of the land and sea, but we need to be able to trade these products too. In doing so, we must ensure that we are protected from the ravages of disease in both the human and animal populations. Whatever action is taken to feed our populations, and to keep them safe, must be sustainable – and that action must be taken together. Sustainability does not mean introducing an approach that is replicated again and again without further improvement. Sustainability is most powerful when it creates a 'mindset', a mindset that involves exploring problems from every angle and seeking new approaches to resolving them – instead of simply relying on old habits. Working together sustainably means forming successful partnerships with aims that are clear to everyone. … A thriving economy, especially a rural economy, is based on trade and is a means to a nation's stability. We must support local economies by promoting safe and sustainable trade among nations.

7.2 Transmission of Animal Diseases by Trade

In the early stages of animal trade the movement of animals followed the transhumance of humans and vice versa, and often pathogens shared these two hosts.

However, the growth of demand for animal protein in developing countries as a result of both increased population and growing affluence has increased trans-boundary trade in livestock, bringing with it an increased risk of disease transmission. This is inherently difficult to quantify, in part because there are multiple entry routes for pathogens and also because there are several stages in the establishment of a disease: introduction, initial dispersal, establishment and spread (de la Rocque *et al.*, 2011). The unregulated nature of most of the trade increases this risk and eventually all regions of the world are likely to host the diseases that are adapted to survive in the local climatic conditions.

Attempts to slow this process centre on the OIE's establishment of reference laboratories around the world, with a reporting system for notification of new outbreaks. The World Trade Organization (WTO) also plays a key role in regulating the sanitary conditions of traded meat and other livestock products. Under the WTO Agreement on the Application of Sanitary and Phytosanitary Measures, sanitary measures are allowed to be imposed on traded commodities to the extent necessary for the protection of human, animal or plant life or health. Import risks have to be carefully and transparently assessed. They take into account the susceptibility of the resident population and the likelihood of contact with imported products, the likelihood of pathogens being infectious, particularly by the oral route, and the prevalence of infectious lesions in the imported meat products. For example, low pathogenicity avian influenza has frequently been detected in samples of chicken meat imported from China to Japan; however, experimental feeding of infected meat to susceptible birds has not so far resulted in transmission of the infectious agent. On the other hand, similar tests to investigate the potential transmission of Newcastle disease virus in poultry concluded that there was a significant risk of disease transmission if they ingested uncooked contaminated meat scraps (Cobb, 2011).

Much can be done to attenuate any risk to importing nations by imposing strict phytosanitary measures. Avian infectious bronchitis is mainly present in the respiratory tract, although significant numbers of pathogens occur in the kidney. Judicious removal of infected body parts can render the risk of transmission negligible. More serious risks occur with the importation of chickens from countries where the chicken flocks are harbouring infectious bursal disease virus (serotype 1). This organism remains viable in muscle for 2–6 days post-infection and can cause high mortality in infected chickens. It can also be transmitted by poultry hatching eggs that are increasingly traded internationally, as can Newcastle disease virus, *Mycoplasma gallisepticum* and *Mycoplasma synoviae*. These organisms are either retained within the reproductive tract or they are able to pass into the egg during formation or storage in the reproductive tract. Not only chicken eggs can transmit diseases; over 1 million bovine embryos are transferred worldwide each year, most from the USA and Europe. Although the risk of vertical transmission is currently assessed as low (Thibier, 2011), and certainly less than trade in live cattle and natural fertilization, the potential exists for diseases to be widely disseminated through this mechanism. Artificial insemination is subject to the same concerns.

The annual Terrestrial Code issued by the OIE provides details of trade risk mitigation for all the major diseases and hosts. Guidelines for the regulation of food products are provided in a Codex Alimentarius, developed by the Food and Agriculture Organization of the United Nations (FAO) and the World Health Organization (WHO). One of the greatest risks occurs with backyard or hobby farmers that may feed contaminated uncooked scraps to their animals. Adequate training, or regulation, of such small farmers is vital in control of disease outbreaks. Another consideration is the presence of intermediate hosts, in particular wild birds and pigs/boar for avian and porcine diseases, respectively. Quarantine procedures must be investigated fully, as these can only contain any disease introduction if the length of quarantine exceeds the incubation period of the disease.

Molecular biology has greatly improved the ability to track disease transmission pathways along trade routes. For example, the recent introduction of West Nile virus into the USA has been traced to an animal carrier from Israel, probably a wild bird (de la Rocque *et al.*, 2011). However, sampling regimes are often deficient in their attempts to generate the field and genetic data to trace the evolution of serotypes. Not only that, the growing livestock trade is important to national economies as well as helping to maintain rural communities, hence countries may be tempted to avoid jeopardizing their revenue by delaying reporting of outbreaks of diseases that would cause other countries to suspend trading with them. Elimination of the disease risk is usually not possible; the strategy adopted can only reduce the risk. The exposure risk tends to increase with the volume of trade, unless quarantine and import/export inspections can effectively detect diseased animals. The increasingly rapid transport times make it easier for pathogens to survive the journey, within live or carcass trade. In the past organisms had to have long incubation periods to successfully survive the transport, such as when heartwater was introduced into the Caribbean in the 1830s by tick-infested cattle that were shipped from Senegal (Uilenberg *et al.*, 1984; de la Rocque *et al.*, 2011). Wars in the past facilitated the spread of disease by, for example, the widespread dispersal of horses causing an outbreak of the African horse sickness virus in Egypt following imports of horses from the Sudan.

Demand for pork in Asia is growing rapidly. In the past the trade in pork or pork products has led to many outbreaks of African swine fever, especially when linked to the feeding of food waste to pigs. Chinese importation of pork and pig products from African nations presents a major risk of infection to their own pork production, which is at its most concentrated in this region of the world (de la Rocque *et al.*, 2011). Religious festivals also present an increased risk, for example the importation of sheep to Saudi Arabia for the Eid ul-Adha festival (worth almost US$1 billion; de la Rocque *et al.*, 2011). The slaughter techniques used, including severance of the jugular blood vessels, enhance the risk of human contamination by Rift Valley fever in particular.

Much of the focus of quarantine services has been on bacterial diseases, but arboviruses spread by arthropods also represent a major threat. In Europe alone there are 12 arboviruses that are potential invaders: Rift Valley fever; Saint Louis encephalitis, California encephalitis, dengue fever, Japanese encephalitis,

Kyasanur forest disease, equine encephalitis, Ross River virus and Colorado tick fever (de la Rocque *et al.*, 2011). Ticks and mosquitoes are the major transmission vectors. The main method of preventing entry is through increased vigilance at entry points.

7.2.1   Foot and mouth disease

Foot and mouth disease (FMD) is a highly contagious viral infection that mainly afflicts cloven-hoofed animals, in particular cattle. It is spread by animal-to-animal contact, often following animal movement, as well as by aerosols and fomites, such as vehicles or people's clothing. FMD is endemic in parts of Africa, Asia and South America, and there are occasional epidemics in developed countries, the UK and the USA in particular, as well as in many developing countries. Following an outbreak it is often necessary to cull large numbers of animals to control the spread of the disease and/or to vaccinate, potentially damaging trade to uninfected areas. Waves of infection pass along well defined trade routes at regular intervals, for example from Afghanistan and Pakistan through Iran to Turkey, and also directly from Pakistan to Saudi Arabia. These disease corridors existed previously for rinderpest, before FMD became so widespread.

Seven major FMD serotypes are recognized and their geographical location and spread through animal trade can be used to trace the sources of infectivity and understand the spread of the disease. The virus itself is not usually fatal but is a painful condition for infected animals, as well as reducing growth and productivity of affected animals and potential for rural income generation.

Border controls are in place, but this also restricts the free passage of animals. In 2014, Syrian refugees from clashes between rival terrorist groups in the north of their country were held up at the border with Turkey because of border restrictions on livestock entry (World Bulletin, 2014). In this case international disaster and emergency management teams were able to negotiate safe passage into Turkey for the livestock and their owners. Many livestock were killed as they approached the heavily mined border territory. The unrest in the region has been partly responsible for a reduction in cattle and sheep keeping in Turkey in recent years, with small farmers having to sell their stock to buy essential supplies (Akbay and Boz, 2005). Reduced red meat consumption locally has been compensated for by increased chicken production and consumption.

Vaccines are available for FMD control but have only temporary effectiveness. Vaccinated animals cannot be distinguished from infected ones, thereby restricting trade. Meat, milk and processed meat products of infected animals can transmit the disease, and so the trade from infected countries, mostly in the developing regions, to FMD-free countries, mostly in the developed regions, is generally restricted. This severely impacts on the ability of developing countries to supply meat to developed countries. The OIE recognizes three FMD statuses of countries, which are used in trade regulation: FMD present, FMD free with vaccination and FMD free without vaccination.

Disease management in Africa and Asia is hampered by the fact that the animal trade is mostly uncontrolled, passing through unofficial border crossings either by trekking or trucks. Large numbers of cattle, sheep and goats travel from the pastoral regions of East Africa, otherwise known as the Horn of Africa and including Sudan, Kenya, Ethiopia and Somalia, to the Arabian peninsula and Gulf States. About 1.7 million sheep and 150,000 cattle made this journey in 2010 (Di Nardo *et al.*, 2011). Even after Saudi Arabia and Yemen banned livestock imports following outbreaks of Rift Valley Fever in 1997/98 there were unconfirmed reports of continued imports. A similar trade exists through northern India's porous borders, mainly focused on illegal cattle exports. The lack of regulatory control of livestock movement is undoubtedly a major factor contributing to the spread of disease in these developing regions of the world.

Pastoralists in much of Africa and Asia operate semi-nomadic grazing systems, moving stock in response to changes in pasture availability and climate change. Often the herds cross international borders in their search for food and water and there is little recourse to veterinary services to treat sick animals. Indeed veterinary services in developing countries are often inadequate, even though there are reviews by the OIE with recommendations for improvement. In the Kenya and Tanzania rangelands pastoralists move up to 30 km daily, with increasing competition with local agriculturalists and the wildlife in an area of exceptional biodiversity. Wild buffalo and impala carry FMD although they do not usually exhibit clinical signs, and contact with livestock is a significant risk because of their malnourished state and the high demands of regular movement. Some of the livestock movement is in response to more favourable trading conditions in neighbouring countries, resulting in movement that unnecessarily exacerbates the risk of disease transmission. In West Africa there is a major trade of cattle into Nigeria to satisfy a growing protein demand for its population, one-fifth of the total African population. Further north there is a significant movement of sheep from Mauritania and Mali to the Mediterranean countries of Algeria and Morocco.

In the Middle East pastoral nomadism of sheep and goats is a conventional way of life that has existed for thousands of years. However, the relatively recent introduction of oil wealth has enabled the development of livestock industries that use vehicles to move live animals rapidly over long distances, potentially exacerbating the spread of disease. The Gulf States are the biggest importers, in particular Saudi Arabia, which imports 3–5 million sheep and 1 million goats annually, many of which are for the Muslim festivals. In total these festivals account for an export of between 10 and 15 million livestock from the Horn of Africa to the Middle East. Live animals are required for the ritual slaughter, hence the region becomes a vast melting pot of FMD virus serotypes at the time of the festival of Eid, with animals coming from Africa, central Asia and Australia. New serotypes constantly evolve, for example the A-Iran-05 lineage, which was first detected in Iran in 2003 and had spread to the whole of the Middle East by 2007 (Di Nardo *et al.*, 2011). Introduction of virulent strains of the disease into the Middle East has been recently traced to the introduction of wild ruminants, including gazelles and sika deer, from India to Dubai for wildlife collections.

In South-east Asia the growth of the economies and liberalization of trade has led to increased livestock trade. Growing populations and a Western-style diet are fuelling demand for animal protein. Large numbers of cattle are transported from India, which has the largest cattle population in the world, to Bangladesh and Myanmar, which in turn export cattle to Thailand and Malaysia. Religious taboos against the consumption of beef in India, price differentials and consumer demand drive the trade. Fortunately FMD is less prevalent here than in the Middle East. Further east, in Vietnam and Laos, pigs move in large numbers to Thailand. China is increasing its export trade, in both pigs and cattle, to South-east Asian countries. Increasingly new pig-adapted type O serotypes are emerging, often originating in China and the Philippines and following the live trade routes. Although not definitively proven, it seems likely that the emergence of this serotype in the 1997 Taipei outbreak followed introduction of pigs smuggled there from the mainland (Drew, 2011). On this occasion almost 1 million pigs were on infected premises alone and the outbreak was estimated to cost US$378 million.

In all of these movements the unregulated nature of the trade facilitates disease transfer. Truck operators often fail to understand the importance of biosecurity, with trucks being inadequately washed out and rarely disinfected. Furthermore, the massive numbers involved in livestock trade in Africa and Asia provide ideal circumstances for the evolution of novel serotypes.

The control strategy for FMD provides a model for other diseases. It has usually involved the following stages:

- effective epidemiological surveillance, providing warning systems able to detect an outbreak in the early stages;
- diagnostic laboratories networked with reference laboratories;
- emergency plans to control any new introduction;
- vaccines certified to comply with OIE standards;
- cold chains to allow use of the vaccines;
- animal identification and traceability; and
- biosecurity measures employed throughout the food chain.

7.2.2   Influenzas

Strains infecting birds typically bind to sialic acid 2,3-galactose receptors, whereas in humans a different receptor, sialic acid 2,6 receptor, is normal. Pigs have both receptors and are therefore potential candidates to be 'mixing vessels' for the virus. The Human AH1N1 virus is believed to have evolved over some years in pigs before infecting humans, followed by reintroduction to pigs and further evolution. Thus close contact between humans and pigs, especially in South-east Asia, is critical to facilitate the spread of the disease and to promote virus evolution during migration to the new host.

7.2.3   Ticks

Ticks are perhaps one of the world's most successful parasites in utilizing trade routes to expand their populations worldwide. Unable to move more than a few centimetres from their host, they have now expanded to pose a danger to extensive meat production industries, particularly those related to beef, across the globe. The situation is deteriorating as a result of the emergence of resistance to acaricides. The tick life cycle in cattle involves them growing on the host over a period of 18–35 days, hence successful transfer to new regions through animal trade requires that the travel period is less than this, that cattle become infected from tick larvae that were produced by ticks from a previous journey, or that bedding infected with larvae was transferred to the destination, where it is able to reinfect cattle.

Tick-borne fever was transported from Asia to Australia in the 19th century, and later it was transferred to New Caledonia (Barré and Uilenberg, 2010). *Rhipicephalus (Boophilus) microplus* has become established in most of the tropical world, indeed almost all of its potential habitat with the exception of a few tropical islands. After reaching northern Australia in 1872, it had spread across the north and east of Australia within 100 years, travelling at an average rate of 45 km/year (Barré and Uilenberg, 2010).

7.3 Risks to Biodiversity

Variability in our animals, wild and domesticated, is our inheritance from millions of years of evolution, in the case of wild animals, and thousands of years in the case of domesticated animals. Variation allows animals to selectively colonize an ecosystem or maintain a presence when the environment changes. Exporting livestock to a new environment will challenge existing wild and captive species. *Bos aurochs* cattle were one of the first victims, outclassed in Europe by the more productive *Bos taurus* cattle almost 400 years ago. In many respects species extinction is a natural process, but humans have undoubtedly accelerated the process considerably faster than they have assisted in the development of new species, resulting in a large negative impact on species diversity. As well, livestock carry with them their microorganisms, parasites and viruses, and these will also compete with those in the receiving country and lead to extinctions that may also negatively impact on our ecosystems. Another takeover by cattle occurred in Africa, where many local breeds were initially replaced by humpless European cattle. Farmers soon found that these cattle did not thrive in hot temperatures with significant disease challenges and replaced them with humped zebu (*Bos indicus*) cattle that were originally from the Indus valley. Neither novel genotypes have the necessary tick and trypanosome resistance, and resistance to chemical control, e.g. by acaricides, is growing and will at some stage render natural resistance a much more essential characteristic of cattle than it is now. Not only do novel cattle genotypes lack resistance to local diseases, they frequently introduce new diseases, such as the rinderpest virus introduced with the movement of cattle from Asia to Africa in the late 19th century (Moutou and Pastoret, 2010). It was from rinderpest that measles developed about 900 years ago to infect humans (Furuse *et al.*, 2010), which had devastating consequences when the Spanish conquistadores introduced it to the naive Aztec population of South America in the 16th century. The rinderpest virus had a high morbidity and mortality in European cattle for centuries, and a new introduction from South African zebu cattle that were resting for 24 h in Antwerp eventually led to a major European outbreak that culminated in the formation of the Office International des Epizooties or OIE in 1924 (Hoffmann, 2010).

The impact of imported high output livestock on biodiversity is at three levels: ecosystem, species and gene (Hoffmann, 2010). At the ecosystem level, livestock are an integral part of many ecosystems, contributing services as diverse as food, fibre, manure and seed dispersal. However, the introduction of high output genetic stock to replace local breeds can change the ecosystem entirely. For example, it might require a change in the feeding system; from hay, which is of relatively low nutritional value, to concentrate and silage, which are high energy and do not usually contain seeds, unlike hay, thereby jeopardizing seed dispersal. Faeces are wetter and not suitable to be used as a fuel source by the rural poor, even if a suitable dispersal mechanism could be found.

Species used for livestock production were carefully selected over many thousands of years by farmers and natural selection pressures. Only a dozen or so are used for most purposes for which livestock are kept: pigs, cattle, goats, sheep, buffalo, rabbits, chickens, turkeys, ducks, geese and guinea fowl (Hoffman, 2010), together with some of local significance, such as camelids and ratites. The increase in live export over the last 50 years has been very much greater in chickens, and to a lesser extent pigs, than in the less commonly eaten cattle, sheep, goats and camels (Table 7.1). Even less common species have actually declined in numbers exported over the last 5 years, emphasizing that there is a concentration of species used for meat production, with a focus on poultry and pigs.

Of the major species used (Table 7.1), 6685 breeds are known, of which 5214 are of local significance, 414 of regional significance and 462 of international significance (Hoffmann, 2010). Whether a genotype constitutes a breed can be a matter of dispute, but it is generally recognized that there are approximately 700 breeds

Table 7.1. Worldwide live exports of common animal species used in agriculture (FAOSTAT, 2014).

Species	Number exported per year		Proportional increase
	1961	2011	
Chickens	8,321,000	1,445,930,000	174.0
Pigs	2,616,304	36,534,853	14.0
Sheep	6,508,924	15,234,284	2.3
Cattle	4,860,845	10,409,329	2.1
Goats	5,879,102	1,277,485	4.6
Camels	81,651	294,702	3.6
Horses	400,563	328,176	0.82
Buffalo	98,760	82,470	0.84
Asses	10,487	2,445	0.23
Mules	5,953	637	0.11

of cattle worldwide (Felius, 1995). There are major differences globally in the proportion of local and international breeds. In North America and the south-west Pacific international breeds are largely used, whereas in Europe, Asia, Africa and the Middle East local or regional breeds predominate. There has also been an influence of colonization, with the countries that colonized large parts of the developing world wanting to perpetrate their high producing animals, without necessarily realizing the multiple functions that the livestock fulfilled in the developing countries.

Despite this, in many developing countries there is still a preponderance of local breeds, which are usually kept for multiple purposes. They are adapted to local conditions and are able to adapt to changes in resource provision, such as food and water availability, climate, pests and diseases (Hoffmann, 2010). They are particularly important for use in marginal ecosystems, since they are more resilient to environmental change. Nevertheless, importation of 'international breeds' from developed countries has expanded rapidly in the dairy and meat chicken sector in particular. Often this is with substantial government and international agency support. The 'send-a-cow' and other campaigns targeting African villagers are an example of this that had some benefit to the local people but also undermined the value of local cattle breeds. The international breeds are often unsuitable because they are specialized for high output of a single product: milk, meat or fibre. They require high levels of resources and offer little flexibility in resource requirement. In particular cheap grain and energy are necessary, and these are the two commodities over which future availability is most in doubt. Nevertheless the production differential between livestock from developed countries that have commercial breeding programmes and the rest of the world that does not is significant. In percentage terms, it has been calculated as 440%, 81% and 53% for milk, beef and eggs, respectively. It is less for sheep, goat and pork meat (20%) and intermediate (31%) for chicken meat (Hoffmann, 2010). The influx of genetic resources from developed countries will eventually cause production levels to converge between the developed and developing world as long as the problems of disease and poor feed quality in the tropics can be solved.

Active proliferation of international breeds has only been possible because of developments in artificial reproduction that enabled vast numbers of offspring to be produced from the highest output stock. Artificial insemination, developed in the mid-20th century, enabled bulls' semen to be frozen and widely used overseas. In the late 20th century embryo transfer was developed, which offered similar possibilities, and more recently cloning offers potential for still further narrowing of the biodiversity pool. Developing countries' eagerness to use these technologies and the willingness of companies in the Western world to exploit this has led to the importation of Western breeds to many situations in which they are unsuited. Transport of chicks has similarly allowed the poultry industry to concentrate on a small genetic stock, with currently less than 6000 great-grandparents to supply the chickens that produce 800 billion eggs, and 15,000 meat chickens to supply the parent stock for chickens that produce 76 million t of meat annually (Hoffmann, 2010). The dangers of such concentration of genetic resource have been known

Table 7.2. Use of major species for meat and milk production and the proportion of breeds at risk of extinction or already extinct (adapted from Hoffmann, 2010).

Species	Meat (%)	Milk (%)	Percentage of breeds at risk or already extinct
Pig	37		35
Cattle	22	84	31
Goat	1.8	2.2	16
Sheep	3.1	1.3	27
Buffalo	1.2	13	8
Rabbit	0.7		22
Chicken	28		37
Turkey	2.2		35
Duck	1.3		27
Goose and guinea fowl	0.8		23

and discussed for at least 40 years, yet the economic imperative has driven this change in worldwide livestock genetic resources.

As well as displacing local breeds of livestock, introduced breeds have also had a major impact on wildlife when left to become feral. This was sometimes for the benefit of future colonizers, when livestock were left on islands for example and became feral. Pigs and goats were both released for this purpose on islands. The Mediterranean wild boar (*Sus scrofa meridionalis*), for example, is presumed to have disappeared from Corsica following the introduction of free-range domestic pigs (Barrat *et al.*, 2010). These islands often had no major predators and goats in particular were able to decimate indigenous flora in their attempts to find suitable food.

Pest animals, such as foxes, sparrows and rabbits, were also taken to the colonies for the provision of animals for hunting and to add variety to an environment considered poor, in some cases decimating the local fauna. The flora too suffered greatly, and the widespread expansion of the herbivorous European rabbit (*Oryctolagus cuniculus*) that competed with introduced livestock in Australia necessitated protection of remaining regions with vast fences, sometimes thousands of kilometres long. Approximately 20–30% of most of the species used for meat and milk production are at risk of extinction or are already extinct (Table 7.2) (Hoffmann, 2010).

7.4 Conclusions

The trade in livestock has seen the transmission of diseases around the world and has probably created the necessary conditions for new and more virulent strains to emerge. Disease transfer has also exposed existing adapted genotypes to novel risks and conversely some newly introduced livestock genotypes have been unable to develop sufficient immunity to endemic diseases. Vigilance and action by the

OIE is helping to control the spread of diseases, but the eventual dispersal of disease organisms to all susceptible areas appears inevitable. The chemical control of the disease organisms, while able to stem the spread currently, seems unlikely to be able to contain it ultimately.

Trade in Horses, Cats and Dogs

8

8.1 Introduction

Horses, cats and dogs share a common usage as companion animals but they can also variously be used as racing animals (horses and dogs), for meat production (horses mostly, sometimes dogs and very occasionally cats), milk production (horses) and fur production (cats and dogs). Because these animals supply specialist markets, not mainstream like cattle and chickens, trade is often local. The trade is often not regulated as well as the livestock trade, frequently covert and sometimes illegal.

8.2 Horses

Horse trading has a long history, with evidence of activity in central Asia around 1000 BCE (Wagner *et al.*, 2011). The close relation between owner and horse makes the transaction very reliant on the owner's report of the characteristics of the horse. The potential for deceit in this activity has given the term 'horse trading' special meaning in relation to business deals.

According to the World Horse Organization (WHO, 2015), there are now approximately 58 million horses worldwide, with 16% in the USA, 13% in China, 11% in Mexico and 10% in Brazil. The racing industry originated in England in the 16th century, expanding up to the formation of the first Jockey Club in 1752 and has since spread to virtually all countries in the world (McManus *et al.*, 2013, p. 45). There are now 60 racecourses in Britain and substantial industries in the USA, Germany, France, Hong Kong and Australia, with major growth in parts of the Middle East and Asia. Australia alone has 360 racecourses, an exceptionally high number for its population. There is a significant international trade in these countries. For example, in Australia there are about 3000 horses imported each year and about 2500 exported (Gordon, 2001). Around 50% are breeding animals, but racehorses brought in for events and live horses exported for meat are included. The contribution to the Australian economy is almost as high as that from the livestock industry, about AU$6.3 billion. As well as traded animals, there is a significant trade in service by stallions, sometimes commanding several hundred thousands of dollars for a top animal, but more often just a few thousand (McManus *et al.*, 2013, p. 50). Although the prize money does not, on average, cover the cost of raising and keeping a racehorse, the potential exists for large sums of money to be made with an outstanding horse. Hence it is a sport dominated by owners and trainers with substantial financial resources. This leads to large sums being paid for horses that may win races, but quickly falling to relatively small amounts paid for average horses. Prize money also focuses on top winners and quickly falls to relatively small amounts. Such inequalities encourage a high wastage rate in the racehorse industry, horses being dispensed with at an early age because they do not have the racing abilities. They are either slaughtered or sold as companion animals.

Many horse fairs have become established in Britain and Ireland, at which horses are traded, often between travelling people. Such fairs represent an historic gathering place for travelling people, even though there are concerns about animal welfare, crime and refuse management. One of the most famous is at Appleby in Cumbria. In British former colonies where the sport has expanded, new horse sales events have been instigated to market the horses professionally to businesspeople, such as the Magic Millions sale on the Gold Coast in Australia.

Given that the chance of breaking even on a racehorse is low, why is the sport so popular? One reason is that the owners are themselves 'gamblers', people willing to take a risk of making money. Secondly, there are tax advantages of owning a racehorse in some countries, e.g. the Stallion Tax Exemption in Ireland, which provided a stimulus to the industry there between 1969 and 2008 (McManus *et al.*, 2013, p. 64). Thirdly, the horse is one of the fastest land mammals in the world over any distance more than a sprint. The close relationship that riders have to have with their horses in order to achieve best performance is appealing to many who desire to see man and animal combinations competing, in preference to sports for just humans, which do not require mastery of an animal.

The jumps racing industry is biggest in the UK, then France and Ireland, which together run about 7000 races annually (McManus *et al.*, 2013, p. 192). The sport is much less popular elsewhere, with Italy, the Czech Republic, the USA, Australia and Japan having some involvement.

Transportation of horses is undertaken for racing and competitions, but also breeding, sales and slaughter. Transportation of horses is relatively common in international racing and jumps, and fortunately they survive long-distance travel well and can compete soon after, for example they are flown to interstate race meetings regularly within Australia. In the 19th and early 20th centuries horses were largely transported by rail, for example within Australia from remote rural properties to be sold in the cities. In the 1980s Australian thoroughbred stallions began to be transported internationally to the northern hemisphere for the spring/summer breeding season.

Dehydration is a major concern in long-distance air travel, as is the development of 'shipping fever' (MacTaggart, 2015). During road transport, loading/unloading and tying of the horses' heads represent the greatest challenges to their welfare. Head ties prevent horses raising and lowering their heads, which prevents drainage of the upper respiratory tract (MacTaggart, 2015). The skill of the driver and quality of the roads are major factors influencing horse welfare during road transit, as they are with all livestock. Recently, competition venues that were traditionally in Europe, North America and Australia have spread to Eastern Europe, South America, Arabia, Asia and Africa (OIE, 2014a). With this has come an increased risk of disease transmission.

The health status of exported horses is of great importance, with the outbreak of equine influenza in Australia in 2007 restricting movement of horses in and out of Australia during that period, and even mustering of cattle in Queensland, which is often conducted on horseback. Most areas were declared free of the disease in early 2008. Equine infectious anaemia and glanders are two diseases that are suspected of having been introduced into many European countries recently, equine infectious anaemia from Romania and glanders from Lebanon (Herholz et al., 2013).

Some countries have standards for racehorse transport, and international transport standards are being developed by the World Organisation for Animal Health (OIE) for a high health-status horse subpopulation for competition, following official agreements between this organization and the International Federation of Horseracing Authorities (IFHA) and Federation Equestre Internationale. In Asia, where there is a nascent horse industry, many countries require horses to be either vaccinated for the major infectious diseases, especially African horse sickness, or certified as free from the disease, including equine infectious anaemia, equine influenza, glanders and piroplasmosis, with tests if the disease is present in the exporting country (OIE, 2014a).

As well as racing, horses are used for companionship and meat and milk production. They evolved naturally to cope with the extreme climate in central Asia, hence they are able to cope well with extreme climates in Australia, Canada and the USA. For many, the horsemeat product is likely to be perceived as using relatively environmentally friendly methods of production. In Australia there is a large population of feral horses in the north and centre of the country, perhaps between 400,000 and 1,000,000 animals, which is subjected to an annual cull of approximately 10%. Most are mustered from the air in Queensland, Western Australia and the Northern Territories and taken to large-scale slaughterhouses. There are a similar number of feral camels, which are treated in a similar way, before being processed for shipping chilled or frozen to Europe, the USA or Canada. The muster, transport and slaughter of both horses and camels attract concern for the welfare of the animals.

There is little uniformity in the trade in horses, both between different countries and over time. The industries are not organized on the scale of the major meat producers, chickens or pigs. As horses are not efficient producers of meat from cereal grain, or even pasture, most trade is in animals for which there is no longer a need for racing rather than being deliberately reared for the purpose of producing meat. Because many countries have taboos on eating horsemeat and demand varies considerably between regions, the international trade is often just with neighbouring countries, such as export of horses from the USA to Mexico. Distances travelled are relatively short. Usually livestock transporters are used, with horses transported loose within the box. Similarly, distances travelled within countries are relatively short, for example, 90% of the 50,000 horses slaughtered in Chile each year travel less than 300 km (Gallo *et al.*, 2004).

The main potential markets for horses are in Western Europe (especially Italy, France and Belgium), Russia, China and central Asia. China as a nation is the leading horsemeat consumer and a major producer. Other key producing countries are Mexico, Mongolia, Argentina and Kazakhstan. The USA is one of the largest exporters, sending approximately 12,000 t abroad, mainly to Mexico and Canada. Informal estimates of the brumby slaughter in Australia suggest that 48,000 are culled annually, producing 24,000 t/year (Forum, 2011). There is also a significant and controversial trade between Poland, where horses are used still for cultivation and farm work, and Italy. The ethnic groups with a taboo against eating horses are often those that have close contact with horses in their everyday lives, such as the Romani people. Anglophone countries usually do not allow the consumption of horsemeat. Following the Eurozone financial crisis of 2009, horses in the Ireland and the UK had little sale value. Horsemeat was detected in burgers by DNA profiling, causing considerable concern because consumption of horsemeat is largely taboo in these two countries. Additional concern surrounded the possible contamination of the horsemeat with drugs used in the horses.

8.3   Cats and Dogs

There are many cats and dogs around the world that are unwanted and are relinquished to a shelter, which people seeking to acquire these animals can visit. Alternatives include pet shops, puppy 'farms', council pounds or purchases via Internet or local media, but these are often believed to result in poorer welfare for the animals. The shelters add value to their sales by ensuring the animals' health and sterilization status, research into the animals' behaviour and hence its suitability to the purchaser, identification and other necessities for successful cat and dog management. Regrettably, many of the relinquished animals, especially cats and large, old dogs, are not able to be sold and have to be euthanized, as do a significant number that are returned to the shelter. A low success rate in sending an animal to a new home has considerable impact on staff, who have a high turnover due to the stress involved. Rather than being a deliberate trade, the transition of cats and dogs from an unwanted home or stray to a shelter and then to a new home often involves several people for whom financial benefit is not an important outcome from the procedure. However, although cat and dog passage through the various outlets involves a purchase/sale of goods and therefore a trade, it must be recognized that shelters at least perform an important social function within the community that helps all members to be satisfied that unwanted animals are being rehomed successfully. A common objective is to reduce numbers in shelters, rather than the increase in trade that has been the objective for the farm animal businesses that we have considered so far. Reducing relinquishment of owned, semi-owned or stray cats indicates that the problems are coming under control. Accepting that there is a social function, a business role must be acknowledged also. Many people present owned cats to shelters as stray animals to avoid paying the surrender fee (Alberthsen *et al.*, 2013).

Most shelters are assisted financially by governments, particularly in the developed world, in support of their ideals of reducing the numbers of stray and unwanted animals in the community, eliminating zoonotic diseases that they might transmit and avoiding the unsightly nuisance that stray animals on the streets create, in their eyes. Stray animals often make up 50% of shelter animals; hence any funding that improves successful adoptions is worthwhile. Funds are also raised by the many animal agencies that operate in this space, but revenue from sales is greatly exceeded by costs. Hence the cat and dog 'problem' is usually managed by government/NGO partnerships, with bodies such as the RSPCA attracting large donations as well as raising revenue from sale of animals.

Western authorities tend to point to irresponsible cat ownership and semi-ownership as the reason for the problem, in which cat caretakers provide a degree of care to the cat, such as feeding it, but without the commitment of assuming ownership. Semi-owners nevertheless have almost as strong a bond with their animals as owners (Zito *et al.*, 2015a,b). Many do not claim ownership because they think someone else owns the cat they are feeding. Despite this, ownership is a value more desired in Western societies, whereas in Eastern societies communal ownership is more accepted. Often this means that the semi-owner does not assume responsibility of controlling the cat's reproduction, allowing it to amplify the problem by regular breeding, and many semi-owners look after cat colonies, rather than individual cats. Despite the enthusiasm of many in the West to collect stray or semi-owned animals and incarcerate them in shelters, it may be primarily because of their fear of not being able to control the stray animal problem that leads them to this action. In many developing countries stray or semi-owned animals have a good life with plenty of company of their kind, unless they fall ill for some reason. They may create a public nuisance by the noise that they make, excreting in public places and scavenging for food, but they also control vermin and give many people pleasure, particularly the young and the old.

Euthanasia rates in Western shelters are usually low for dogs but often exceed one-third of cats, sometimes up to 70% (Alberthsen *et al.*, 2013), even though the cats are mostly suitable for rehoming. There is pressure from the public for shelters to adopt a no-kill policy, even if it means that intake is selective, depending on whether it is felt that the animals can be sold from the shelter. However, in part due to stress levels in the shelters, disease levels are high and many animals are euthanized because they display the symptoms of disease acquired in the shelter. Many shelters are now transferring animals between shelters at peak periods to try to equate supply with local demand. The transfers may be over long distances, for example from distant regions of Queensland or British Columbia to the state capitals. If by car, the animals usually survive with little damage providing the thermal environment is made suitable. If by aeroplane, as with humans, respiratory infections often thrive after the event, which themselves may result in euthanasia or a long period of rehabilitation.

Alternatives to shelters that governments could adopt, such as trap and euthanize, are sometimes more expensive than sheltering because of the public support and sale possibilities for the latter. Subsidized sterilization for cats from low-income cat owners is one policy that can be effective at reducing shelter intakes and euthanasia rates. Encouraging early age desexing of both cats and dogs, before unwanted litters appear, trap-neuter and return schemes, and cat confinement are other methods of potentially reducing numbers in shelters. Strategies to increase adoption rates from shelters may also reduce occupancy rates: better marketing, animal sales at reduced price, improving the image of the shelter, e.g. as a clean environment and providing a happy atmosphere for cats and dogs, and its portrayal of animals to the public, e.g. referring to animals as lost rather than stray. Predictably, given that people do not just view shelters as places to buy cats and dogs but have some social responsibility, elasticity of demand is low for cats (Zito *et al.*, 2015a). In the situation where price is rather arbitrarily set and does not reflect the cost of producing the goods, purchasers probably expect prices based mainly on their past experiences.

As well as companion animals, dogs are also traded as racing animals. Greyhounds are usually used for this purpose. Greyhound racing industries are in worldwide decline, particularly as serious welfare and ethical concerns have come to light. Dogs were encouraged to be aggressive in their chase by the use of live lures in some clubs, at least in Australia. Piglets and other small animals were tied to the mechanical lures and dogs goaded to pursue and destroy them. The other concern with the industry is an ethical one: the high wastage rate, with only a small minority of dogs born that are then registered for racing. The rest are often destroyed as their temperament makes them unsuitable for retirement as companion animals. The same issue pervades the horseracing industry (Doughty *et al.*, 2009), although in this case many horses are successfully retired to become companions. In the case of greyhounds, Australia, which has arguably one of the biggest greyhound industries in the world, is reported to be still exporting animals to Macau, despite attempts at regulatory control of this practice, and to New Zealand. In Macau there are no animal welfare standards enforced for greyhounds, and conditions for keeping the dogs are believed to be of low quality (AA, 2015). Other greyhounds are sent to veterinary colleges where they are used by students. The Australian greyhound racing industry itself is largely self-regulated. It is unclear whether Australia would be in breach of World Trade Organization (WTO) rules if it bans export of domestic animals to just one country on account of animal welfare concerns.

Dogs are traded for meat in many parts of the world, but most commonly in China and Korea (Podberscek, 2009). In many regions, however, eating dog meat is taboo, especially in Muslim cultures. In places where dogs are regularly eaten they are sometimes farmed, but pet dogs may also be stolen for this purpose. Dogs and cats are also slaughtered for their fur, but many developed countries have banned importation of this product. Activist groups report that pets and strays are used for this purpose in Asia (HSIA, 2015). Pedigree dogs are also traded internationally but, unlike the livestock industries, numbers are not documented and there is little legislative control of the trade. This trade is supported by international dog shows and fairs. There are reports of many pedigree dogs being bred in Eastern Europe for lucrative sale in the West, but with little attention to welfare standards (Schiessl, 2010).

8.4 Conclusions

The trade in horses, dogs and cats is highly variable, both between countries and over time. The purposes for which they are used are also varied, and sometimes not easily quantified without taking into account the social benefit. Racing is often associated with gambling, and the high value of some horses and dogs has encouraged unethical practices. The use of these species for meat is taboo in some countries, and the use of cats and dogs for fur is also taboo and actually illegal in some advanced countries. Trade is less documented than for livestock, but is still considerable for some species. The future survival of horses and dogs in racing to a large extent depends on their ability to ensure the industries are free of drugs, cruelty and high wastage rates.

Trade in Wildlife and Exotic Species

9

9.1 Introduction

Wildlife animals have been traded for millennia, probably even before the domestication of animal species for the production of food and clothing. Yet despite the development of a small number of domesticated species to provide for most of our needs, we have continued to harvest and trade in wildlife and exotic species. Exotic species are those that are not indigenous to the region, which usually precludes the domestic livestock species. These are kept by zoos, for the entertainment of the public and increasingly for conservation and for scientific purposes. Their use for entertainment in circuses is diminishing as public recognition of associated cruel practices in training and transport between venues has increased, creating public pressure for legislative control. They are also kept by a growing number of members of the public for display and a variety of other reasons that will be outlined later. Wildlife animals are harvested for food as well and may be traded with other regions because their exotic and novel nature encourages people to try eating them. The biggest harvest of wild animals, indeed the biggest of any food animals, is that of fish from the oceans. However, many other animals are harvested from the oceans and our scant knowledge of populations in the past has led to many manmade catastrophes, with populations decimated because of high demand for the products and mechanized harvesting of ever increasing efficiency.

Even more concerning has been the growth in harvesting of animals for little advantage for the human population, such as for medicinal purposes, especially in Asia. Under the guise of supporting centuries-old rituals, those that can afford it and desire the envy of others demonstrate their wealth by purchasing products from ruthlessly exploited animals. An extreme example is sharks that are slaughtered for their fins to make soup for wealthy Chinese, an ingredient that adds only texture, not even taste. Another is the killing of tigers for their parts, including penises and bones, to be ingredients in Chinese medicine. Although the motivations for such pointless killing may be many and hard to discern, not a small part may be a desire to dominate nature, boosting the self-esteem of those doubting man's ability to do this. Similar motives may be ascribed to the hunting of iconic wild animals, so-called trophy hunting, which is not considered in detail here because the kill is usually not for trade purposes. It should be investigated, though, whether people's engagement in these senseless activities, and the potential harm caused to animal populations, is akin to the peacock developing a tail display that bears significant cost to its survival. Are the perpetrators of such animal destruction actually dragging humanity down the path of supreme self-confidence, which says 'we can survive as a species even if we eradicate other species around us in a spate of senseless slaughter'?

The risks to native wildlife of importation of exotic species include the diseases against which native species may not have protection. These risks are greatest for importation into islands with many endemic species, such as Australia, New Zealand and Japan. In particular, there are risks to ecosystems, human safety, agriculture, forestry and fisheries. Control of alien species takes several forms: assessing their potential impact on ecosystems, taking control measures when introduced and encouraging the use of native species wherever possible (Goka, 2010). Arguments have been made in favour of using native wild ruminants in Africa and kangaroos in Australia as alternatives to the ubiquitous cattle for meat production. However, 'farming' native wild ruminants is likely to impose constraints on their movement and natural behaviour. Such animals naturally migrate, at least locally, and control of wildlife movements could thwart the attempts of adaptable species to survive by migrating to novel areas, a vital strategy to overcome the damaging effects of climatic extremes – including adapting to climate change – escaping from fire or pollution.

9.2   Historical Development of Trading in Exotic Animals for Display

Ancient civilizations began a trade in exotic animals that was to remain one of the trademarks of the early explorers for centuries. The ancient Greeks, under Alexander the Great, returned parakeets from the Far East to Europe as early as the 4th century BCE (Chamberlain, 2015). The Romans introduced other parrot species from North Africa and India. A more horrific example of trading exotic animals was for the spectacle of animal torture that ancient civilizations, and particularly the Romans, delighted in between the 1st and 4th centuries AD. Roman emperors paid for the animals to be imported, which were used as a demonstration of their own wealth and power. Alexandria on the Egyptian shores of the Mediterranean became the centre of an exotic animal trade, which by the Middle Ages became a major wild beast market, lasting until the 12th century. Exotic animals were brought from as far away as India to provide a challenge for gladiators, thereby both entertaining the public and ensuring the Roman Empire would have a notorious legacy. One celebrated 3rd-century procession had chariots pulled by elephants, goats, antelopes, oryx, hartebeest, ostriches and wild asses (Wilson, 2015).

In the 15th and 16th centuries European explorers brought back American and Asian parrot species, and in the 18th century they brought back many Australian exotic species. These included parakeets and the celebrated platypus that many believed at the time was so bizarre that it must have been artificially constructed by the colonists.

The Victorians in Britain were therefore not the first to trade in exotic species but they were particularly fascinated by the natural world and acquired some major collections of exotic specimens. Roualeyn Gordon Cumming was a well-known Scottish Victorian explorer, who typified their attitudes to collecting and trading in exotic animal parts. In the words of historian Hancock (2006):

> Cumming ... describes the love of ivory as characteristic of industrialised or 'civilised' nations, which fashioned items like piano keys, knife handles, and billiard balls from this durable and versatile material. As a hunter and trader, Cumming valued elephant tusks as both trophies and commodities, though he claimed that he allowed his profit-motive to become a secondary consideration to adorning his collection. Cumming viewed an 'ordinary' bull elephant in terms of how many pounds and shillings he could get for its tusks, which typically weighed around fifty pounds each; at four shillings and sixpence a pound, such a pair would bring him twenty-two pounds. ... He represents his achievement through sheer numbers. During his final expedition, Cumming was so prolific that he ran out of room for his trophies and often had to settle for a small part of the animal, a synecdochic practice he had adopted earlier as an expedient for taking souvenirs from giraffes and elephants. Thus he contents himself with just the head of a crocodile, rather than 'the entire skin', and he preserves 'only the nails and tail of a lion'. At journey's end, he inspects his spoils on a farm ...: 'Here I found nine heavily-laden wagons drawn up ... my valuable collection of trophies and my Cape wagon, weighing all together upwards of thirty tons, were then carefully shipped'. ... In 1845, Cumming ... put on a show at Colesberg. 'All the forenoon I was busy off-loading two of the wagons. We spread out the curiosities ... It was truly a very remarkable sight, and struck all beholders with astonishment.'

> After his return to Britain in 1848, Cumming took advantage of the commercial possibilities of his collection ... through the exhibition of his trophies. Though some critics repudiated Cumming's blood lust as inhumane, others celebrated it as a component of British national identity ... a sign and support of imperial destiny. ... 'The immense variety of tusks, antlers, horns, bones, skulls, teeth, etc. are interesting to the sportsman, to the naturalist, and to the everyday observer. Each of these represents a select specimen of some fierce and formidable, or shy and wary animal, and most of them were obtained by undergoing extraordinary perils, hardships, and fatigues.'

Cumming was not alone in his fascination with ivory; King Leopold II of Belgium enslaved huge numbers of Congolese workers and used them to develop a trade that plundered the country's vast store of ivory (Simpson, 2008). Thousands of elephants were slaughtered to make piano keys between 1885 and 1920. This was ably documented by the Anglo-French journalist Edmund Morel and a British consul in the Congo, the Irishman Roger Casement, who revealed the horrors of this trade before he was hanged for treason for helping the Germans to plot an invasion of Ireland in the First World War. The lust for ivory led to a lucrative trade in mammoth ivory in the 18th and 19th centuries. Preserved in the icy wastes of Siberia, it is reported that 46,000 sets of mammoth bones and ivory had been exhumed and sold to supply the Western demand for the product by 1913 (Haynes, 1991). Regrettably, the desire to sell the ivory has made it rare for whole carcass discoveries to be reported to the authorities.

Such exploitation of wildlife must have appealed to the British sense of domination of the globe, which had grown over the 17th, 18th and 19th centuries until they came to rule one-quarter of the world's land mass and one-fifth of its population. In so doing they had encountered many new species, and the growing middle class in Britain delighted in exhibiting dead specimens of the most elaborate of these, as well as adorning themselves with exotic animals' body parts, such as the feathers of the birds of paradise, for which there was a prodigious market. Alfred Wallace was one such Victorian who had a fascination for the equatorial fauna, and he planned to fund his exploration by selling specimens in England. His first trip to the Amazon lasted 4 years, but it ended in disaster when his ship caught fire on his return journey and all the carefully prepared specimens were lost. Undeterred, his next trip was successful, not least for prompting him to liaise with Charles Darwin on how to release their theory of natural selection, so bringing it to the world in an exemplary manner (and earlier than would have happened if Darwin had not been concerned that his own work on this topic would be unrecognized). On his return from the Malay Archipelago, as Wallace called it, he sold a couple of birds of paradise to London Zoo for £150 and was able to auction many of the 125,000 specimens he had collected on the voyage.

At the very time that Wallace was flogging dead animals to fund his forays to South-east Asia, his shared theory of evolution with Darwin was severely challenging views on the supremacy of humans over other animals. It is therefore ironic that the Victorians turned to animal specimen collecting to reinforce their sense of domination over nature, the elevated status of humans, and a fervent belief in God's entrustment of the management of nature to humans that was outlined in the Bible. The Industrial Revolution was testament to a range of new human achievements that confirmed this attitude. It was a new age of confidence in human abilities to master nature that was advertised prolifically through a trade in exotic animals.

The Victorians' penchant for stuffed animals was testament to their ready embrace of consumerism following the Industrial Revolution, which brought the rise in living standards amongst the middle classes to enable them to buy specimens. In 1881 no less than 400,000 hummingbirds were sold in an auction to enable the ladies to adorn their hats with these beautiful birds. Even more treasured were cabinets full of stuffed birds and mammals, grouped together in unnatural proximity and numbers, but demonstrating the owner's wealth and mastery over the natural world. Cabinets with drawers of specimens were another favourite, showing numerous variations of beetles, butterflies etc. Was this simply a delight in the variety of the natural world? Perhaps it was, but in a rather perverse voyeuristic fashion. The true revelations of the marvels of the natural world were to come later, perhaps first and foremost by the likes of Jane Goodall, who dared to suggest, albeit rather unscientifically, that chimpanzees have individual personalities. Above all, the Victorian obsession with decorating their houses with stuffed animals from the farthest corners of the globe can be ultimately considered an expression of their supposed mastery of all things natural.

Was it a search for a cleaner, purer nature that was rapidly disappearing at home? The Welsh valleys no longer resounded to the call of the blackbird, as coal became king and turned the valleys into an industrial landscape reminiscent of inner city squalor. There were backlashes to these worrying trends – the Quaker movement and Protestantism more generally – but the Victorian fascination with exotic animals and passion for displaying them persisted well into the 20th century.

9.3 Trade in Live Animals

At the same time as the trade in exotic animal specimens grew, there emerged a trade in live animals to support sales of interesting animals, such as tigers, to zoos, menageries and private parks. Animal trainers employed a variety of punishment skills to make the animals perform unnatural acts. A tiger costing US$500 could be worth US$5000 after 2 years' training (Wilson, 2015). Others engaged solely in the sale of exotic animals, such as M. Wombwell, who advertised the following above his shop: 'Wild Beast Merchant, Commercial Road, London. All sorts of Foreign Animals, Birds, &c, bought, sold, or exchanged, at the Repository, or the Travelling Menagerie' (Wilson, 2015). This was probably linked to George Wombwell's travelling wild animal menagerie of approximately 500 animals that operated in the early 1800s. Performing animals were taught all manner of tricks, mainly through the use of punishment, and were then set to earn money for their owners in travelling shows and theatres. William Snyder, who acquired an elephant, Hattie, from Carl Hagenbeck and trained it for New York's Central Park Zoo admitted to doing so by beating it (Wilson, 2015, p. 84). Also of concern were the humiliating acts that they were trained to do, e.g. chimpanzees acting as drunks, which reinforced people's perceptions of animals as 'dumb brutes', and the declawing of animals such as lions. In 1921 *Punch* included a poem about a wild-caught hippopotamus that appeared on the stage, which included the line: 'He must have been a most repulsive brute who marked thee down as profitable loot' (Algol, 1921). Acquisition of young animals from the wild frequently required the fatal wounding of the parents if they defended their young, e.g. by cutting the Achilles tendons of lions so that young cubs could be captured (Wilson, 2015, p. 95). Elephants were particularly in demand, with Barnum and Forepaugh Circuses capturing 67 in Ceylon in 1883 alone (Wilson, 2015, p. 95). Transferring captured animals to Europe, initially on foot and then by ship, had high mortality rates, often in excess of 50% (Wilson, 2015, p. 95). Broken limbs were common and many succumbed to capture myopathy. Managers of wildlife shows often preferred wild-caught animals to those bred in the menagerie, believing them to be more tractable through fear of their novel environment than those with familiarity (and contempt) for their environment. In one recorded incident in the 1920s, three 6-month-old tigers were caught in Malaysia and incarcerated in a 2 × 1.3 m box. Two months later they were shipped to England, during which voyage one died, and another shortly after arrival, leaving only one survivor (Wilson, 2015, p. 161). Money was usually the motivation and led trainers to cut corners to achieve rapid training. 'The training of performing animals is a trade, ... as the man who trains animals to perform generally lets them out on hire as soon as they are "broken", it follows that his main desire is to train them as quickly as possible' (Wilson, 2015, p. 133). Animals going to the USA usually had to pass through brokers in London, before enduring a long and arduous journey. Many succumbed to respiratory disease, the risk of which was no doubt exacerbated by the stress of transport. As a result prices rose, up to £5000 for a boxing kangaroo, buoyed up by the high earning capacity of the animals (Wilson, 2015, p. 139). In this respect one could be forgiven for thinking that nothing has changed, boxing kangaroos are still exhibited in circuses in the USA, although some shows have been stopped following an outcry from the Australian public (Keene, 2013).

The demise of the trade in performing animals was accelerated in the 1920s and 1930s with the decline of the music hall. As the music hall gave way to cinema and the 'talkies', so animals came to be used more for film and then later television. However, before standards became established for these new forms of entertainment, some macabre fights between wild animals were staged in the 1930s. One film actually cost US$95,000 in slain animals alone (Wilson, 2015, p. 195). A major supplier in the latter half of the 20th century was Brelands Animal Behavior Enterprises, which trained over 15,000 animals of 150 species over a period of almost 50 years, apparently using scientific principles (Wilson, 2015, p. 200). The services offered by the Brelands were described early in their business development plan as follows (Breland and Breland, 1951):

> the biggest applications exist in the entertainment world. Here we can take over the formal animal training involved in the standard animal act for stage, circus, and movies, and do it faster, cheaper, better, and in multiple units. It is possible to create new acts, whole new circuses, in fact, using unusual animals and unusual acts, and again do it cheaply, quickly, and in numbers limited only by time and production facilities. Television offers unusual opportunities. We can invade the field of night-club entertainment with novel small animals. We can sell or rent trained animal units to hospitals, doctors' offices, waiting rooms of various sorts, or even to private individuals, supplying instructions on care and maintenance.

Opposition began to grow, slowly at first but rising to a crescendo by the early 21st century. As early as the First World War, parliamentarians complained vigorously about use of merchant shipping for transport of performing animals, including a consignment of apes and eight pandas (Wilson, 2015). Later there were major concerns about the cruel training of performing animals in the music halls, the stage and in circuses. The biggest animal dealer in the world at the time, German Carl Hagenbeck, was convicted for allowing one of his employees, an Indian mahout, to injure an elephant so badly during training that blood ran down its legs (Wilson, 2015, p. 75).

In the late Victorian and Edwardian eras major concerns about the treatment of performing animals began to be voiced in England (Wilson, 2015), as well as cruelty during the production of furs, skins and feathers in female adornment.

The opposition may have been suppressed by the need for attention to human cruelty during the war years of the first half of the 20th century. However, the campaigns renewed with vigour in the second half of the century, in particular during the cultural revolution of the 1960s and 1970s.

9.4   Wildlife for Food

9.4.1   Marine animals

Whaling, sealing and mutton-bird industries
Attempts to exploit exotic wildlife on a widespread scale may have started with the expanding European colonization movement of the 18th and 19th centuries. British acquisition, or in the case of Australia requisition, of territory in the southern hemisphere had to be justified economically, providing benefit for those outlaying funds for the colonization. Whales and seals were just two of the primary resources plundered in the southern hemisphere by the European colonizers.

Although the colonizers may not have known or indeed cared, the aboriginal people of the southern lands had hunted and traded in sea mammals for centuries, focusing their efforts in times of the year when they were plentiful. For example, the Melukerdee and Mouheneene tribes of south-east Tasmania met several times a year to trade in sealskins, mutton-birds and swan eggs. In the late 18th century the arrival of Europeans provided a much expanded market for seal furs, and commercial sealing began in this region along the lines of the seal trade that had spread in the North Atlantic in the 17th and 18th centuries and the South Atlantic in the late 18th century. Sealing gangs terrorized the local aboriginal population in Tasmania. Through regular raids on the tribes, they captured women to work for them as slaves or secured them in exchange for dogs, which were much valued by the aborigines. Each sealer had two to three women to help him in his work. Fur seals were clubbed to death and stripped of their pelts; occasionally elephant seals were stripped of their blubber. Between 1800 and 1806 over 100,000 seal skins were exported from Sydney.

The vulnerability of the seal populations resulted in numbers being decimated in their native lands. Within just 5 years of the start of the industry, in 1803, Governor King reported to London that the industry was in jeopardy. By 1830 it was almost all over. This had a devastating effect on the region. For example, in Chatham Island, 870 km south-east of Christchurch, New Zealand, lived a peaceful people, the Moriori, who had over a period of about 500 years gained a good understanding of the balance of nature and the numbers of seals that they could take annually. The arrival of the British in 1791 brought the near extinction of not only the seals but also the Moriori themselves. After initial hostile approaches by the British invaders, the island was taken possession in the name of George III and within a few years there was an influx of whalers and sealers. Seal furs were particularly valued in China, with pelts fetching 15 shillings each in Canton.[1] By 1830 the seals were gone and the Moriori people had lost their source of food, oil and warm clothing. As if this was not bad enough, cats and rats that jumped ship from the traders' ships wiped out many of the seabirds by eating their eggs, and Western diseases added to the misery of the Moriori people. Finally, invasion by the cannibalistic Maori, themselves suffering from the British invasion, reduced the population of pure Moriori people from 1500 in 1835 to just 101 in 1862. It took over 100 years for the seal population to rebuild.

Sealers lost in the southern ocean found Macquarie Island in 1810, a rich breeding ground for more than 100,000 seals. Ten years later fur seals had been exterminated, but it took a further 50 years for most (70%) of the elephant seal population to be wiped out.[2] Penguins were targeted next, at least until 1911 when Antarctic pioneer Douglas Mawson won his battle to stop the slaughter and the penguin 'digesters' were shut down.

The decline of the seal industry brought a search for new animal products to export from the southern lands. A whaling industry started in the early 19th century, and the First Fleet contained two whaling vessels. Demand for whale oil and baleen (whalebone) was growing in the expanding and increasingly affluent population of Britain. The blubber was boiled down and the oil stored in barrels, ready to be shipped for oil lamps and soap manufacture. Up to the mid-19th century the economic value of the whaling industry in southern Australia and New Zealand rivalled the pastoral industries in these regions, but the herds of southern right whales were much depleted. Attention turned to sperm whales in deeper waters, but by the end of the century the industry was largely abandoned due to depleted stock.

Some recovery was evident in the decades that followed and by 1931 large numbers of whaling boats were again in the northern and southern oceans, and international regulations were introduced to control the harvest. In 1946 the International Convention for the Regulation of Whaling was signed by many countries, with the aim of protecting whales from overhunting and introducing international regulations for that purpose. Quotas were later established by the International Whaling Commission, a voluntary body 'to provide for the conservation, development, and optimum utilization of the whale resources'. In the mid-1980s a moratorium on whale slaughter was agreed, except for small quotas for aboriginal subsistence and slaughter for scientific purposes. Since then countries that support whaling, led by Japan, have been entrenched in battle with anti-whaling countries, such as the USA, the UK, New Zealand and Australia (see Chapter 3).

Another easily harvested marine animal that was exploited when seal stocks declined, though not to the same extent as the whale, was the mutton-bird (short-tailed shearwaters). These were harvested, salted and packed into barrels before shipment overseas. The harvest over, entrepreneurs in the southern lands moved on to the Gold Rushes in the early 19th century or timber logging. These birds are still legally harvested during a hunting season in some 36 New Zealand islands (Lyver *et al.*, 2012) and in Tasmania, Australia, where there are still more than 200,000 harvested commercially under licence each year (McLeod, 2013). They are used for their down and feathers, oil and flesh. The oil is used as an additive for racehorse food, down and feathers for pillows and preserved meat for human consumption, which resembles mutton (McLeod, 2013).

The exploitation of the abundant resources of the new southern colonies in the early 19th century destroyed an aboriginal culture and almost destroyed an entire ecosystem. The British were mostly to blame. Americans were also heavily involved but now have a ban on seal hunting by anyone except the indigenous population in the Arctic regions. The motivation of the colonizers was not just exploitation of the land's resources; preventing rival powers, especially France, from obtaining new territories was also very important. If Britain had not defeated France in Europe in the Napoleonic Wars of the early 19th century, colonization of the southern lands, New Zealand and Australia in particular, would very likely have been the subject of much more competition between the superpowers of the day.

Nowadays, sealing is mostly confined to Atlantic waters, especially by Canada, which retains a commercial industry that is highly disputed for its impact on the welfare of the seals. Several hundred harp seals are clubbed to death each year, which is probably around 5% of the population in the region. Defendants argue that the seal's death is more humane than other culling procedures adopted for free-ranging land mammals or farm animals, but an absolute rather than relative consideration of the humaneness of the action would be better. Some still argue that seals reduce the stock of fish, in particular cod, but this is not universally accepted. In 2010 the EU banned the importation of seal products from Canada, except those produced by Inuit and other aboriginal communities. For some years after, Canada was locked in dispute with the EU, after appealing to the WTO. However, in 2014 a landmark ruling by the WTO stated that the EU ban was legitimate on the grounds of public concern of EU citizens about the morality of the slaughter methods. This potentially sets a precedent for animal welfare to be considered in other trade disputes.

In the southern hemisphere, Namibia has a significant commercial seal cull to protect fisheries that it wishes to exploit. However, worldwide demand for seal-skins is falling since the EU banned their import in 2009.

Exploitation of other marine animals

Wild-caught fish represent the largest use of natural stocks of animals for food in the world. Annual global kills of wildlife include 70 billion wild-caught fish, with an additional 10 billion by-catch (Phillips, 2009). For comparison, there are approximately 12 billion cat-kills and 1 billion road-kills annually, and of the farm animals killed annually chickens are most numerous at approximately 15 billion (Phillips, 2009). More terrestrial wild animals are lost by habitat destruction. Most of the fish are for trading purposes, often internationally, with the harvesting being undertaken mainly by professional teams. Recreational fishing is a further source of harvesting fish, but not usually for trading. Numbers are hard to define but it has been estimated that 139 million aquatic animals are taken in recreational fishing in Australia (DoE, 2015).

Aquatic mammals are also harvested in large numbers and often have more iconic status than fish. Turtles have been eaten by indigenous peoples for centuries, and this practice has come to be considered their cultural heritage. One of the delicacies from the oceans that was most favoured by wealthy and discerning consumers, particularly in China and America, was turtle soup. In the early 20th century a company called Masters Food used turtles harvested in north Queensland, Australia, to make canned soup, with the following instructions for use:

> Real turtle soup is truly the aristocrat of soups. Empty contents into saucepan. Add
> equal quantity of water. Heat with lid on – do not boil. Garnish each bowl with a
> fine slice of lemon. Additional sherry or Madeira wine may be added if desired.
> Serve iced if preferred. Ingredients: Australian Green turtles, vegetables, sherry
> wine, salt, sugar, herbs, spices and seasoning.

As early as 1929, it was realized that the turtle numbers were becoming depleted, and in 1950 legislation was passed that banned the harvest. Harvesting of both turtles and dugongs is still allowed by indigenous people in Australia, and up until 2012 they were exempt from the State of Queensland cruelty legislation. This was largely because the communities that have traditionally harvested these animals, for example the communities of the Torres Strait Islands, did not have the means to kill and preserve the animals before eating them. Traditionally turtles were taken from the sea and kept on their backs on shore, with body parts removed as required from the live animal.

Dugongs were, and still are, killed by drowning, holding them underwater until they expire. Exploitative harvesting for oil, accidental capture in fishing nets and boat strikes have depleted their numbers massively over the last hundred years. The exemption of indigenous Queenslanders has now been removed and this and other forms of cruel slaughter, admittedly only perpetrated by a small number of individuals, will probably eventually be brought under control. However, native title acts still allow indigenous people to harvest turtles and dugongs. More specifically the Aboriginal and Torres Strait Islander Communities Act (1984) allows resident members of a community government area to take marine fauna by traditional means for consumption by members of the community. Similarly under the Aurukun and Mornington Shire Leases Act 1978, a resident may kill and consume native wildlife as necessary for sustenance. Thus harvesting for home consumption is generally permitted, even if it is cruel, but harvesting for trading purposes is not.

World heritage agreements under UNESCO provide some protection of such cultural heritage. Thus the recent repeal of exemption from cruelty legislation in Queensland is not without its difficulties, in that this brings it into conflict with earlier legislation protecting indigenous people's rights. However, this is potentially a landmark ruling, demonstrating that claiming that a practice is a tradition or cultural heritage will not always allow indigenous people to cruelly treat animals. Currently this is claimed all around the world, for example to justify Inuit slaughter of seals, Spanish bullfighting and South African slaughter of bulls by Zulu warriors. Some practices, such as the Spanish throwing of goats from towers during festivals, have been recently banned, demonstrating that such claims are currently questioned. There is a danger that criticisms of the people doing these abhorrent practices are motivated more by racial prejudices and a desire to persecute ethnic minorities than by controlling cruelty. The counter-argument is made that other forms of institutionalized cruelty are supported by those seeking to outlaw the practices, by consuming eggs from caged birds, for example. However, other cruel practices, such as infanticide, cannibalism and slavery, which could have been defended on the grounds of cultural heritage, have been outlawed, especially when injustices to humans were involved. This weakens the argument that cruel practices to animals can be preserved on the grounds of cultural heritage.

Sharks are another marine animal whose exploitation has been ruthless at several time points over the course of the last century, including one of them right now. In the 1930s and 1940s a trade emerged in shark liver oil, but this dwindled as artificial substitutes were found. More recently this has been replaced by a harvest that angers conservationists and animal welfarists alike: the taking of sharks' fins for the making of soup. Favoured by the wealthy Chinese, the making of this soup is also claimed to be a cultural heritage, yet ironically the addition of shark's fin to a soup adds little to its flavour. The threat to shark populations, and some concern for the animal's welfare, has led to emergence of a movement that decries the use of shark's fin for celebratory meals and seeks the use of alternatives. Not least, the harvest is deplored because of its waste, with fishermen removing just the fins of captured sharks, which can be worth tens of thousands of dollars, before discarding the rest of the body. Another major issue, apart from the depletion of shark stocks, is the welfare of sharks that are left to die in the ocean with fins removed. A lucrative trade is under threat, but the growing Chinese middle class is leading to rapid expansion of demand for this cruelly-harvested product. Yet of the 546 species of shark assessed by the World Conservation Union, 100 are classified as endangered, threatened or vulnerable. Modern fishing techniques make mass harvesting of sharks possible and a recent estimate suggests that between 26 and 73 million sharks are traded each year, with an increase in trade in fins from 4900 t in 1987 to 13,600 t in 2004 (WildAid, 2007). As well as for their fins, many sharks are slaughtered for their meat, which forms a staple for many coastal communities, as well as a replacement for depleted stocks of other fish, such as cod.

Our fascination with this top predator has also led to wildlife experiences being offered, in which sharks are lured to interact with humans in cages by provision of meat. The so-called cage diving of white sharks has been criticized for familiarizing sharks to human presence and luring them with the smell of blood without them being able to capture the lure.

9.4.2   Land animal harvesting – the growth of poaching in Britain

Shooting wildlife first became popular in Britain in the early 18th century, by which time firearms had become sufficiently accurate and affordable to be used for this purpose. Field sports evolved over the course of the next century, with regular competitions between landowners to see who could slaughter the most animals on one of their estates. Partridges, pheasants, snipe, woodcocks, hares and rabbits were all fair game, as well as animals considered to be vermin: foxes, stoats, hawks and wild cats (Cuming, 1913, p. 18). Prizes were given for the most animals killed in 6 days in the shooting season, which usually ran into thousands. Farming methods at the time supported wildlife and many saw shooting as the only way to control them. Many landowners fed the birds to increase numbers and support their field sports. However, their spoils were not usually sold; what was not needed for the household was given away.

Trade in game developed in Britain because the widespread poverty of the agricultural workers tempted many to poach these animals to support their meagre existence on the farm, which frequently brought them into conflict with the estates' gamekeepers, often with fatal consequences. It had been illegal since 1603 to kill partridges, pheasants, grouse and hares (Cuming, 1913, p. 6). Fines were levied that were divided between the gamekeepers and the poor of the parish. However, there was a lucrative market for these animals, especially in London, where the markets were principally supplied by poachers. The common areas also provided opportunities for shooting and fishing to augment their haul on the estates, in particular the seashores where wild duck, geese and all kinds of shorebirds were hunted, not by 'gentlemen' (Edie, 1772) but by 'commoners' who were in need of the income from this quarry. The British coast was a regular stopping place for migratory birds, as well as providing a habitat for many resident birds. Often working from the cover of a punt, the wildfowl shooter had to understand the behaviour of shorebirds well to score a kill, as the migrant birds in particular were aware of the dangers on land.

9.4.3   The kangaroo trade

Australia has a large resident population of kangaroos, with few predators and the population controlled fundamentally by climatic extremes. A trade in kangaroos and their body parts emerged out of suspicion that they were eating grass that could be sustaining the large cattle and sheep population and later as a source of meat that was cheap, for pet food, and unusual, to be served in restaurants. The trade rapidly became one of the largest harvests of wild animals that are legally traded internationally. Between 1877 and 1907 approximately 8 million macropods were harvested for submission to the Queensland Government to collect bounty money (Pople and Grigg, 1999). In the late 20th century the threat to the populations by harvesting was becoming apparent and restrictive legislation was put in place (Population Assessment Unit, 1992).

The export of kangaroo products is now licensed by Australian Federal and State governments and is largely justified on the grounds of reducing agricultural damage, yet allowing kangaroos to be maintained in their normal home range (Population Assessment Unit, 1992). Most meat is used for pet food, and the skins are used as a cheap substitute for other hides. Over the last 30 years, the Australian kangaroo industry has killed and processed approximately 3 million kangaroos annually, much greater than previously, supported by better management of grazing conditions for livestock, including provision of water. Better control of disease risks exists than in the illegal bush-meat trade, where wild kangaroos are shot in the paddocks at night and partially eviscerated in the field, and then the carcasses are transferred to cold storage units until they are sent to meat processing plants. In addition there is a code of practice for kangaroo shooters, which attempts to guarantee that all animals will die instantly by a shot to the head and females with young at foot will not be targeted. There are, however, doubts about shooters' ability to guarantee the latter. Despite this level of control, Russia, which was the major importer of Australian kangaroo exports, banned imports of kangaroo meat in 2009 due to bacterial contamination. Since then it has been selective as to which companies are authorized to import meat. The commercial value of the trade is estimated at AU\$200 million, with employment of 4000 people (Ben-Ami *et al.*, 2014).

9.4.4 The bush-meat trade

Meat from wild animals originating in Africa, Asia and Central/South America is commonly referred to as bush meat. Such meat fetches a premium in developed countries because of its exotic nature, being considered a delicacy and adding variety to the diet (Falk *et al.*, 2013). Approximately 70% is dried, smoked or otherwise processed, making it difficult to determine the species (Falk *et al.*, 2013). Nevertheless the illegal trade in bush meat poses a significant threat to endangered species and to human health, being linked to diseases such as ebola and HIV/AIDS. Many primates are hunted, including chimpanzees, orang-utans, red colobus monkeys, wild herbivores and cats, and reptiles, such as snakes, crocodiles and tortoises (Falk *et al.*, 2013). Primates provide the greatest threat of disease transmission, not just because they are physiologically similar to humans but also because they come from hot, humid climates that foster pathogen growth and there is frequently no refrigeration during transportation of the meat. Most comes in by air freight, but some enters by road into smaller states, having been initially transported from developing regions by air. Estimates of tonnages of bush meat entering Europe are difficult to make but extrapolating from figures provided in Falk *et al.* (2013) it is likely that from 50,000 t to 100,000 t are coming in annually. Clearly illegal imports of bush meat into Western countries is a trade that should be eradicated, but limited checks in airports and difficulties in determining species of processed meats greatly hinders this process.

9.5 Exotic Animals for Pets

A fascination with unusual animals as pets emerged in Victorian times, but there is currently resurgence in interest. Animals used for this purpose are prized for their unique and unusual features, such as blue-tongued lizards for their unusual tongue colour, or for their ferociousness or the danger that they pose, such as lions and tigers.

The trade in exotic species is growing rapidly. To describe them as pets or companion animals may be somewhat of a misnomer, as they often perform quite different functions from traditional animals kept for pets. Although some authors (e.g. Slater, 2014) suggest that a major motive for exotic pet ownership is power assertion, a fascination for and admiration of nature must also be a strong motivator for many. Developing collections is clearly a motivation for others, perhaps a reflection on our obsession with ownership in a materialistic society. In the growing competition in society today, obtaining something different from the normal pet dog or cat, to make the owner stand out, inspires many. Some get a taste for ownership of 'different' animals when they start out as carers for wildlife. Others are rewarded psychologically by the helpless animals being dependent on them, even to the extent of believing that they are helping to maintain an endangered species, like tigers, of which there are at least 5000 in captivity worldwide (Slater, 2014). Or it may be the challenge of taming a wild creature, since even the most dangerous species learn subjugation by humans if they use punishment as a means of shaping the animal's behaviour. This breeds resentment, however, and sometimes retribution by the animals, in the form of uncontrolled bouts of aggression with often disastrous results, occurs in exotic pet ownership just as it does in zoos and companion animals.

There are some exotic-animal owners, who, just like companion-animal owners, treat their animals as surrogate children or simply could not resist them when they were offered for sale as juveniles. In the USA exotic animal auctions are held in many states, and the high prices encourage illegal wildlife capture and transport, often from developing countries, but also countries such as Australia with its unique fauna. The quest for the exotic has led some breeders to develop animal crosses that are often malformed and malfunctioning, the liger for example. These are bred from the union of a male lion and a tigress, are nearly always infertile and pose a risk to the tigress during birth. Such unnatural breeding is banned by many zoos but poses a fascination for some private collectors. Not surprisingly, this fascination started in 19th-century Britain, with Darwin amongst others being a leading reporter on the ligers that he had observed and heard about in Victorian collections.

One of the most commonly traded exotic pets is the psittacines or parrots. Although there are over 350 species of parrots, a relatively small number are kept as pets, including budgerigars, African grey parrots, macaws and cockatoos (Kalmar et al., 2010). The birds are particularly prized for their vocalizations, cognitive abilities and colourful appearance. Cockatoos are valued especially for their erectile crest. Most come from the southern hemisphere, particularly the tropical regions in central and southern America and the subtropical regions of Australia. The most commonly kept psittacine, the budgerigar, comes from Australia. In the USA they are the most popular pet, estimated at 10.1 million in 2002 (AVMA, 2002). The psittacines are also the most endangered birds in the world, with most species listed by the Convention of International Trade in Endangered Species of Wild Fauna and Flora (CITES; see below) as endangered, threatened or potentially in danger. Fifty-one psittacine species are listed in CITES Appendix I, that is approximately one-third of all listed avian species, and nearly all of the remaining two-thirds are in Appendix II (CITES, 2014). The welfare of captive parrots is generally a concern, particularly because their capture and trade as companion animals is relatively recent. Although parrots have long been returned to Western countries by explorers, their widespread trade has been facilitated by the growth in popularity of exotic pets in recent times.

There are many arguments against the keeping of exotic pets, which cannot be explored here in detail: the capture of many of the animals from the wild and the risk of extinction that this poses; the health and welfare risks to the animals, with very high mortality rates (typically 2–3%, but as high as 75% for certain animals and some species of reptile; Endcap, 2012) reported during and following transport; the risks to human health and safety, the environment and indigenous species from accidental release of exotic species; and the financial cost of controlling exotic species that were accidentally released (Endcap, 2012). Mortality rates for birds are less than for reptiles, with the latter estimated to contribute 69% of the total trade by the wildlife monitoring network TRAFFIC (Mancera *et al.*, 2014). There is pressure to control the problem at source, i.e. stemming the trade, rather than attempting to fix the problems that have been caused. Special restrictions are in place in many countries for the keeping of primates, which has been banned in seven southern and eastern European countries, as well as the Netherlands (Endcap, 2012). In others licences are often required for some species, although non-compliance is believed to be high.

9.6   The Transport Process

The exotic animal trade often involves intercontinental transport, from tropical or subtropical locations to temperate regions, in particular from Africa, Asia and South America to Europe, Japan and the USA, but also from Africa, India and South America to Far-Eastern markets. The numbers are staggering, especially when it is considered that as many as 50 animals may be captured or bred for each animal actually kept as a pet, e.g. it has been estimated that in 2009 between 5 and 10 million live reptiles were imported into the EU, which is a rapid growth for a trade that only started in the 1990s (RSPCA, 2010; Mancera *et al.*, 2014). Much of the trade is illegal, perhaps as much as 25%, making the worldwide trade in wildlife species second only to weapons and drug trafficking in value (Endcap, 2012). Border controls in Europe seize many animals, estimated at 1.7 million wildlife specimens per year in 3500 seizures in 2003/04. Numbers of ornamental fish that are traded worldwide are said to be as many as 1.5 billion per year, exported from over 100 countries mostly to the EU (Endcap, 2012). The numbers of ornamental fish kept often exceeds the number of cats and dogs, with over 50 million imported annually into Japan alone (Goka, 2010). This number has declined by about 3% per year recently, probably as a result of better enforcement of regulatory control of importation and growing awareness of the risks of disease importation (Goka, 2010).

Exotic animals are transported mainly in vehicles and by air. Itinerant wildlife traders at markets utilize vehicles, often hiding their animals under the floors of trucks, in car and caravan body compartments and hidden in with luggage if the animals are being traded illegally. In air transport, animals and in particular reptiles may be hidden in luggage or sent by post. During transport the animals are subjected to many stresses, including extreme temperatures, noise and vibration from vehicles and inadequate food, water and space. Poikilothermic animals such as lizards, which cannot regulate body temperature physiologically, are vulnerable to extremes of temperature and humidity. Low temperatures damage cells, which can freeze, and high temperatures cause muscle spasms, erratic breathing and heart rate. Both reduce the ability to capture prey, although this is obviously rarely possible during transport. Following transport, many are offered for sale in markets, of which there are at least 100 in Europe alone, with several hundred events annually (Endcap, 2012). The growth of Internet marketing has almost certainly increased sales of exotic animals.

9.7   Marketing of Exotic Animals for Pets

More common exotic animals are sold through pet stores and at markets, especially in developing countries with little regulation of the trade. Private collections are sources of the larger species such as big cats. The unregulated nature of Internet trading of exotic animals has contributed to the increased sales of these animals by this means. There are many exotic animal sales in countries such as France, but increased regulation established in 2004 is threatening these (Gerard, 2014). Infringing the regulatory standards carries a 6-month prison sentence, or a €9000 fine. Exotic animal auctions are also held in the USA, with zebras, camels, llamas and snakes all on offer. The United States Department of Agriculture regulates these sales and state laws must also be complied with. Animals travelling interstate must have health certificates and abide by the state wildlife laws. Exotic livestock, elk, sika deer and pot-belly pigs are popular for ranches. There is a distinction between this sort of exotic animal ranching and entrepreneurs who aim to be the first to breed novel species, such as emus, llamas and guanacos, to supply a market for alternative animals and products.

9.8   Regulatory Control of Trade in Exotic Animals

As a result of an international agreement between 180 governments, CITES was established in 1973 to ensure that international trade in specimens of wild animals and plants does not threaten their survival. Under the treaty, endangered and at-risk species are classified and the import and export of wild fauna, including living or dead animals and their products and tissues, is regulated. Imports and exports covered by the treaty are licensed through Management Authorities within each country, which is supported by a Scientific Authority to advise them on the effects of trade on the status of a species (CITES, 2014). Three appendices list the approximately 5000 species that are at various degrees of risk:

- Appendix I details species threatened with extinction. Trade is only allowed in exceptional circumstances, such as for scientific purposes.
- Appendix II details species not necessarily threatened with extinction, but requiring trade control to avoid over-utilization that might threaten their survival.
- Appendix III includes species that are protected in at least one country, which requests control of the trade.

Some species are split-listed. For example, the African elephant has some populations listed under Appendix I and those in Botswana, Namibia, Zimbabwe and South Africa under Appendix II to enable trade in elephant ivory from these countries (see also Chapter 3).

Changes to Appendices I and II are agreed by a supreme body, the Conference of the Parties, whereas changes to Appendix III can be unilaterally introduced by just one country.

CITES only covers a small proportion of the total number of species, e.g. about 8% of the 7700 known species of reptile (RSPCA, 2010). Unregulated species have higher mortality rates when they are transported, almost certainly because the conditions are worse (Mancera *et al.*, 2014).

Most countries do not have animal health import requirements for exotic pets, unless they are controlled by CITES. For example, in the UK it is just required that they are accompanied by their owner and that there is a letter from a vet or the owner stating that the animals are fit and healthy to complete the journey. Groups of more than five pets entering from countries outside the EU constitute a commercial consignment and are subject to EU legislation (DEFRA, 2014). In Australia many native species are protected under the Nature Conservation Act 2002. For example, the Tasmanian devil is protected as a native species in Tasmania, making it an offence to take, buy, sell or possess any live animal or part or product of the species without a permit. In May 2008 it was officially listed as 'Endangered' by the Tasmanian Government under the Threatened Species Protection Act 1995.

9.9 Conclusions

Exotic animals and wildlife are traded in many forms, dead and alive, and for many reasons, principally as food, for display and for entertainment. The trades have evolved over many centuries and built up to a peak about 100 years ago, causing many concerns about sustainability and the impact on the receiving country, as well as concerns about the welfare and conservation of the animals. In some cases trade in wildlife devastated natural stocks within just a few years, in other cases an incipient flow of animals led to the gradual demise of the local populations. However, as a result of widespread concerns about the ethics of trade in exotic animals and wildlife in the last 100 years, local and national controls have gradually been introduced and in some cases international agreements are in place. Although these measures can be criticized for being too little too late, in some cases numbers of local populations have been restored and the publicity given to the issues has led to markets diminishing.

Notes

[1] *Whalers and Free Men – Life in Tasmanian Colonial Whaling Stations* (Whaling resource file); Allonah History Room, Bruny Island, Tasmania.
[2] Antarctic House, Hobart Botanic Garden, Tasmania.

The Future of Animal Trade **10**

10.1 Introduction

The past has seen some dramatic changes in world trade in animals. This chapter considers what will shape the future of the animal trade and what changes in the trade are likely. Continuation of current trends does not seem to be an option. Worldwide meat and milk production have been growing, as outlined in Chapters 4 and 5, respectively. Even taking into account increasing population, meat availability per capita has been increasing steadily over the last 50 years to approximately double what it was at the beginning of the 1960s; milk availability per capita has increased by about 20% over the last 10 years (Fig. 10.1). The increasing livestock production requires prodigious quantities of feed grain and there is still potential for meat consumption to increase in many developing regions of the world, e.g. sub-Saharan Africa. The steadily increasing trajectory for meat availability per capita has been consistent over the last 50 years (Fig. 10.1), and it will therefore take extreme measures if this is to be changed.

However, the gradual increase in world meat consumption hides very different patterns of change in different countries, most reflecting economic situations. In some countries, such as China, there has been a steady increase in recent years (Fig. 10.2). Amongst others, Guyomard *et al.* (2013) recently predicted that meat consumption would decline in developed countries, and there is evidence of this in some countries, for example recently in the USA and since the late 1980s in Germany (FAOSTAT, 2015; USDA, 2015). Factors involved in this decline are economical, ethical and human health. Some convergence of the lines seems likely, at about 200 g/capita/day, but the time to achieve this is uncertain. For China, whose meat availability per capita increased at 4.4 g/day over the last 20 years, this should happen in 10 years if the recent trajectory is maintained.

It is likely that there will be increased trade between countries with surplus agricultural products (principally OECD, Latin American and former Soviet Union countries) and those with deficits (mainly those in Asia, the Middle East and Africa). Such increased trade should come with better control of the disease transmission risks, protection of the environment and animal welfare. This requires competent international agencies, with advanced capacity for monitoring

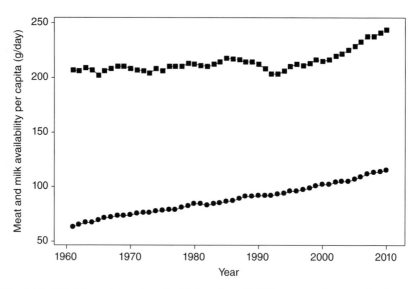

Fig. 10.1. World meat (●—●) and milk (■—■) availability per capita over the last 50 years (FAOSTAT, 2015).

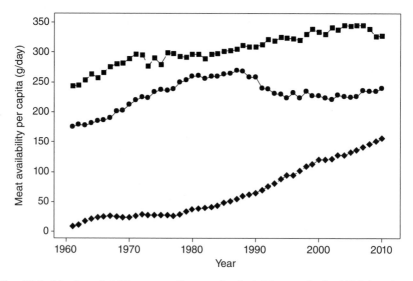

Fig. 10.2. Meat availability per capita over the last 50 years in the USA (■—■), Germany (●—●) and China (◆—◆) (FAOSTAT, 2015).

trade in particular, but also for agricultural research. Sufficient support from the major countries involved is essential. Such agencies are emerging, in the form of the World Trade Organization (WTO), the World Organisation for Animal Health (Office International des Epizooties; OIE), the Food and Agriculture

Organization of the United Nations (FAO) and World Animal Protection (WAP), but major challenges to world food security could test their resolve and abilities. To maintain meat and milk supply the world will have to feed a greater proportion of its cereals to livestock, which is estimated to be one-third of total cereal production (Steinfeld, 2006). Approximately an extra billion tonnes of cereal grain would need to be grown by 2050 (IAASTD, 2009). Much of this will be utilized in developing countries that currently do not have the potential to produce sufficient grain, yet demands for meat and milk are increasing (Figs 10.3 and 10.4). This has led in the past to an increasing proportion of cereal grain used for animal feed, for example in China it increased from 7% in 1960 to 22% in 2007 (FAOSTAT, 2013). Such expansion of livestock production is likely to be achieved from imported grain, mostly used for pig and poultry production (Fig. 10.3). Currently almost 1 billion t of feed grain are traded annually (Alltech, 2014), a figure that may grow substantially if anticipated growth in animal production systems in developing countries eventuates. Unless grain production can be dramatically increased, which seems unlikely, this worrying scenario can only be sustained by growing inequality of wealth. Currently more than 1 billion people do not have enough to eat, yet the wealthiest 1% of people will own more than the other 99% by 2016 if the current rich/poor divide continues to grow at the current rate. Such inequality in wealth will enable the demand for meat consumption to be maintained in the face of escalating cereal prices as a result of increasing global population.

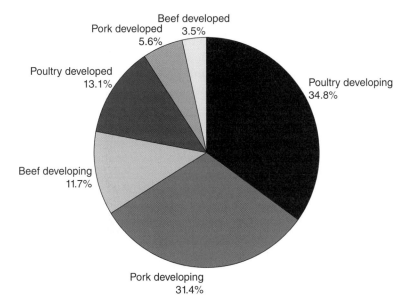

Fig. 10.3. Predicted growth in meat production in developing and developed countries in the various meat production sectors between 2011 and 2020 of +2% or 60 million t, one-half of which will be exported (OECD-FAO, 2011).

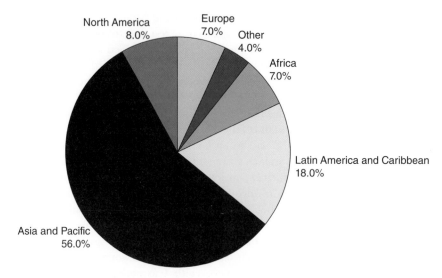

Fig. 10.4. Predicted growth in meat production in the various regions of the world between 2011 and 2020 (OECD-FAO, 2011).

10.2   Free Trade

Trade liberalization has demonstrable benefits as we move towards a global economy. Removal of trade barriers, which has been a focus of the late 20th and early 21st centuries, enables goods to be produced in the most suitable places using the most appropriate methods. The motive for trade restriction is usually to internalize markets in countries with relatively high labour costs in the face of competition from countries with lower labour costs. It can also be to protect markets, in order to sustain practices that would otherwise be unviable in a free market, such as small-scale production using antiquated methods. The transition to a global economy is bound to result in some painful restrictions on income for farmers in developed countries with high labour costs, as well as some advantages for farmers in developing countries, as markets selling to consumers that can afford to pay higher prices become accessible. This transition process has to be carefully managed, as the lessons of history are that food producers are a vulnerable and somewhat volatile sector of the populace. This volatility may stem from a feeling of isolation: from each other, from government and from their markets.

Providing the transition to a global economy can be managed effectively, there are long-term benefits to increased trade: in efficiencies of production, product accessibility to a larger consumer population and harmonized relations between trading nations. However, the quality of production is at greater risk if goods are exchanged between nations, which in the case of animal products includes the methods used for producing and processing the products. Global standards are slow to emerge and it is often difficult to guarantee compliance. This may change, but in the meantime securing animal welfare is only possible with strict national safeguards, which can operate until a better global standards system exists.

Multimedia advances mean that people will be better aware of how their meat is produced compared with today. An Australian sustainable fisheries group, for example, has introduced a barcode that is provided with fish at the point of sale. This can be scanned to provide details of the fishermen that caught the fish and the methods that they used (King, 2014). This could create a new market for ethical food production if consumers are able to choose between different methods of production. If farmers do not volunteer this information, activist groups may obtain it, even if there are legislative attempts to prevent them from doing so. The currently proposed Ag-gag laws, if passed, would limit the options for activists to obtain footage of animal cruelty. However, these attempts to enable farmers to limit public understanding of their production methods are unlikely to be successful as the public want to know this information. Information on animal production methods tends to become distorted at some point and a better in-formed public could drive ethical production more effectively. For example, most of the Australian public believe that meat chickens are reared in battery cages (Erian *et al.*, unpublished information), whereas they are actually reared in large groups on shed floors. A message of cruelty is getting across to the public, but not always one that is accurate.

There are many reasons to believe that there are increasing numbers of animals suffering worldwide for food production:

- increased world meat and milk consumption;
- more reliance on small animals for food production, especially chickens;
- more intensive production systems, especially of poultry and cattle;
- increased live trade; and
- increased animal production in developing countries without animal welfare standards.

Evidence of increased live trade in animals is rapidly emerging. Major air travel is anticipated, particularly with a shortage of shipping containers and mounting concerns about the effects of long journeys on livestock welfare. In 2016 JFK airport in New York will open the first terminal just for animals, up to 70,000/year, for pets, livestock, birds and horses. The terminal will be equipped with climate-controlled rooms for the animals, a vet clinic and an aviary. Toowoomba in Australia has just opened a new airport to convey agricultural produce to China. Growth in animal trade is clearly anticipated by businesses.

10.3   Future Political Models for Animal Management

The world is still struggling to find a workable political ideology, and this influences how people think about their purchasing of animal products. The capitalism that

emerged in many European countries after the social revolutions of the 17th to
the 19th centuries in Europe might be suspected to support a buoyant animal
trade. Its support for individual enterprise encourages investment of people's time
and energy, as well as planning and appropriate risk taking. This may all be beneficial when it comes to caring for animals, which require meticulous management
if their welfare is to be safeguarded. However, as outlined in the Introduction, the
capitalist system also encourages individuals to expand their enterprises, making
it less likely that there will be the close human–animal bonds that usually benefit
the animals. Large enterprises tend to make financial returns their focus, whereas
the small-farm model that has been perpetuated in much of western Europe has
animal welfare as a central tenet, because animals tend to grow well, lactate pro-
fusely and reproduce rapidly if they are being looked after by someone that is
personally bonded to them and committed to looking after their well-being. The
trade in animal products in such small enterprises requires the assistance of governments, which through the course of the 20th century established management
bodies, such as the Milk Marketing Board of the UK, to benefit the farmers.
However, the inefficiencies of small-scale farming, especially in labour use, require government support for farmers to persist. Such government support would
allow the enterprises to be steered towards a sustainable farming system, with
control of emissions, aesthetic appeal of the farms, preservation of cultural heritage and maintenance of high standards of animal welfare. This model might
well be heralded as optimal were it not for the significant cost to taxpayers, many
of whom have little understanding of where their food comes from. Support for
free enterprise has also led to major retailers taking advantage of the disparate
nature of farms, which has forced prices paid to farmers down to unsustainable
levels, as well as being highly volatile. The European Union (EU) is emerging with
a mixed model of control of farm trade. On the one hand, farmers are still given
support in return for maintaining acceptable standards of farming that will ensure
long-term sustainability; on the other, consumers are becoming prepared to pay
more to support even better standards. Both are having an impact, and European
farming systems are arguably some of the most sustainable and responsible in the
world, as well as providing a satisfying existence for more farmers than would be
the case if government did not support them directly. The competition from big
farm enterprises outside of Europe is fierce, but the EU attempts to restrict imports with trade barriers. Often these are ostensibly on quality grounds, but have
ethical implications, such as the banning of imports with productivity enhancers
administered to livestock. Reciprocal trade barriers are sometimes imposed by
potential exporters to the EU, together with involvement of the WTO in an increasing number of trade disputes.

   The EU model may not work in other parts of the world for a host of
reasons. There may be no cultural heritage of small farms, no great desire on
the part of the consumers to support improved animal welfare or the majority
may live in cities with little connection to farms. The massive experiment that
was communism in the 20th century had at its heart an ideology of sharing and
fair trade. However, by the end of the century it was clear that it had failed

miserably, mainly because of mismanagement and corruption. The human involvement in free enterprise is the glue that holds the Western European farming system together and this was largely absent in the communist cooperative and state farms. If people do not own their animals and do not receive any direct benefit from doing the job well, they invest less in their work and may do the job less well. Such is the nature of animal farming, that a close union between person and animal is necessary. The skill of a good animal manager cannot easily be replaced by machines, or by top-heavy management systems. Ownership confers responsibility on animal managers and is a very necessary part of successful systems. Ownership of farm animals is now limited to a small proportion of the population, corporations or governments.

At the same time as capitalism evolved into the consumer-focused ideologue that it has become today, the democracies of Europe also diminished their reliance on Christianity, from divinely appointed monarchs of the 17th century to the secular leadership we have today. Christianity had as one of its central tenets that animals are put on Earth for the benefit of humankind, which allowed people to use them as they wished. Starting with the emerging recognition that humans are not different from animals in any way, and that they are in fact animals themselves, there has been a growing recognition that humans are just a small part of some very complex ecosystems. These ecosystems have been demonstrated to be extremely fragile, and our ignorance of that has led to many disasters, such as the collapse of agricultural systems, extinction of animal and plant species and, more recently, anthropogenic manipulation of the climate. This has led to a growing ideology of concern for ecosystem health, with movements against using animals exploitatively for food, pets and other purposes. The Internet has become the people's 'church' to discuss and act upon these concerns, sharing information and raising awareness around the world. This movement is reviling against industrial animal production and the large-scale trade that supports it. However, it is by no means clear that this growing concern will overcome the capitalist ideal of more goods at low price, which has produced the growth in intensive animal farming and trading.

To find the answer to how the animal trade will develop, we have to look at the evidence that people's ideals will influence their purchasing of animal products. People are more likely to want to pay extra for more respectfully and sustainably produced animal products if they are affluent. We can assume a growing dissatisfaction of the majority with the unequal wealth distribution that is emerging in the 21st century. However, most of those worst affected are not currently in democratic countries with capitalist ideals and this seems unlikely to change rapidly. They will be in totalitarian regimes in Africa or Asia, limiting their opportunities to find political solutions to their plight. Food shortages predicted by the FAO will be most keenly felt in developing countries in these regions, as the enhanced trade in agricultural goods exacerbates the food shortages there. Animal products, like oil, will be the source of intense international negotiations in the most optimistic scenario. In the most pessimistic scenario, and one that follows from national food shortages, it will be the source of

civil unrest in the countries supplying the products, as the food requirements of the people are pitted against the opportunity for foreign revenue from overseas trade. In Thailand for example, where 13% of the population is in poverty (World Bank, 2015), there is growing use of grain to support a burgeoning poultry industry. Unrest over food supplies has been growing in recent years, in Egypt for example, which imports most of its cereal grain (Sjerven and Donley, 2011). If history repeats itself, civil unrest will grow if grain shortages limit basic food supplies. If intensive systems of animal production are a cause of that, governments will have to control their growth.

The green movement, with its already growing ability to influence policy in democracies, can be expected to respond vigorously to emerging problems of an animal trade based on unsustainable production in developing countries with serious food supply problems of their own. Images of starving people in developing countries first found their way into the hearts and minds of Western nations via our television screens in the Bangladesh famines of the 1970s. Then it was not clear that the public could do anything about the crisis other than to voice their concerns and donate money for relief supplies. In the case of a trade in animal products that prevents people in the country of origin having adequate food for themselves, it may be restricted by media campaigns as part of the growing green movement. Exhortations to boycott fast-food outlets purveying such goods are likely to succeed in the same way that boycotting of South African goods helped change the regime's policy, and indeed the regime, in the 1960s to the 1980s.

A common response to such concerns by the consumer is for fast-food chains, or governments, to attempt to persuade the consumer that their concerns are covered by appropriate standards. For example, during the beef export crisis of 2011 in Australia, when activist revelations of cruel beef slaughter practices in Indonesia caused a public outcry, the government chose to defend its support for the trade by saying that OIE standards for animal welfare were being abided by, or, if they were not, a supply chain assurance scheme had been put in place to guarantee that they would be abided by in future. This elevation of guidelines, which were meant to cover the then 174 signatories to the WAH (OIE) organization, to the position of robust and enforceable standards led many to believe that the problem had been solved. However, it was subsequently demonstrated that the guidelines were sometimes neither sufficiently robust nor enforceable and the problem remained.

10.4   Public Responsibility

Can the public be excused for not knowing about and acting upon the circumstances of food animal production? They were first warned about the inhumanity of using animals as machines over 50 years ago (Harrison, 1964), but dietary habits change slowly. Then intensive animal production was in its infancy.

Now most of us live in cities and animals are crowded into sheds far away, and the public rely mostly on the media rather than first-hand knowledge for information about farming. Just as we usually do not know the details of how the car that we drive works, so the public are largely ignorant of the way in which animals are kept for meat and milk production.

Fifty years ago people could be excused for thinking that making cheap meat available to people that had none would be a good thing, especially when we were emerging from a half century of wars that threatened to starve large populations. However, the widespread availability of cheap meat products has contributed to people struggling to contain their appetite. Overconsumption of highly digestible meat is now leading to epidemic-scale obesity and the related diseases of diabetes, gastrointestinal cancer and cardiovascular disease. The truth is that humans, although not designed to eat raw meat, depended for their survival over millions of years of evolution on selection and consumption of the most nutritious foods. Meat, cheese and milk are all highly nutritious and, when confronted with the opportunity to buy as much as we can eat, many people struggle to balance their nutrient intake with their needs.

Even though the public is often unaware, governments are well aware of the massive growth in intensive poultry and pig production, with rising consumption worldwide. They are also aware of the high levels of public concern for animal welfare, but vested interests in maintaining an economically viable agriculture in the face of cheap imports mitigate against strict regulatory control of animal welfare in intensive agriculture. Hence the systems used continue to offer minimal space, as well as an environment devoid of the animal's natural needs, the same food every day, and not even sunlight in which to stretch their limbs. The scale of production growth will cause unprecedented pollution, human and animal health problems and a chronic waste of resources. In an attempt to further increase production, scientists have bred chickens and pigs that grow faster, cows that produce more milk and sheep that produce more lambs, until the animals are little more than commodity-producing machines. This has led to major welfare issues for the animals: joint distortion from the rapid growth, painful mastitis in the cows' udders. If we experienced just a little of the pain that they go through in their very short lives, we would surely do something about it. We could give them at least a bit more space, some natural light and a variety of foods. This might be as much for our own feelings of self-worth as for the animals' benefit, helping us to feel better about the way we look after the animals. Ghandi said that the greatness of a country could be seen from the way it looks after its animals. This is also true for every one of us. We too can be great in what we do for animals simply by what we choose to eat. We might even rekindle that respect for animals that our ancestors had, reserving meat consumption just for special occasions. But as long as governments ignore the cruelty and the public is unaware of what the animals have had to endure to produce the food that they eat, history will not judge us to have been a great civilization.

Case study: Australia and Asia, two contrasting neighbours.

The challenges for meat-producing nations over the next few decades are no-where as well illustrated as with Australia and its developing country neighbours in Asia. Australia is conservative, has a low population density of predominantly white Christian people that are mostly relatively recent immigrants. Its developing neighbours in southern Asia are highly populated, yet they have ancient cultures and systems of doing things that make people easily offended if their traditions are challenged.

Australia is one of the world's major food exporters; exports in 2012/13 were valued at AU$32 billion compared with just AU$11.6 billion spent on imports (DA, 2012–13). Meat is the most important agricultural export commodity, worth about AU$5 billion. Whereas previously most meat was processed and sent to Europe and the USA, about 20% is now exported as livestock to Asia, with cattle going mainly to South-east Asia and sheep to the Middle East. Despite the industry's attempts to ensure adequate welfare of the animals in transit, the length of the journey 'from paddock to plate' and the lack of control in recipient countries make welfare issues almost inevitable (see Chapter 6).

Australians' ability to demonstrate a collective responsibility for the live export trade stems from the liberal democratic processes that allow freedom of expression and an ability to create change, which does not exist in many Asian countries. The Export Supply Chain Assurance Scheme temporarily abated criticisms about the trade. However, although Australians are more vocal about the issues than people in the countries receiving the animals, many Asian people are also offended. Nevertheless, increased prosperity and population of Asian people is increasing demand for livestock products, and there is little or no opportunity or desire to buy meat that has been produced under guaranteed high-welfare standards.

Exporting livestock has created an opportunity to extend and improve trade relations with countries such as Indonesia and Saudi Arabia, which have very different cultures from that in Australia. But the differences in welfare standards are profound. For example, in these Muslim countries there is a requirement to kill animals by a cut to the throat, whereas in Australia nearly all animals are stunned before slaughter. Frequently the trade has had to be suspended by the Australian government because of animal welfare concerns (see Chapter 6). This understandably damages relations, and encourages recipient countries to source their meat from other countries or develop their own production capacity.

These cultural sensitivities threaten Australia's dominance of the world's meat trade, which evolved because of its natural advantages for the raising of livestock. Increasing meat production capacity in Asia will require destruction of rainforest and is likely to reduce staple crop production for the ever-expanding human population (Rutherford, 1999).

The changes in commodity trade that will take place over the course of this century are hard to predict, even more so for sensitive commodities like livestock, but one choice is clear: Australia can try to retain a small but wealthy economy in a distant corner of the world or share its resources and development with its neighbours and develop into a major force for good in the region. Australia

Continued

Case study. Continued.

already has a major shortage of skills in areas of sensitive exports, mining and agriculture in particular. Developing a skilled labour force in conjunction with its neighbours could be a priority, and it fosters growth in another of Australia's great industries – agricultural education. Sharing resources and cooperation with neighbours will be vital for success in the 21st century. Australia is well placed to demonstrate this, having already developed into a multicultural nation that demonstrates considerable tolerance compared to other countries. This need to share resources and development with neighbours is all the more pressing as Asian population growth is foreshadowing major food shortages (FAO *et al.*, 2012), which coupled with climate change could further widen the economic gap between Australia and the Asian continent.

As Australia is vastly underpopulated compared with its Asian neighbours, population expansion and development could be facilitated by using its agricultural resources in collaboration with its Asian neighbours, rather than producing animals to sell them overseas. Fewer livestock would be exported to Asia. Australia could be using its resources to produce food locally for an expanded multicultural population. The carbon footprint of its agricultural product transport would considerably decline, remembering that agriculture is a major contributor to global climate change. The ethical problems associated with animal export would be largely avoided.

As the century evolves it is likely that raising cattle and sheep extensively on Australian rangelands will diminish in importance, as food production technologies develop to allow production of large quantities of high-quality food from agrarian farming. This process has already started in parts of the tropical north of Australia, where there is good water supply and adequate temperatures for year-round crop growth. For example, the Ord River has been dammed, making irrigation water available for 117 km^2 for the production of melons, sandalwood and sugarcane. In the 1880s and 1890s the land had been settled with cattle and sheep by the pioneering Durack family. Within 50 years the sheep had gone, unable to survive in the face of predators and spear grasses that burrowed into their flesh. Land used for cattle grazing was badly eroded, especially around the riverbanks. In the 1960s and 1970s a progressive destocking occurred, together with attempts to rehabilitate the land, for example with kapok bush brought in from overseas. Finally completed in 1971, the Ord River dam created a lake, Argyle, which enabled a large area to be cropped. Although it was originally conceived to support livestock production, testing of suitable crops allowed more profitable horticultural production to be developed. Expansion of the irrigation system was recently evaluated and is highly likely (DSD, 2011).

The current century will bring opportunities for Australia to develop into a modern global society that will be the shape of future successful societies. Australia's good fortune in having the resources to develop in this way has remained largely unrealized until recently, but the inefficient use of high-quality land for livestock production and strong concerns about the export of live animals (Tiplady *et al.*, 2012) may encourage a new direction in utilization of agricultural resources in this century. A transition from widespread use of land

Continued

Case study. Continued.

for intensive livestock production to more efficient use of land for human food production is at first sight almost inevitable in the face of growing world demand for food. This would have considerable inferences for animal welfare, with livestock production confined to areas where natural resources are unsuitable for agrarian production of human food. Intensive systems utilizing grain feeding to livestock in buildings or corralled into yards would be discontinued/decrease, avoiding the welfare problems associated with these systems.

But what if global political systems were to allow suppression of the provision of food for the poor, using free-market economics to concentrate resource use in areas of highest profit? Although the proportion of malnourished people worldwide has been declining (FAO *et al.*, 2014), the actual number is increasing and they will remain unable to afford animal products in their diet. However, the burgeoning middle class in Asia, for example, with their growing demand for meat in their diet, will be able to pay high prices for meat (FAO, 2011). Widespread expansion of intensive animal production systems is possible under this scenario, with catastrophic effects on food availability for the poor. If governments can pay scant regard to human well-being, they can also do the same for animal welfare. A major expansion of animal farming in intensive production systems would force large numbers of animals into systems with acknowledged poor welfare (McInerney, 2004). In the past such inequalities in food supply to the rich and poor would have triggered riots, revolutions and rebellion, but the most likely outcome in the 21st century is economic migration. Strong, just government and support for food production systems that recognize the human and animal implications of intensive animal production systems are required.

As well as expansion of food production in Australia, there are opportunities in underutilized parts of central Asia. For the most part the development of central Asian livestock systems has proceeded along the lines of settlement and the lifestyle support to the nomads outlined for the Kirghiz in Chapter 1. However, there has been little recognition of the ecological superiority of the nomadic system, with central planning leading to many having to seek employment elsewhere. Despite this, there has been a general increase in livestock productivity, with fewer animals kept at a low productivity and more-productive animals making up the majority. This can be achieved in part by using supplements for the animals, which can prevent overgrazing of pastures, but also by improving the health status of animals, controlling parasites and infectious diseases. Such developments are essential if pastoralists are to manage the challenges posed by climate change and population increases. Pastoralists can be changed into 'landscape managers', with supplementary payments for reductions in flock sizes to manageable levels and increases in productivity per animal. Rather than wholescale removal of pastoralists from fragile mountain pastures, modern controls could focus on working with pastoralists and their vast store of local knowledge to develop a sustainable system for pasture utilization. Indigenous knowledge is critical for the development. Imposing such systems from a central means of control is less effective than utilizing the pastoralists to develop improved systems, with their local knowledge facilitating the process.

10.5 World Food Production in 50 Years' Time

Let us fast forward to 2050, within the lifetime of most of us. The world population has expanded to 9 billion, and food production must increase by 70% from today's levels. But this is only a part of the problem that is looming, like dark clouds gathering on the horizon. Most of the population expansion has occurred in developing countries, and especially sub-Saharan Africa, where there are expanding food requirements but without the growing wealth that characterizes the Asian newly developed countries, like India and China. As these newly developed countries became more affluent, they have embraced a Western diet as avidly as Western music and television. Thus the big multinational agricultural corporations have a ready overseas market in the developed world for the now intensively produced animals for meat. Australia's long acknowledged potential to act as the food bowl for Asia has been realized. The north of Australia has been tamed, the plentiful water supply and warm climate used to create vast fields of lush grazing for breeding cattle. Weaners come down en masse to the feedlots in central east and west Australia, where they are fattened on grain produced in the southern states, before being processed and sent overseas as vacuum-packed beef.

Back in 2011 there were about 1 billion people in the world that were chronically undernourished out of a total population of 7 billion, or 14%. To reduce this number food production has increased considerably, in fact by 70% compared with 2011, which reduced the numbers of chronically undernourished people to 0.4 billion or 5%. However, in parts of sub-Saharan Africa it is 15% of the population. The people there are not able to afford the luxury of meat, or even the cereals that are used to feed the cattle. Widespread famines are predisposing to unrest. Just as how over the course of history major inequities in food supply led to revolts by the disadvantaged, which eventually put the power back in the hands of the masses, there is major disruption in Africa today. People are rebelling against their Chinese masters that manage much of food production there, producing food that is conveyed to China rather than being available at home. In the past, food production was largely internalized within a country and wealth redistribution was an achievable target for a revolution. Now that food production is globalized and international travel is easy, people are increasingly turning to an easier alternative, economic migration. Europe and the USA are experiencing pressure on their southern borders as never before, with massive economic migration. Their economies in disarray, world economic growth is firmly rooted in Asia, especially the east and south-east, where living standards are now the highest in the world.

There is now essentially a global labour market. Although there will remain differences in distribution of ethnic groups, labour cost distortions no longer support a trade from one part of the world to another simply because the labour costs are lower in the producing country. Intensification of the livestock industries has been almost completed, with cattle and sheep production largely phased out because of their inefficiencies compared with chicken and pig production.

10.6   Future Scenarios for Companion Animals

In this new world scenario, is there a need for companion animals? Here an element of doubt exists. They are hugely wasteful of resources and emit many pollutants, but the continued breakdown of the cohesive family unit has continued, and animals provide much of the essential companionship to people living alone. This breakdown resulted from the need and capacity for people to work in different places, coming together to reproduce if necessary. Human longevity has continued to increase, to the extent that regular reproduction may not be necessary and may even come to be centrally managed. The Chinese one-child policy has come to be seen as just the initial major experiment in human reproduction management. Humans will always have a big need for social interaction – we evolved that way. The most satisfying social relationships will always be between humans, but if these prove difficult companion animals provide a good second best. In a larger, more intensive human living environment eventually there will be little room for companion animals. Humans will evolve that cope well with that environment. Companionship will be less related, or eventually unrelated to the family unit, with mother, father and children. So in the end we may have little use for our domesticated animals and trade in these animals will certainly become a thing of the past. Some exchange of wild animals between natural reserves may be necessary to retain flexibility in the gene pool, in the event of climate change, which has a natural element as well as a controllable human component. But before the animal trade essentially ends we have a lot to do to control and regulate its impact, the suffering of the animals, the pollutants they emit and the diseases they transmit.

10.7   Towards Solutions for the World's Future Food Production Problems

There are several possible solutions to the world's looming food inequity problem; all require action that might seem difficult now, but with proper planning could be put in place before 2050. Further agricultural research and development to increase output even more than 70% would be one option, but all the signs suggest that the rate of growth in output is declining. Even where the research is successful it may bring unwanted side effects in terms of damage to the environment, breakdown of biosecurity or poor animal welfare. For example, intensification of meat production through the use of beef cattle with a double muscling gene causes welfare problems of purebred animals being less fit than normal cattle. The development of more intensive animal production systems will do little to help the chronically undernourished in rural Africa.

Another potential solution would be changing the type of food production systems we operate. As long as they use land that could be used for production of other types of human food, beef cattle are generally acknowledged to be one of the least efficient agricultural converters of resources into food, with high levels of energy and water use and emissions output compared to food production from plants. Conversion of some of north Australia's agricultural production to salad and vegetable crops has already started, for example the Ord River scheme outlined in the case study, which could be expanded in similar tropical regions with the necessary infrastructural investment. This will increase food production potential, which if adopted worldwide could have a significant impact on food availability.

How will the big multinational companies trading in animal products serve the disaffected developing world population when the food crisis escalates? They offer the advantage over small farming systems in the degree of control that they have over their enterprises. During drought, for example, cattle can be moved from one property to another with more fodder available. However, they answer primarily to their shareholders, who may not want to see their investment risked in novel ventures to alleviate the plight of the poor, who have limited ability to pay for the food they need. Will the multinational companies invest in the infrastructure and technologies necessary to feed the world's poor when their first-world consumers are feeding the voracious demands of their shareholders for profits? 'Cash is king', as Warren Staley, the former CEO of the food company Cargill, said in 2002.

The other problem with multinational companies is that they think big. Many people believe that the world's food security problems can only be solved by integrated farming systems that combine crops or crops and animals, better utilizing the land and input resources than production systems focused on one commodity. Such systems minimize risk, for example of diseases and commodity price volatility. However, the multinational companies want to streamline production, processing and marketing, which means that dealing with multiple commodities is not easily accommodated.

One solution will be for the developed nations of the world to collaborate more intensively with those still developing to look after the food supply for the growing sector that is unable to feed itself. This could be on a latitudinal basis: the USA and Canada working with countries in South and Latin America, European nations with Africa, and Australia and New Zealand having a major role in the Asia/Pacific regions. The FAO will offer guidance and limited support, but is nowhere near powerful enough to take on this significant challenge alone. Multinational trading partner agreements have been established since the Second World War, which range from those with a degree of political unity, as in the EU, to more loose-knit groups of countries, as in the newly formed Eurasian Economic Union, an attempt to ultimately reconstruct a union of Soviet-linked countries in Europe and Asia. In the latter case there is understandable nervousness on the part of some countries, such as Belarus, to joining the union. Although about 50% of Belarus' trade is with Russia, the volatility of the Russian economy and the way in which they have used their military power in the past produces concerns about closer union. Similar trading unions exist in pan-Pacific countries and the Americas. Such multilateral political unions may be necessary to enable governments to have a greater control over the ever-expanding multinational companies. Conglomerates like the Cargill Empire, which emerged in the 'land of the free', increasingly dominate trade and must be made to align their interests with those of the populations they serve. At a broad level this exists through consumer purchasing power, but some of the concerns about the trades perpetuated by major multinational companies are unlikely to be controlled by consumer power alone – the impact of animal production systems on global warming, their efficiency in feeding the world's poor, their contribution to global inequalities in food purchasing power.

The trade agreements being brokered between leading Western nations and major developing nations, such as between the USA and India, focus not on the agricultural sector, where the need is greatest, but on arms. The USA currently supplies arms to Pakistan, and India obtains arms mainly from Russia, but if the USA expands its arms sales to India, it would be in the invidious position of supplying arms to two potentially warring nations. India currently has approximately 90 million farming households and another 28 million agricultural labour households, with widespread malnutrition amongst children and women of reproductive age. Investments in food processing, packaging and trade would help to create a sustainable agriculture. This could embrace agroforestry systems, with the trees helping to alleviate the widespread pollution that is reducing life expectancy and quality of life for a disaffected but powerless sector of society. Developing the small-farming sector, so beloved by Mahatma Gandhi, could enable it to stem the rural depopulation that contributes to urban pollution and could provide surplus produce that can be traded in response for necessities. Small famers could contribute mainly to local production and consumption of food. In the West a new movement is emerging, espousing the virtues of 'Slow Food', which are the production of good, clean and fair food in communities practising small-scale and sustainable production. There is now a substantial network of people – chefs, activists, farmers and fishermen in particular – supporting the movement.

The growth in the intensity and scale of the international trade in animal products is just part of the industrialization of human living that will eventually poison us in our own towns and cities unless we can control it. Whereas local development in productivity can lead to better living standards for the rural poor, the emerging international trades of industrially produced animal products will only accentuate the growing pollution problems that the world is facing today.

Despite these concerns, the retention of many livestock for the maintenance of the rural poor is inevitable, at least until mid-21st century, if a human tragedy is to be avoided. About 70% of the rural poor currently depend on livestock (Hoffmann, 2010). The animals fulfil many diverse functions – food, fibre, manure for fertilizer and fuel, nutrient cycling and seed dispersal – within their complex ecosystem. Some of these functions can be easily replaced by other animals, e.g. locally adapted wild herbivores to disperse seeds. However, other functions cannot be so easily replaced – the use of livestock as capital in Africa, for example. There is already considerable pressure on nomadic pastoralists to relinquish their stock and develop settled agricultural practices. They are blamed for denuding the land by overgrazing and, in times of rapidly increasing populations in Africa, settled agriculture is more manageable by governments. Similar pressures exist at the forest fringes due to encroachment of graziers into forest territory traditionally managed by local tribesmen. For example, in India there has been an active re-afforestation programme, but uncontrolled grazing by local cattle jeopardizes the establishment of these forests. Concentrating cattle production into high-output farms could alleviate much of this pressure, but would bring associated problems of pollution, poor animal welfare, dispersal of manure and other fringe benefits of the cattle to the rural poor. Similar tensions exist in eastern Amazonia, where the forest fringes are often inhabited by smallholders that use cattle in silvo-pastoral systems to establish dairy units. Selected high-value trees are retained, particularly if they will yield building materials later, but the sustainability of farming systems that integrate livestock, forest and pasture has not yet been fully evaluated. Some farmers recognize the need to conserve soil fertility and land and water quality by not overstocking, but others do not and there is nothing to stop them from getting short-term gain from overstocking with their cattle or logging to exploit the soil fertility that has accumulated over centuries.

Whatever the opportunity costs, it seems likely that combatting environmental pollution, and in particular climate change, by modifying our diet to reduce consumption of animal products is likely to be easier than reducing fossil fuel consumption or other means of tackling one of the most challenging threats to our society in the near future. Maintaining the international fossil-fuel trade has already caused large-scale corruption and war even though it is evidently unsustainable and a major contributor to climate change. Eventually animal production growth will be curtailed, and probably reversed, by a need to control pollution. The pollution of the aerial, ground and water environment from animal systems will become of increasing concern as the overall pollution of the environment places a brake on human development and lifestyle. Already the major cities in the world are choking with aerial pollutants, with groundwater and soil faring only a little better. Even though the major animal production units are outside of the cities, the contribution to the shared atmospheric pollution will probably be the major factor requiring a reduction in animal production. Peak animal pollution may be seen sometime this century before it is reduced in the interest of maintaining a healthy environment for humans.

There will be growing awareness of the need to act on environmental issues when our emissions are maximized to a point when further emissions would create an unacceptable impact on our lifestyle. This will also be the driving force behind the demise of animal agriculture at some stage in the future. Animals are hugely wasteful in terms of resource utilization and are massive emitters of pollutants. Currently 26% of the world's ice-free regions are in grazing lands and one-third of the land used to grow crops is used to feed livestock. They emit 18% of greenhouse gases, more than planes, trains and cars combined. Farm animals harbour a huge reservoir of diseases that can and do threaten humans. Synthetics are waiting to take the place of animal products, and this is already a rapidly growing market. We do not need to keep a pig in a pen to make pork or bacon; it is already possible to synthesize the taste and texture, all that is needed is to make it economical to do so (van der Weele and Tramper, 2014). The cost of the growth medium and the need for high standards of laboratory cleanliness for the growth process are major limiting factors at present.

When natural resources are limiting, the price of meat will increase and it will be humans that drive animals from the land; we are inherently speciesist, as are all animals. We want to perpetuate our species, even if it means the demise of others. Humans want space to live and the competition for resources will intensify as long as humans enjoy living. Our technological developments in the last century have ensured that high quality of life is increasingly achievable for all new humans born on the planet. Although animal agriculture will eventually end, our fascination and pride in the past and pleasure in viewing other animals will ensure that wild places remain, with their natural fauna. Zoos are already heading that way (Maple and Perdue, 2013), but these will be specific for each region and the need for trade will be very limited. Each natural place will need to be self-sustaining, large enough for a viable population of the major animal species to exist, yet close enough to centres of human population that they can be enjoyed on a regular basis, taking into account the undoubted ease of long-distance travel in future.

10.8   The Role of Multinational Companies

The emergence of a new world order of major multinational companies governing all aspects of our food production systems seems inevitable. Certainly nowhere is the recent emergence of major industrial enterprise more evident than in our food production industry. The development of the broiler industries in Brazil and Thailand over the last 20 years are prime examples. These industries are not demonstrating any altruistic concerns for food ethics; indeed they could be accused of engaging in brinkmanship to minimize their commitment to the environment, biosecurity and animal welfare. Large industries command the support of governments, which can easily ignore the people's wishes. For example, Australian people's wishes to end the live export of animals to slaughter overseas are consistently ignored by the Australian government because the major financial implications to the industry are evident.

Multinational companies bring the promise of profits, growth and secure food for the developed world, gaining them government support. But there are human, animal and environmental costs to be paid. In the challenging times ahead we need strong governments that are able to control the multinational companies and are prepared to take the hard decisions to invest in the future of global food supplies and hence regional peace, security and prosperity.

Multinational companies are targeting our foibles, and the very appetites that evolved because of their importance for the maintenance of the human body are now exploited to poison our bodies – sugar for short-term energy, fat for long-term energy, salt for ionic homoeostasis. Food manufacturers use brain imaging to detect human responses in fine detail, for example the flavour burst produced by salt (with Cargill being the world's largest producer of this commodity). The prolonged aromatic and sensory flavours from high-fat cheeses are well known and exploited. The human cost in suffering of the victims that are predisposed to non-communicable diseases (NCDs) by what they eat is very large. The animal cost is rarely considered, but is also significant as it includes both food animals and laboratory animals to produce the medicines to treat the NCDs. Last year alone over 2000 scientific articles using mice or rats to address the burgeoning problem of diabetes were published in journals recognized by the Web of Science. Even if a conservative 50 animals were used per study and only one-half of the work that was done ended up being published in Web of Science journals, that is still 200,0000 rodents used in 1 year and millions of dollars in research funding. Yet more mice were used in the production of suitable genetic models that were susceptible to the disease. While few can doubt that progress is being made in the diagnosis and treatment of the disease, if a fraction of the money used for these studies was used to educate the public about management of their diet, people's quality of life would improve and fewer research animals would be needed.

10.9　Conclusions

The world will face major food shortages this century, and increasingly intensive animal production systems is the dominant response to growing demand, particularly in rapidly developing parts of the world. Schematically, the possible effects of these increasingly intensive animal production systems are shown in Fig. 10.5. In this scenario, the growing inequality in socio-economic status will

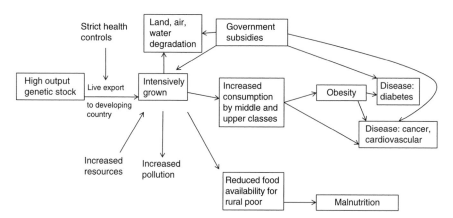

Fig. 10.5. Possible consequences of further intensification of animal production industries.

enable privileged sectors of the population to continue to increase their meat consumption, using products from developing regions. Further growth in intensive meat production systems will contribute to the growing pollution problems, of the atmosphere, water and soil. Human health will further deteriorate through the spread of NCDs. Meanwhile there will be increasing shortages of staple foods for under-developed regions of the world, with a major proportion of the world's grain used for livestock feeding. Reducing the international trade in intensively produced meat animals will be the most effective mechanism to combat both environmental and human health challenges.

We end our look into the future with a look towards the past. Two hundred and fifty years ago the celebrated essayist and moralist Dr Samuel Johnson added the words 'Trade's proud empire hastes to swift decay' to Oliver Goldsmith's poem 'The Deserted Village', which condemned the pursuit of excessive wealth in cities by people deserting the villages. Has Johnson's prediction been proven correct? Has society decayed because of modern trading activities? What would the world look like if the energies that were put into the arms trade, the slave trade, people trafficking, trade in ivory, animal and human body parts and live animals since Johnson's day had instead been devoted to the development of sustainable local societies? Probably it would be a much better and safer place to live. But trade in some goods has brought undoubted benefits to society, in medicines and foods for example, but the greatest benefit has been in the exchange of ideas, thoughts, discoveries, dreams. The human race must cooperate to survive, and all that is needed is a means of ensuring that humanity, and the ecosystem that we live in, benefits from our trading exchanges. The growth in scale of the animal trade in our society could not have been foretold by anyone even 50 years ago, and its impact on society must now be carefully scrutinized for signs that it is causing moral decay.

References

Abbas, B., Yousif, M.A. and Nur, H.M. (2014) Animal health constraints to livestock exports from the Horn of Africa. *Revue Scientifique et Technique (International Office of Epizootics)* 33, 711–721.

AHAW (2011) Scientific opinion concerning the welfare of animals during transport. *European Food Safety Authority Journal* 9, 1–125.

Akbay, C. and Boz, I. (2005) Turkey's livestock sector: production, consumption and policies. *Livestock Research for Rural Development* 17, paper 105. Available at: http://www.lrrd.org/lrrd17/9/akba17105.htm (accessed 30 September 2015).

Alberthsen, C., Rand, J., Bennett, P., Paterson, M., Lawrie, M. and Morton, J. (2013) Cat admissions to RSPCA shelters in Queensland, Australia: description of cats and risk factors for euthanasia after entry. *Australian Veterinary Journal* 91, 35–42.

Algol (1921) To a performing hippopotamus. *Punch* 160, 23 March, p. 22.

Alltech (2014) Alltech global feed survey summary. Alltech, Nicholasville, Kentucky. Available at: http://www.alltech.com/sites/default/files/alltechglobalfeedsummary2014.pdf (accessed 17 April 2015).

American Veterinary Medical Association (AVMA) (2002) *US Pet Ownership and Demographics Sourcebook*. American Veterinary Medical Association, Schaumburg, Illinois.

Animal Welfare Standards (AWS) (2015) Key messages. Available at: http://www.animalwelfarestandards.org (accessed 23 February 2015).

Animals Australia (AA) (2015) Save greyhounds from live export. Available at: http://www.animalsaustralia.org/take_action/save-greyhounds-from-export (accessed 17 February 2015).

Anon. (2008) Meat by numbers. *The Guardian* 7 September. Available at: http://www.theguardian.com/environment/2008/sep/07/food.beef (accessed 22 January 2014).

Anon. (2010) Who the Dongria Kondh are, what Niyamgiri is to them? Available at: https://makanaka.wordpress.com/2010/08/26/who-the-dongria-kondh-are-what-niyamgiri-is-to-them (accessed 23 February 2015).

Anon. (2011a) Tibet under communist China. Available at: http://tibet.net/wp-content/uploads/2011/08/TibetUnderCommunistChine-50Years.pdf (accessed 23 February 2015).

Anon. (2011b) Exclusionary rule. Available at: http://defensewiki.ibj.org/index.php/Exclusionary_Rule (accessed 20 May 2015).

Anon. (2013) DAFF labelled 'out of touch' over exports. *The Veterinarian* 9 March. Available at: http://theveterinarian.com.au/?tag=lloyd-reeve-johnson (accessed 23 February 2015).

Anon. (n.d.) *List of Abattoirs Currently on the Cause for Concern List as at 2nd March*. Food Standards Agency, UK.

Astley, M. (2014) Milk quota abolition will create North European 'production belt'. *Dairy Reporter* 18 March. Available at: http://www.dairyreporter.com/Markets/Milk-quota-abolition-will-create-North-European-production-belt (accessed 23 February 2015).

Australian Centre for International Agricultural Research (ACIAR) (2011) Final Report (C. Delitz) 2011 – Benchmarking the beef supply chain in eastern Indonesia project SMAR/2007/202. Local co-authors/collaborators: Teddy Kristedi, Prajogo U. Hadi, Joko Triastono, Ketut Puspadi and Nasrullah. ACIAR, Canberra.

Australian Standards for the Export of Livestock (ASEL) (2011) Version 2.3, April, 2011. Commonwealth of Australia, Australian Government, Department of Agriculture, Fisheries and Forestry, Canberra.

Aw-Hassan, A., Shomo, F. and Iniguez, L. (2010) Trends in small ruminant meat production-consumption gaps in West Asia and North Africa Implications for intra-regional trade. *Outlook on Agriculture* 39, 41–47.

Barber, N. (1965) *The Black Hole of Calcutta*. Tower Publications, New York, pp. 179–198.

Barrat, J., Richomme, C. and Moinet, M. (2010) The accidental release of exotic species from breeding colonies and zoological collections. *Revue Scientifique et Technique (International Office of Epizootics)* 29, 113–122.

Barré, N. and Uilenberg, G. (2010) Spread of parasites transported with their hosts: case study of two species of cattle tick. *Revue Scientifique et Technique (International Office of Epizootics)* 29, 149–160.

Basset-Mens, C., Ledgard, S. and Boyes, M. (2009) Eco-efficiency of intensification scenarios for milk production in New Zealand. *Ecological Economics* 68, 1615–1625.

Beato, M.S. and Capua, I. (2011) Transboundary spread of highly pathogenic avian influenza through poultry commodities and wild birds: a review. *Revue Scientifique et Technique (International Office of Epizootics)* 30, 51–61.

Beatty, D.T., Barnes, A., Taylor, E., Pethick, D., McCarthy, M. and Maloney, S.K. (2006) Physiological responses of *Bos taurus* and *Bos indicus* cattle to prolonged, continuous heat and humidity. *Journal of Animal Science* 84, 972–985.

Beatty, D.T., Barnes, A., Taplin, R., McCarthy, M. and Maloney, S.K. (2007) Electrolyte supplementation of live export cattle to the Middle East. *Australian Journal of Experimental Agriculture* 47, 119–124.

Beijing Shennong Kexin Agribusiness Consulting (2013) China monthly dairy market report, February 2013. Available at: http://www.bjsn110.com/upload/CaseData/bxite-SP2013031513220001.pdf (accessed 15 January 2014).

Beloff, N. (1973) *The Observer* 15 July. Cited in: Ritson (1977).

Ben-Ami, D., Boom, K., Boronyak, L., Townend, C., Ramp, D., Croft, D. and Bekoff, M. (2014) The welfare ethics of the commercial killing of free-ranging kangaroos: an evaluation of the benefits and costs of the industry. *Animal Welfare* 23, 1–10.

Black, H., Matthews, L.R. and Bremner, K.J. (1991) The welfare of sheep during sea transport. *Proceedings of the New Zealand Society of Animal Production* 51, 41–42.

Brambell, F.W.R. (1965) *Report of the Technical Committee to Enquire into the Welfare of Animals Kept Under Intensive Husbandry Systems*. Command Report 2836, Her Majesty's Stationery Office, London.

Breland, K. and Breland, M. (1951) A field of applied animal psychology. *American Psychologist* 6, 202–204.

Browning, L.M. and Jebb, S.A. (2006) Nutritional influences on inflammation and type 2 diabetes risk. *Diabetes Technology and Therapeutics* 8, 45–54.

Bruinsma, J. (2003) *World Agriculture: Towards 2015/2030: An FAO Perspective*. Earthscan, London.

Burke, M., Oleson, K., McCullough, E. and Gaskell, J. (2009) A global model tracking water, nitrogen, and land inputs and virtual transfers from industrialized meat production and trade. *Environmental Modelling and Assessment* 14, 179–193.

Buscu, D. and Catavencu, A. (2010) Old Ion Ratiu and the Union. Romanian Cultural Centre, London. Available at: http://www.romanianculturalcentre.org.uk/post.php?id=2605&v=1 (accessed 16 December 2014).

Caro, D., LoPresti, A., Davis, S.J., Bastianoni, S. and Caldeira, K. (2014) CH_4 and N_2O emissions embodied in international trade of meat. *Environmental Research Letters* 9, 1–13.

Caulfield, M.P., Cambridge, H., Foster, S.F. and McGreevy, P.D. (2013) Heat stress: a major contributor to poor animal welfare associated with long-haul live export voyages. *The Veterinary Journal* 199, 223–228.

Cernicchiaro, N., White, B.J., Renter, D.G., Babcock, A.H., Kelly, L. and Slattery, R. (2012) Associations between the distance traveled from sale barns to commercial feedlots in the United States and overall performance, risk of respiratory disease, and cumulative mortality in feeder cattle during 1997 to 2009. *Journal of Animal Science* 90, 1929–1939.

Chamberlain, S. (2015) Parrot history: yesterday and today. Bird Channel.com. Available at: http://www.birdchannel.com/bird-news/bird-entertainment/bird-history.aspx (accessed 14 April 2015).

Chambers, J.D. and Mingay, G.E. (1966) *The Agricultural Revolution, 1750–1880*. BT Batsford Ltd, London.

Chepstow-Lusty, A.J., Frogley, M.R., Bauer, B.S., Leng, M.J., Cundy, A.B., Boessenkool, K.P. and Gioda, A. (2007) Evaluating socio-economic change in the Andes using oribatid mite abundances as indicators of domestic animal densities. *Journal of Archaeological Science* 34, 1178–1186.

Churchill, W.S. (1964) *A Churchill Anthology, Selections from the Writings and Speeches of Sir Winston Churchill*. Odhams Press Limited, London.

Cobb, S.P. (2011) The spread of pathogens through trade in poultry meat: overview and recent developments. *Revue Scientifique et Technique (International Office of Epizootics)* 30, 149–164.

Cockram, M.S., Baxter, E.M., Smith, L.A., Bell, S., Howard, C.M., Prescott, R.J. and Mitchell, M.A. (2004) Effect of driver behaviour, driving events and road type on the stability and resting behaviour of sheep in transit. *Animal Science* 79, 165–176.

Cohn, R.L. and Jensen, R.A. (1982) Mortality in the Atlantic slave trade. *The Journal of Interdisciplinary History* 13, 317–329.

Collins, E.J.T. (1978) *The Economy of Upland Britain, 1750–1950: an illustrated review*. Centre for Agricultural Strategy Paper 4, May 1978, CAS, University of Reading.

Convention of International Trade in Endangered Species of Wild Fauna and Flora (CITES) (2014) How CITES works. Available at: http://www.cites.org/eng/disc/how.php (accessed 15 September 2014).

Council of Hemispheric Affairs (CHA) (2011) The great Peruvian guano bonanza: rise, fall, and legacy. Available at: http://www.coha.org/the-great-peruvian-guano-bonanza-rise-fall-and-legacy (accessed 24 February 2015).

Council Regulation (EC) No 1/2005 (2005) On the protection of animals during transport and related operations and amending Directives 64/432/EEC and 93/119/EC and Regulation (EC) No 1255/97. *Official Journal of the European Union* L 3/44. Available at: http://eur-lex.europa.eu/LexUriServ/site/en/oj/2005/l_003/l_00320050105en00010044.pdf (accessed 21 January 2014).

Cuming, E.D. (1913) *Covert and Field Sport*. Hodder and Stoughton, London.

Darwin, C. (1859) *On the Origin of Species by Means of Natural Selection, or the Preservation of Favoured Races in the Struggle for Life*, 1st edn. John Murray, London.

Davey, A. (2013) Economic impact of phasing out the live sheep export trade. Report to World Society for Protection of Animals by the Sapere Research Group. Available at: http://www.srgexpert.com/wp-content/uploads/2015/08/Economic_impact_of_phasing_out_the_live_sheep_export_trade.pdf (accessed 3 August 2015).

De la Rocque, S., Balenghien, T., Halso, L., Dietze, K., Claes, F., Ferrari, G., Guberti, V. and Slingenbergh, J. (2011) A review of trends in the distribution of vector-borne diseases: is international trade contributing to their spread? *Revue Scientifique et Technique (International Office of Epizootics)* 30, 119–130.

Delgardo, C.L., Clare, A.N. and Marites, M.T. (2003) *Policy, Technical and Environmental Determinants and Implications of the Scaling-up of Livestock Production in Four Fast-growing Developing Countries: a Synthesis.* International Food Policy Research Institute and FAO, Rome.

Department for Environment, Food and Rural Affairs (DEFRA) (2014) Pet invertebrates, amphibians and reptiles. Available at: http://www.defra.gov.uk/animal-trade/imports-non-eu/iins/live-animals/iins-other-animals-balai/iin-bllv-8 (accessed 2 October 2014).

Department of Agriculture, Australian Government (DA) (2012–13) Australian food statistics 2012–13. Department of Agriculture, Canberra, Australia, p. 8. Available at: http://www.agriculture.gov.au/SiteCollectionDocuments/ag-food/publications/food-stats/australian-food-statistics-2012-13.pdf (accessed 17 April 2015).

Department of State Development (DSD) (2011) Ord River Irrigation Expansion Project. Available at: http://www.dsd.wa.gov.au/state-development-projects/agrifood/ord-river-irrigation-expansion-project (accessed 15 April 2015).

Department of the Environment, Australian Government (DoE) (2015) Estimated numbers of marine animals harvested by recreational fishers. The National Recreational and Indigenous Fishing Survey. Available at: http://www.environment.gov.au/system/files/pages/d408c11f-1c20-4797-8b75-3618322f118d/files/co62nationalrecreationalfishingsurvey.pdf (accessed 3 August 2015).

Di Nardo, A., Knowles, N.J. and Paton, D.J. (2011) Combining livestock trade patterns with phylogenetics to help understand the spread of foot and mouth disease in sub-Saharan Africa, the Middle East and Southeast Asia. *Revue Scientifique et Technique (International Office of Epizootics)* 30, 63–85.

Doughty, A., Cross, N., Robins, A. and Phillips, C.J.C. (2009) The origin, dentition and foot condition of slaughtered horses in Australia. *Equine Veterinary Journal* 41, 808–811.

Drew, T.W. (2011) The emergence and evolution of swine viral diseases: to what extent have husbandry systems and global trade contributed to their distribution and diversity. *Revue Scientifique et Technique (International Office of Epizootics)* 30, 95–106.

Earley, B. and Murray, M. (2010) The effect of road and sea transport on inflammatory, adrenocortical, metabolic and behavioural responses of weanling heifers. *BioMedical Central Veterinary Research* 6, 1–13.

Earley, B., McDonnell, B., Murray, M., Prendiville, D.J. and Crowe, M.A. (2011) The effect of sea transport from Ireland to the Lebanon on inflammatory, adrenocortical, metabolic and behavioural responses of bulls. *Research in Veterinary Science* 91, 454–464.

Earley, B., Murray, M., Prendiville, D.J., Pintado, B., Borque, C. and Canali, E. (2012) The effect of transport by road and sea on physiology, immunity and behaviour of beef cattle. *Research in Veterinary Science* 92, 531–541.

Edie, G. (1772) *Treatise on English Shooting.* J. Cooke, London.

Edwards, A. and Rogers, A. (1974) *Agricultural Resources.* Faber and Faber, London.

Elam, T.E. (2006) Projections of global meat production through 2050. Available at: http://www.farmecon.com/Documents/Projections%20of%20Global%20Meat%20Production%20Through%202050.pdf (accessed 12 February 2015).

Eldridge, G.A. and Winfield, C.G. (1988) The behaviour and bruising of cattle during transport at different space allowances. *Australian Journal of Experimental Agriculture* 28, 695–698.

Endcap (2012) Wild pets in the European Union. *Report* 0812. Available at: http://endcap. eu/wp-content/uploads/2013/02/Report-Wild-Pets-in-the-European-Union.pdf (accessed 1 October 2014).

European Commission (2010) General guidance on EU import and transit rules for live animals and animal products from third countries. European Commission, Health and Consumers Directorate-General, Brussels. Available at: http://ec.europa.eu/food/ international/trade/guide_thirdcountries2009_en.pdf (accessed 21 January 2014).

Everitt, A.V., Hilmer, S.N., Brand-Miller, J.C., Jamieson, H.A., Truswell, A.S., Sharma, A.P., Mason, R.S., Morris, B.J. and Le Couteur, D.G. (2006) Dietary approaches that delay age-related diseases. *Clinical Interventions in Aging* 1, 11–31.

Falk, H., Durr, S., Hauser, R., Wod, K., Tenger, B., Lortscher, M. and Schupback-Regula, G. (2013) Illegal import of bushmeat and other meat products into Switzerland on commercial passenger flights. *Revue Scientifique et Technique (International Office of Epizootics)* 32, 727–739.

Farnes, N. (2003) *Spike – an Intimate Memoir*. Fourth Estate, London, p. 95.

Felius, M. (1995) *Cattle Breeds: an Encyclopaedia*. Misset, Doetinchem, The Netherlands.

Fine, L.B. and Davidson, B.C. (2008) Comparison of lipid and fatty acid profiles of commercially raised pigs with laboratory pigs and wild-ranging warthogs. *South African Journal of Science* 104, 314–316.

FAO (Food and Agricultural Organization of the United Nations) (2008) *World Review of Fisheries and Aquaculture*. FAO, Rome, 6 pp.

FAO (Food and Agricultural Organization of the United Nations) (2011) World livestock 2011 – livestock in food security. FAO, Rome. Available at: http://www.fao.org/ docrep/014/i2373e/i2373e00.htm (accessed 17 April 2015).

FAO (Food and Agricultural Organization of the United Nations) (2014) *Milk and Milk Product Trade Update*, Issue 3, November, 2014.

FAO, WFP and IFAD (2012) *The State of Food Insecurity in the World 2012: Economic Growth is Necessary But Not Sufficient to Accelerate Reduction of Hunger and Malnutrition*. FAO, Rome.

FAO, IFAD and WFP (2014) *The State of Food Insecurity in the World 2014. Strengthening the Enabling Environment for Food Security and Nutrition*. FAO, Rome.

FAOSTAT (2013) FAO statistical yearbook, 2013. FAO, Rome. Available at: http://www.fao. org/docrep/018/i3107e/i3107e03.pdf (accessed 21 January 2014).

FAOSTAT (2014) FAOSTAT statistical data. Available at: http://faostat.fao.org/site/535/ DesktopDefault.aspx?PageID=535 (accessed December 2014).

FAOSTAT (2015) FAOSTAT statistical data. Available at: http://faostat3.fao.org/home/E (accessed February 2015).

Forum (2011) Australia slaughters Brumby for export profit. Available at: http://forum. onlineopinion.com.au/thread.asp?discussion=4210 (accessed 17 February 2015).

Fur Commission USA (2010) World mink production. Available at: http://www. furcommission.com/world-mink-production (accessed 23 February 2015).

Furuse, Y., Suzuki, A. and Oshitani, H. (2010) Origin of measles virus: divergence from rinderpest virus between the 11th and 12th centuries. *Virology Journal* 7, 52.

Furuseth, O.J. (1987) Public attitudes toward local farmland protection programs. *Growth and Change* 18, 49–61.

Gallo, C., Caraves, M. and Villanueva, I. (2004) Antecedentes preliminaries sobre bienestar en los equinos beneficiados en mataderos chilenos. In: Gallo, C., Tadich, N. and Allende, R. (eds) *Resumenes Seminario 'Produccion Animal de Calidad Contemplando Bienestar*

Animal'. Facultad de Ciencias Agrarias de la Universidad Austral de Chile (UACh), Valdivia, Chile, pp. 70–77.

Galloway, J.N., Burke, M., Bradford, G.E., Naylor, R., Falcon, W., Chapagain, A.K., Gaskell, J.C., McCullough, E., Mooney, H.A., Oleson, K.L., Steinfeld, H., Wassenaar, T. and Smil, V. (2007) International trade in meat: the tip of the pork chop. *AMBIO: A Journal of the Human Environment* 36, 622–629.

Gerard, P. (2014) Vers la fin des bourses. *Reptil Mag* 56, 58–60.

Ghosh, P. (2014) Cattle smuggling: a dangerous, illegal and highly profitable trade between India And Bangladesh. *International Business Times*, 4 February 2014. Available at: http://www.ibtimes.com/cattle-smuggling-dangerous-illegal-highly-profitable-trade-between-india-bangladesh-1553155 (accessed 10 April 2015).

Gille, Z. (2011) The Hungarian foie gras boycott: struggles for moral sovereignty in postsocialist Europe. *East European Politics & Societies* 25, 114–128.

Goka, K. (2010) Biosecurity measures to prevent the incursion of invasive alien species into Japan and to mitigate their impact. *Revue Scientifique et Technique (International Office of Epizootics)* 29, 299–310.

Gordon, J. (2001) *The Horse Industry, Contributing to the Australian Economy*. Report to the Rural Industries Research and Development Corporation. RIRDC Publication No 01/083.

Grandin, T. (2013) Animal Welfare Audits for Cattle, Pigs, and Chickens that use the HACCP Principles of Critical Control Points with Animal Based Outcome Measures. Available at: http://www.grandin.com/welfare.audit.using.haccp.html (accessed 3 October 2014).

Guyomard, H., Manceron, S. and Peyraud, J.-L. (2013) Trade in feed grains, animals, and animal products: Current trends, future prospects, and main issues. *Animal Frontiers* 3, 14–18.

Haley, M.M. (2001) Changing consumer demand for meat: the US example, 1970–2010. *Changing Structure of Global Food Consumption and Trade/WRS-01-1*, pp. 41–48.

Hall, S.J.G., Broom, D.M., Goode, J.A., Lloyd, D.M., Parrott, R.F. and Rodway, R.G. (1999) Physiological responses of sheep during long road journeys involving ferry crossings. *Animal Science* 69, 19–27.

Hancock, M.W. (2006) Layard's Assyria and Cumming's Africa: travel narratives and imperial exhibitions at mid-century. In: Boffin's Books and Darwin's Finches: Victorian Cultures of Collecting. PhD thesis, University of Kansas, pp. 17–76.

Harrison, R. (1964) *Animal Machines: The New Factory Farming Industry*. Vincent Stuart, London.

Hartung, T., Blaauboer, B.J., Bosgra, S., Carney, E., Coenen, J., Conolly, R.B., Corsini, E., Green, S., Faustman, E.M., Gaspari, A., Hayashi, M., Wallace Hayes, A., Hengstler, J.G., Knudsen, L.E., Knudsen, T.B., McKim, J.M., Pfaller, W. and Roggen, E.L. (2011) An expert consortium review of the EC-commissioned report 'Alternative (non-animal) methods for cosmetics testing: current status and future prospects-2010'. *ALTEX – Alternatives to Animal Experimentation* 28, 183–209.

Haynes, G. (1991) *Mammoths, Mastodonts and Elephants, Biology, Behaviour and the Fossil Record*. Cambridge University Press, Cambridge, UK, pp. 47, 55.

Herholz, C., Schwermer, H., Fuessel, A.-E., Perler, L., Binggeli, M., Tschan, D.B., Kennel, R. and Wohlfender, F. (2013) International horse movements and spread of equine diseases: Equine Infectious Anaemia and Glanders – two examples. *Pferdeheilkunde* 29, 445–450.

Hoffmann, I. (2010) Livestock biodiversity. *Revue Scientifique et Technique (International Office of Epizootics)* 29, 73–86.

Huang, S. and Show, C. (2011) An analysis of Taiwanese meat demand within domestic and imported upon entering into World Trade Organization (WTO). *African Journal of Business Management* 5, 9059–9066.

Humane Society International Australia (HSIA) (2015) Dog and cat fur. Available at: http://www.hsi.org.au/go/to/160/the-fur-trade-dog-and-cat-fur-.html (accessed 19 February 2015).

Ibrahim, R.A. and Grace, I.M. (2010) Modeling of ship roll dynamics and its coupling with heave and pitch. *Mathematical Problems in Engineering* 2010, Article ID 934714.

International Assessment of Agricultural Knowledge, Science and Technology for Development (IAASTD) (2009) McIntyre, B.D., Herren, H.R., Wakhungu, J. and Watson, R.T. (eds) Synthesis report: agriculture at a crossroads. Available at: http://www.unep.org/dewa/agassessment/reports/IAASTD/EN/Agriculture%20at%20a%20Crossroads_Synthesis%20Report%20(English).pdf (accessed 3 August 2015).

Johnson, D.G. (1973) *World Agriculture in Disarray*. Fontana/Collins in association with the Trade Policy Research Centre, London.

Jones, T.A., Waitt, C. and Dawkins, M.S. (2010) Sheep lose balance, slip and fall less when loosely packed in transit where they stand close to but not touching their neighbours. *Applied Animal Behaviour Science* 123, 16–23.

Kahn, S. and Varas, M. (2014) OIE animal welfare standards and the multilateral trade policy framework. In: *Proceedings of the 3rd Global Conference on Animal Welfare*, 6–8 November, 2012, Kuala Lumpur. OIE, Paris, pp. 5–13.

Kalmar, I.D., Janssens, G.P.J. and Moons, C.P.H. (2010) Guidelines and ethical considerations for housing and management of psittacine birds used in research. *Institute of Laboratory Animal Resources Journal* 51, 409–423.

Keene, N. (2013) US Stardust Circus to put real-life boxing kangaroos in the ring. *Daily Telegraph*, 18 January. Available at: http://www.dailytelegraph.com.au/news/national/us-stardust-circus-to-put-real-life-boxing-kangaroos-in-the-ring/story-fncvk70o-1226556310903?nk=efb3e7c3536990715a70ee2c0b8e5a90 (accessed 2 October 2014).

King, S. (2014) Scan a fish for facts, it'll have you hooked. *The Australian*, 22 November. Available at: http://www.theaustralian.com.au/news/nation/scan-a-fish-for-facts-with-oceanwatch-itll-have-you-hooked/story-e6frg6nf-1227131195271 (accessed 23 February 2015).

Kremen, C., Niles, J.O., Dalton, M.G., Daily, G.C., Ehrlich, P.R., Fay, J.P., Grewal, D. and Guillery, R.P. (2000) Economic incentives for rain forest conservation across scales. *Science* 288, 1828–1832.

Kreutzmann, H. (2013) Transformation of high altitude livestock-keeping in China's mountainous western periphery. *Études Mongoles et Sibériennes, Centrasiatiques et Tibétaines* 43–44; DOI: 10.4000/emscat.2141.

Langewiesche, W. (2010) The outlaw sea. In: Bradley, J. (ed.) *The Penguin Book of the Ocean*. Penguin Group, Camberwell, Australia, pp. 415–443.

Leach, G. (1976) *Energy and Food Production*. IPC Science and Technology Press, Guildford, UK.

Ling, A.W. and Egdell, J.W. (1941) Milk production in war-time. In: *Articles on War Time Agriculture*, Pamplet No. 3, June 1941. Bath and West and Southern Counties Society, Bath, UK.

Livecorp (2014) Industry statistics. Available at: https://www.livecorp.com.au/industry-statistics; http://faostat3.fao.org/download/T/*/E (accessed October 2014).

Lyver, P., Newman, J. and the Rakiura Tītī Islands Administering Body (2012) 'Tītī – muttonbirding – Muttonbirding in New Zealand', Te Ara – the Encyclopedia of New Zealand, updated 22 September 2012. Available at: http://www.TeAra.govt.nz/en/titi-muttonbirding/page-1 (accessed 23 February 2015).

MacTaggart, A. (2015) Creation of a welfare index for thoroughbred racehorses. PhD thesis, Faculty of Science, University of Queensland, Australia. [Submitted.]

Malaysian Standard (2004) *Halal Food; Production, Preparation, Handling and Storage, General Guidelines, First Revision*. Department of Standards, Malaysia.

Mancera, K.F., Murray, P.J., Gao, Y.N., Lisle, A. and Phillips, C.J.C. (2014) The effects of simulated transport on the behaviour of Eastern Blue Tongued Lizards, *Tiliqua scincoides*. *Animal Welfare* 23, 239–249.

Maple, T. and Perdue, B.M. (2013) *Zoo Animal Welfare*. Springer, Dordrecht, the Netherlands.

Marson, J. and Jargon, J. (2014) Russia Closes Four McDonald's Branches in Moscow. *Wall Street Journal*, 14 August. Available at: http://www.wsj.com/articles/russia-closes-four-mcdonalds-in-moscow-mcd-1408568948 (accessed 16 December 2014).

Masri, A.B.A. (2007) *Animal Welfare in Islam*. The Islamic Foundation, Markfield, Leicestershire, UK.

Mazoyer, M. and Roudart, L. (2006) *A History of World Agriculture*. Translated by J.H. Membrez. Earthscan, London.

McDonald, C.L., Rowe, J.B., Gittins, S.P. and Smith, J.A.W. (1988) Feed additives for attracting sheep to eat a pelleted diet during assembly for live export. *Australian Journal of Experimental Agriculture* 28, 719–723.

McInerney, J.P. (2004) *Animal Welfare, Economics and Policy*. Study undertaken for the Farm & Animal Health Economics Division of Department for Environment, Food and Rural Affairs, UK. DEFRA, London.

McLeod, A. (2013) Shearwater wreck. In: *Friends of Stradbroke Island*, Issue 67, December 2013.

McManus, P., Albrecht, G. and Graham, R. (2013) *The Global Horseracing Industry: Social, Economic, Environmental and Ethical Perspectives*. Routledge, New York.

Meat and Livestock, Australia (MLA) (2013) *Australian Livestock Export Industry Statistical Review*. Meat and Livestock, Australia, Sydney.

Menczer, K. (2008) Africa. In: Appleby, M.C., Cussen, V.A., Garcés, L., Lambert, L.A. and Turner, J. (eds) *Long Distance Transport and Welfare of Farm Animals*. CAB International, Wallingford, UK, pp. 182–211.

Milton, K. (2000) Hunter-gatherer diets – a different perspective. *American Journal of Clinical Nutrition* 71, 665–667.

Ministry of Agriculture, Fisheries and Food (MAFF) (1955) *Poultry Housing. Bulletin No. 56*. Her Majesty's Stationery Office, London.

Ministry of Information (1945) *Land at War*. Her Majesty's Stationery Office, London.

Montonen, J., Boeing, H., Steffen, A., Lehmann, R., Fritsche, A., Joost, H.G. *et al.* (2012) Body iron stores and risk of type 2 diabetes: results from the European Prospective Investigation into Cancer and Nutrition (EPIC)-Potsdam study. *Diabetologia* 55, 2613–2621.

Moran, J.B. (2012) Calf and heifer mortalities in the tropics. In: *Rearing Young Stock on Tropical Farms in Asia*. CSIRO, Collingwood, Victoria.

Moran, J.B. and Doyle, R. (2015) *Cow Talk: Understanding Dairy Cow Behaviour to Improve their Welfare on Asian Farms*. CSIRO Publishing, Sydney.

Moutou, F. and Pastoret, P.-P. (2010) Defining an invasive species. *Revue Scientifique et Technique (International Office of Epizootics)* 29, 37–45.

Narrod, C., Tiongco, M. and Scott, R. (2011) Current and predicted trends in the production, consumption and trade of live animals and their products. *Revue Scientifique et Technique (International Office of Epizootics)* 30, 31–49.

Nationmaster (2013) Health statistics, obesity (most recent) by country. Available at: http://www.nationmaster.com/graph/hea_obe-health-obesity (accessed 22 January 2014).

Norris, R.T. (2005) Transport of animals by sea. *Revue Scientifique et Technique (International Office of Epizootics)* 24, 673–681.

Organisation for Economic Co-operation and Development and Food and Agriculture (OECD-FAO) (2011) Meat. In: *OECD-FAO Agricultural Outlook 2011–2020*. OECD-FAO, p.135. Available at: http://dx.doi.org/10.1787/888932427075 (accessed 20 March 2015).

Organisation Internationale Epizootie (OIE) (2012) Transport of animals by sea. In: World Organisation for Animal Health Terrestrial Animal Health Code. Available at: http://www.oie.int/en/international-standard-setting/terrestrial-code/access-online (accessed 2 September 2012).

Organisation Internationale Epizootie (OIE) (2013) Terrestrial animal health code – slaughter of animals, 22nd edn, p. 306. Available at: http://www.oie.int/fileadmin/Home/eng/Health_standards/tahc/2010/chapitre_aw_slaughter.pdf (accessed 10 August 2015).

Organisation Internationale Epizootie (OIE) (2014a) *Analysis of Regulatory Requirements for the Importation of Horses in Asia*. A questionnaire survey. Final report, Regional Workshop for Asia, Far East and Oceania, Hong Kong, 18–20 February 2014.

Organisation Internationale Epizootie (OIE) (2014b) The transport of animals by sea. Available at: http://www.oie.int/index.php?id=169&L=0&htmfile=chapitre_aw_sea_transpt.htm (accessed 20 July 2014).

Paarlberg, R.L. (1980) Lessons of the grain embargo. *Foreign Affairs*, Fall Issue. Available at: http://www.foreignaffairs.com/articles/34274/robert-l-paarlberg/lessons-of-the-grain-embargo (accessed 2 October 2014).

Paradice, J. and Thornber, P. (2014) Facilitating the use of the OIE standards for the transport of animals by sea and by land. In: *Proceedings of the 3rd Global Conference on Animal Welfare*, 6–8 November, 2012, Kuala Lumpur. OIE, Paris, pp. 45–51.

People for the Ethical Treatment of Animals (PETA) (2014) The pain behind foie gras. Available at: http://www.peta.org/issues/animals-used-for-food/animals-used-food-factsheets/pain-behind-foie-gras (accessed 23 February 2015).

Peterson, L.A. (2010) Detailed discussion of fur animals and fur production. Animal Legal and Historical Center. Available at: https://www.animallaw.info/article/detailed-discussion-fur-animals-and-fur-production (accessed 23 February 2015).

Petherick, J.C. and Phillips, C.J.C. (2009) Space allowances for confined livestock and their determination from allometric principles. *Applied Animal Behaviour Science* 117, 1–12.

Phillips, C.J.C. (2008) The welfare of livestock during sea transport. In: Appleby, M., Cussen, V., Garces, L., Lambert, L.A. and Turner, J. (eds) *Long Distance Transport and Welfare of Farm Animals*. CAB International, Wallingford, UK, pp. 137–156.

Phillips, C.J.C. (2009) *The Welfare of Animals: The Silent Majority*. Springer, Dordrecht, the Netherlands.

Phillips, C.J.C. and Santurtun, E. (2013) The welfare of livestock transported by ship. *The Veterinary Journal* 196, 309–314.

Phillips, C.J.C., Pines, M.K., Latter, M., Muller, T., Petherick, J.C., Norman, S.T. and Gaughan, J.B. (2010) The physiological and behavioral responses of steers to gaseous ammonia in simulated long distance transport by ship. *Journal of Animal Science* 88, 3579–3589.

Phillips, C.J.C., Pines, M.K., Latter, M., Muller, T., Petherick, J.C., Norman, S.T. and Gaughan, J.B. (2012a) The physiological and behavioral responses of sheep to gaseous ammonia. *Journal of Animal Science* 90, 1562–1569.

Phillips, C.J.C., Pines, M. and Muller, T. (2012b) The avoidance of ammonia by sheep, with investigation of effects of prior exposure. *Journal of Veterinary Behaviour: Clinical Applications and Research* 7, 43–48.

Pines, M. and Phillips, C.J.C. (2011) Accumulation of ammonia and other potentially noxious gases on live export shipments from Australia to the Middle East. *Journal of Environmental Monitoring* 13, 2798–2807.

Pines, M.K. and Phillips, C.J.C. (2013) Microclimatic conditions and their effects on sheep behavior during a live export shipment from Australia to the Middle East. *Journal of Animal Science* 91, 4406–4416.

Pines, M., Petherick, J.C., Gaughan, J.B. and Phillips, C.J.C. (2007) Stakeholders' assessment of welfare indicators for sheep and cattle exported by sea from Australia. *Animal Welfare* 16, 489–498.

Podberscek, A.L. (2009) Good to pet and eat: the keeping and consuming of dogs and cats in South Korea. *Journal of Social Issues* 65, 615–632.

Pople, T. and Grigg, G. (1999) The kangaroo industry past and present. In: *Commercial Harvesting of Kangaroos in Australia*. Department of Zoology, The University of Queensland, for Environment Australia.

Population Assessment Unit (1992) *Overview of Background Information for Kangaroo Management in Australia*. Australian Nature Conservation Agency, Australia.

Porter, M. (1961) *Overture to Victoria*. Longmans, Green and Co., Toronto.

Randall, J.M. and Bradshaw, R.H. (1998) Vehicle motion and motion sickness in pigs. *Animal Science* 66, 239–245.

Reiter, P. (2010) The standardised freight container: vector of vectors and vector-borne diseases. *Revue Scientifique et Technique (International Office of Epizootics)* 29, 57–64.

Richards, R.B., Norris, R.T., Dunlop, R.H. and McQuade, N.C. (1989) Causes of death in sheep exported live by sea. *Australian Veterinary Journal* 66, 33–38.

Ritson, C. (1977) *Agricultural Economics: Principles and Policy*. Granada Publishing Ltd, London.

Robins, A., Pleiter, H., Latter, M. and Phillips, C.J.C. (2014) The efficacy of pulsed ultra-high current for the stunning of cattle prior to slaughter. *Meat Science* 96, 1201–1209.

Rothman, M.S. (2004) Studying the development of complex society: Mesopotamia in the late fifth and fourth millennia BC. *Journal of Archaeological Research* 12, 75–119.

Round, M.H. (1986) Influence of pellet composition on the performance of export wethers. *Proceedings of the Australian Society of Animal Production* 16, 43–44.

Royal Society for the Prevention of Cruelty to Animals (RSPCA) (2010) The Welfare State: Five years measuring animal welfare in the UK 2005–2009. Available at: http://www.rspca.org.uk/utilities/aboutus/reports/animalwelfareindicators (accessed 23 February 2015).

Royal Society for the Prevention of Cruelty to Animals (RSPCA) (2012) Are animals used for cosmetics testing in Australia? Available at: http://kb.rspca.org.au/Are-animals-used-for-cosmetics-testing-in-Australia_399.html (accessed 10 August 2014).

Rutherford, A.S. (1999) Meat and milk self-sufficiency in Asia: forecast trends and implications. *Agricultural Economics* 21, 21–39.

Santilli, M., Moutinho, U., Schwartzman, S., Nepstad, D., Curran, L. and Nobre, C. (2008) Tropical deforestation and the Kyoto Protocol: an editorial essay. *Climate Change* 71, 267–276.

Santurtun, E. and Phillips, C.J.C. (2015) The impact of vehicle motion during transport on animal welfare. *Research in Veterinary Science* 100, 303–308.

Santurtun, E., Moreau, V. and Phillips, C.J.C. (2013) Behavioural responses of sheep to simulated sea transport motion. In: *Proceedings of the 47th Congress of the International Society for Applied Ethology*, Brazil.

Santurtun, E., Moreau, M., Marchant-Forde, J.N. and Phillips, C.J.C. (2015) Physiological and behavioral responses of sheep to simulated sea transport motions. *Journal of Animal Science*, in press.

Schiessl, M. (2010) The puppy mafia: black market in dogs big business in Germany. Spiegel Online International June 09 2010. Available at: http://www.spiegel.de/international/europe/the-puppy-mafia-black-market-in-dogs-big-business-in-germany-a-699228.html (accessed 19 February 2015).

Schultz-Altmann, A.G.T. (2008) Engineering and design of vessels for sea transport of animals: the Australian design regulations for livestock carriers. *Veterinaria Italiana* 44, 247–258.

Shaw, F.D., Bager, R. and Devine, C.E. (1990) The role of the vertebral arteries in maintaining electrocortical activity after electrical stunning and slaughter in calves. *New Zealand Veterinary Journal* 38, 14–16.

Sidhom, P. (2003) Welfare of cattle transported from Australia to Egypt. Letter to the Editor. *Australian Veterinary Journal* 81, 364–365.

Simpson, J. (2008) *Not Quite World's End, a Traveller's Tales.* Pan Books, London.

Singer, P. (1975) *Animal Liberation: A New Ethics for our Treatment of Animals.* New York Review/Random House, New York.

Siri-Tarino, P.W., Sun, Q., Hu, F.B. and Krauss, R.M. (2010) Saturated fatty acids and risk of coronary heart disease: modulation by replacement nutrients. *Current Atherosclerosis Reports* 12, 384–390.

Sjerven, J. and Donley, A. (2011) Unrest in Egypt. Available at: http://www.world-grain.com/News/News%20Home/Features/2011/4/Unrest%20in%20Egypt.aspx?cck=1 (accessed 23 February 2015).

Slater, L. (2014) Wild obsession. *National Geographic* 225, 96–115.

Smith, K.R., Clayton, P., Stuart, B., Myers, K. and Seng, P.M. (2005) The vital role of science in global policy decision-making: An analysis of past, current, and forecasted trends and issues in global red meat trade and policy. *Meat Science* 71, 150–157.

Standing Committee on Agriculture (SCA) (2013) *Australian Animal Welfare Standards and Guidelines for Cattle.* Pre-public consultation version, Standing Committee on Agriculture, Canberra, January 2013.

Steinfeld, H., Gerber, P., Wassenaar, T., Castel, V., Rosales, M. and de Haan, C. (2006) *Livestock's Long Shadow: Environmental Issues and Options.* Food and Agriculture Organization (FAO), Rome.

Stockman, C.A., Barnes, A.L., Maloney, S.K., Taylor, E., McCarthy, M. and Pethick, D. (2011) Effect of prolonged exposure to continuous heat and humidity similar to long haul live export voyages in Merino wethers. *Animal Production Science* 51, 135–143.

Tadich, N., Gallo, C., Brito, M.L. and Broom, D.M. (2009) Effects of weaning and 48 h transport by road and ferry on some blood indicators of welfare in lambs. *Livestock Science* 121, 132–136.

Tarrant, P.V., Kenny, F.J. and Harrington, D. (1988) The effect of stocking density during 4 hours of transport to slaughter, on behaviour, blood constituents and carcass bruising in Friesian steers. *Meat Science* 24, 209–222.

Tarrant, P.V., Kenny, F.J., Harrington, D. and Murphy, M. (1992) Long distance transportation of steers to slaughter: effect of spatial allowance on physiology, behavior and carcass quality. *Livestock Production Science* 30, 223–238.

Tasmania Times (2014) Live export shame Tasmania. Available at: http://tasmaniantimes.com/index.php/article/live-export-shame-tasmania (accessed 24 October 2014).

Thibier, M. (2011) Embryo transfer: a comparative biosecurity advantage in international movements of germplasm. *Revue Scientifique et Technique (International Office of Epizootics)* 30, 177–188.

Thow, A.M., Annan, R., Mensah, L. and Chowdhury, S.N. (2014) Development, implementation and outcome of standards to restrict fatty meat in the food supply and prevent NCDs: learning from an innovative trade/food policy in Ghana. *BMC Public Health* 14, DOI:10.1186/1471-2458-14-249.

Times News Network (TNN) (2015) India wants to keep US chicken legs out. *Times of India*, 28 January, Times Business.

Tiplady, C., Walsh, D.B. and Phillips, C.J.C. (2012) Cruelty to Australian cattle in Indonesian abattoirs - how the public responded to media coverage. *Journal of Agricultural and Environmental Ethics* 26, 869–885.

Uilenberg, G., Barre, N., Camus, E., Burridge, M.J. and Garris, G.I. (1984) Heartwater in the Caribbean. *Preventive Veterinary Medicine* 2, 255–267.

United Nations Development Programme (UNDP) (2006) *Human Development Report 2006*. Palgrave Macmillan, New York.

United States Department of Agriculture (USDA) (2015) Overview. Available at: http://www.ers.usda.gov/data-products/food-availability-%28per-capita%29-data-system.aspx (accessed 17 February 2015).

Van der Weele, C. and Tramper, J. (2014) Cultured meat: every village its own factory? *Trends in Biotechnology* 32, 294–296.

Vang, A., Singh, P.N., Lee, J.W., Haddad, E.H. and Brinegar, C.H. (2008) Meats, processed meats, obesity, weight gain and occurrence of diabetes among adults: findings from Adventist Health Studies. *Annals of Nutrition and Metabolism* 52, 96–104.

Vérité, M. (1961) *Animal Travellers. The Wonderful Story of Migration*. Odhams Press, London.

Wadham, S., Wilson, R.K. and Wood, J. (1964) *Land Utilisation in Australia*. Melbourne University Press.

Waghorn, G.C., Davis, G.B. and Harcombe, M.J. (1995) Specification of pen rail spacing and trough heights to prevent escape and enable good access to feed by sheep during sea shipments from New Zealand. *New Zealand Veterinary Journal* 43, 219–224.

Wagner, M., Wu, X.-H., Tarasov, P., Aisha, A., Ramsey, C., Bronk, M., Schmidt-Schultz, T. and Gresky, J. (2011) Radiocarbon-dated archaeological record of early first millennium BC mounted pastoralists in the Kunlun Mountains, China. *Proceedings of the National Academy of Sciences USA* 108, 15733–15738.

Wall Street Journal (WSJ) (2014) Authorities to destroy huge stockpile. *Cited by The Australian, 25–26 January* 2014.

Wang, J., Zhou, Z. and Cox, R.J. (2005) Animal product consumption trends in China. *Australasian Agribusiness Review* 13, 1–28.

Wang, Y. and Beydoun, M.A. (2009) Meat consumption is associated with obesity and central obesity among US adults. *International Journal of Obesity (London)* 33, 621–628.

Wasserstein, B. (2007) *Barberism and Civilization*. Oxford University Press, Oxford, UK.

Wieck, C., Schlueter, S.W. and Britz, W. (2012) Assessment of the impact of avian influenza-related regulatory policies on poultry meat trade and welfare. *World Economy* 35, 1037–1052.

WildAid (2007) *The End of the Line*, 2nd edn. Available at: http://www.wildaid.org/sites/default/EndOfTheLine2007US.pdf (accessed 24 December 2014).

Wilson, D.A.H. (2015) *The Welfare of Performing Animals, a Historical Perspective*. Springer, Dordrecht, the Netherlands.

World Bank (2015) Thailand, poverty head count. Available at: http://data.worldbank.org/country/thailand (accessed 20 February 2015).

World Bank Group (WBG) (2015) Population growth rate. Available at: http://www.worldbank.org/depweb/english/modules/social/pgr (accessed 13 April 2015).

World Bulletin (2014) Turkey pledges to save Syrian refugees' livestock. 23rd September, 2014. Available at: http://www.worldbulletin.net/news/144979/turkey-pledges-to-save-syrian-refugees-livestock (accessed 30 September 2014).

World Horse Organization (WHO) (2015) World horse populations – gathering accurate information. Available at: http://www.worldhorse.org/public/World-Horse-Populations-Gathering-Accurate-Information-2.cfm (accessed 18 February 2015).

World Society for Protection of Animals (WSPA) (2013) *Report to Indonesian Veterinary Medical Association/Government of Indonesia on Inter-Island Livestock Transport – April 2013*. WSPA, London.

Zito, S., Paterson, M., Vankan, D., Morton, J., Bennett, P. and Phillips, C.J.C. (2015a) Determinants of cat choice and outcomes for adult cats and kittens adopted from an Australian animal shelter. *Animals* 5, 276–314.

Zito, S., Paterson, M., Stephens, D., Morton, J., Rand, J. and Phillips, C.J.C. (2015b) Cross-sectional study of characteristics of owners and non-owners surrendering cats to four Australian animal shelters. *Journal of Applied Animal Welfare Science*, in press.

Index